KU-794-801

Learning Theories in
Childhood

⑤SAGE | 50 YEARS

SAGE was founded in 1965 by Sara Miller McCune to support the dissemination of usable knowledge by publishing innovative and high-quality research and teaching content. Today, we publish more than 850 journals, including those of more than 300 learned societies, more than 800 new books per year, and a growing range of library products including archives, data, case studies, reports, and video. SAGE remains majority-owned by our founder, and after Sara's lifetime will become owned by a charitable trust that secures our continued independence.

Los Angeles | London | New Delhi | Singapore | Washington DC

2ND EDITION

Learning Theories in
Childhood

COLETTE GRAY AND SEAN MACBLAIN

Los Angeles | London | New Delhi
Singapore | Washington DC

Los Angeles | London | New Delhi
Singapore | Washington DC

SAGE Publications Ltd
1 Oliver's Yard
55 City Road
London EC1Y 1SP

SAGE Publications Inc.
2455 Teller Road
Thousand Oaks, California 91320

SAGE Publications India Pvt Ltd
B 1/I 1 Mohan Cooperative Industrial Area
Mathura Road
New Delhi 110 044

SAGE Publications Asia-Pacific Pte Ltd
3 Church Street
#10-04 Samsung Hub
Singapore 049483

Editor: Jude Bowen
Editorial assistant: George Knowles
Production editor: Nicola Marshall
Copyeditor: Solveig Gardner Servian
Proofreader: Sarah Cooke
Indexer: Silvia Benvenuto
Marketing manager: Lorna Patkai
Cover design: Wendy Scott
Typeset by: C&M Digitals (P) Ltd, Chennai, India
Printed and bound in Great Britain by Ashford
Colour Press Ltd

© Colette Gray and Sean MacBlain 2015

First edition published 2012. Reprinted 2012 (twice) & 2014 (twice).

This second edition published 2015

Apart from any fair dealing for the purposes of research or private study, or criticism or review, as permitted under the Copyright, Designs and Patents Act, 1988, this publication may be reproduced, stored or transmitted in any form, or by any means, only with the prior permission in writing of the publishers, or in the case of reprographic reproduction, in accordance with the terms of licences issued by the Copyright Licensing Agency. Enquiries concerning reproduction outside those terms should be sent to the publishers.

All material on the accompanying website can be printed off and photocopied by the purchaser/user of the book. The web material itself may not be reproduced in its entirety for use by others without prior written permission from SAGE. The web material may not be distributed or sold separately from the book without the prior written permission of SAGE. Should anyone wish to use the materials from the website for conference purposes, they would require separate permission from us. All material is © Colette Gray and Sean MacBlain, 2015.

Library of Congress Control Number: 2015933520

British Library Cataloguing in Publication data

A catalogue record for this book is available from the British Library

ISBN 978-1-47390-645-7
ISBN 978-1-47390-646-4 (pbk)

MIX
Paper from
responsible sources
FSC
www.fsc.org   FSC® C011748

At SAGE we take sustainability seriously. Most of our products are printed in the UK using FSC papers and boards. When we print overseas we ensure sustainable papers are used as measured by the Egmont grading system. We undertake an annual audit to monitor our sustainability.

Colette Gray:
For my family.

Sean MacBlain:
For my brother Brian.

ABOUT THE COMPANION WEBSITE

The second edition of *Learning Theories in Childhood* is supported by a wealth of online resources to aid study for students, which are available at **https://study.sagepub.com/grayandmacblain2e**

- Read more widely! A selection of open access **SAGE journal articles** to help expand knowledge and reinforce your learning of key topics.
- Hear it from an expert! Listen to **podcasts** from the book's authors discussing the key concepts in each chapter to help you think more critically.
- **Weblinks** direct you to relevant resources to deepen your understanding of chapter topics with visual examples.

CONTENTS

LIST OF FIGURES AND TABLES

FIGURES

TABLES

ABOUT THE AUTHORS

Dr Colette Gray is a Chartered Developmental Psychologist at Stranmillis University College, a College of Queen's University Belfast. She is a Principal Lecturer working with students on the BA (Hons) Early Childhood Studies degree and MA and MEd pathways. Until very recently she was Head of Research Development and a Visiting Professor (Child Development & Education) to the University of St Mark & St John Plymouth. Editor of the *International Journal of Early Years Education*, she continues to develop her research interests with young children and marginalized groups. She co-chairs the participatory research special interest group at EECERA that seeks to give children a voice in matters that affect their lives. With Pascal and Bertram she was a key architect in the production of the first ethical guidelines for practitioners working with children and vulnerable groups (EECERA, 2014). Married to Norman, she is a proud mother and grandmother.

Dr Sean MacBlain is Reader in Child Development and Disability at the University of St Mark and St John. Before taking up his current position Sean worked as a Senior Lecturer in Education and Developmental Psychology at Stranmillis University College, a College of Queen's University Belfast. Prior to working as an academic, Sean worked as an educational psychologist in Belfast and Somerset, and continues in this field in his own private practice, SMB Associates SW LTD (enquiries@seanmacblain.com). Sean's research interests include the professional development of teachers and Early Years practitioners and the social and emotional development of children and young people with special educational needs and disabilities. Sean is married to Angela and lives in Somerset, England.

FOREWORD

Learning is complex, multifaceted and informed by factors within and without our control. The development of the cognitive architecture [e.g. memory, attention, information processing and intelligence] necessary to support learning begins within three weeks of conception. More than ten years ago Bjorklund, Lindahl and Plug (2005) found evidence that a poor prenatal environment can lead to poor social, educational and physical outcomes in later life. Similar conclusions were drawn by Ludwig and Currie (2010), who note the long-term negative effects of maternal smoking and drinking on the foetus. Smoking is also correlated with low birth weight. Seemingly innocuous, the importance of low birth weight was noted in a Norweigan study by Black et al. (2007). Linking birth data to adult education, earnings and IQ, they concluded that a 10 per cent increase in birth weight may increase future earnings, the probability of finishing secondary school, and IQ by approximately 1 per cent.

Whilst it is beyond our gift to change the child's prenatal experience, in partnership with parents and external agencies, we can level the playing field by providing every child with an enriched early years experience. Compelling evidence suggests that a quality learning experience requires a well-qualified workforce, who are skilled and knowledgeable (Nutbrown, 2012; EYFS Statutory framework, 2014).

This book seeks to develop your knowledge and understanding of children's learning. The first edition, published in 2012, was the result of our frustration with the lack of a suitable text for students which addressed pertinent learning theories (including Pavlov, Skinner, Piaget, Vygotsky, Bronfenbrenner and Bruner) and the contribution of philosophers (e.g. Locke, Rousseau, Steiner) to early years education. This led us to write a book with the notion of supporting our own students' learning. We were pleased to note that others found it similarly useful and delighted to reach an international audience; our first edition has been translated into Malay and Chinese.

When SAGE requested a second edition we examined the reviews of the first book and sought information from a range of academics on how it might be improved. This edition is the result of extensive consultation. The book retains the balance between theory and practice but is enhanced by the addition of two new chapters (see Chapters 2 and 11). Several chapters are extended, whilst others are updated to include evidence from neural imaging and international studies that seek to identify the processes underpinning children's learning. The recommended reading list at the end of each chapter is updated and has been carefully chosen from the literature in the field to enhance your knowledge and understanding of the issues discussed in the chapter. On the Companion Website for the new edition, you will find a selection of SAGE journal articles relevant to each chapter, which can all be viewed in open access (these are also listed at the end of each chapter). Additionally, YouTube clips popular with our students are included in the chapters and listed on the book's Companion Website to allow you to view visual examples of children's learning. Podcasts for each chapter are also available on the Companion Website for the new edition, to offer insight into our thinking. Importantly, however, from the inception of the first edition through to this latest effort, we remain committed to the belief that no single theory can fully explain children's learning. Instead elements of most theories are frequently seen at work, and there remains much to discover. To test your knowledge of theory and gain an insight into your preferred learning style complete the exercises included in Chapter 2. Then consider how pedagogy can be modified to meet the learning styles of the children in your setting.

Your journey of discovery will be well advanced if, at the end of the book, you find that opinions of learning are influenced by a multitude of factors including the theoretical lens utilized to examine specific forms of behaviour. Viewed simply and without consideration for the multiple factors that impact learning, explanations may be simplistic, unsubstantiated and devoid of the richness and complexity that truly reflects the *how, why* and *when* of learning. In the final analysis, we hope your investigations provoke more questions than answers. As Confucius so wisely noted:

To know what you know and what you do not know, that is true knowledge.

REFERENCE

Bjorklund, A., Lindahl, M. and Plug, E. (2005). The Origins of Intergenerational Associations: Lessons from Swedish Adoption Data. IZA Discussion Papers, No. 1739. Available at: http://hdl.handle.net/10419/33381

Black S.E., Devereux, P.J. and Salvanes, K.G. (2007). From the Cradle to the Labor Market? The Effect of Birth Weight on Adult Outcomes. *Quarterly Journal of Economics, 122,* 1, 409–439.

EECERA (2014) Ethical guidelines for early childhood researchers. Available at: www.eecera.org/documents/pdf/organisation/EECERA-Ethical-Code.pdf (accessed 11.4.15).

EYFS Statutory framework for the early years foundation stage (2014). Setting the standards for learning, development and care for children from birth to five. Reference: DFE-00337-2014.

Ludwig, D.S. and Curry, J. (2010) 'The association between pregnancy weight gain and birth-weight: a within-family comparison. *Lancet,* Sept 18; 376 (9745): 984–990.

Nutbrown, C. (2012). *Foundations for quality.* The independent review of early education and childcare qualifications. Crown copyright.

AN INTRODUCTION TO LEARNING THEORIES

This chapter aims to:

- familiarize the reader with the organization and structure of the book
- provide a brief synopsis of each chapter.

More than thirty years ago, seminal studies conducted by DeCasper and Fifer (1980) and Hepper (1996) offered the first tangible proof that learning precedes birth. From the third tremester, DeCasper and Fifer had mothers read aloud the Dr Seuss story *The Cat in the Hat* at regular intervals before birth. Immediately after birth, they exposed babies to a nonneutritive nipple. Sucking on the nipple activated a recording of the story read by the baby's mother or another female. In all instances, babies suckled harder and faster to hear their mother's voice. Hepper's (1996) relaxation study revealed that babies could make associations prior to birth (see Gray and MacBlain, 2012). More recently, Moon et al. (2012) identified 30 weeks (a time when the sensory and brain mechanisms for hearing are intact) as a critical period for learning. Their research suggests that exposure to complex sounds 10 weeks prior to birth can be learned and remembered up to six months after birth.

These findings and evidence from non-invasive brain imaging studies provide important insights into the course of cognitive development. For example, synaptic formation, necessary for the development of complex neural connections, occurs in the first years of life, whereas the central cortex, which plays a key role in memory, attention, perceptual awareness, thought and language, continues to develop throughout adolescence and early adulthood (Stiles and Jernigan, 2010). Experience and the environment are also central to brain development (Robson, 2012). Greenough et al. (1987) coined the terms *'experience-expectant'* and *'experience-dependent'*. The former refers to the critical role of experience in brain development during the early post-natal stage of life. The latter captures the essential role of learning in neural development. It is argued that an enriched learning environment can have a dramatic effect on the complexity and functioning of the developing brain (Stiles and Jernigan, 2010).

Some learning is incidental, effortless and undirected, whilst other learning is effortful, purposeful, directed, creative and reflective. For example, you might settle down to show a toddler how Lego Duplo® bricks fit together (directed learning) but find their attention drawn to an activity at the writing table (incidental learning). By the end of the session, the child might report the sounding out words used in the writing activity, 'S is a snake, a slithering snake', but have no clue about putting Lego Duplo bricks together. This situation reflects the sheer complexity of human learning. It also highlights how distraction can degrade learning. Indeed, the negative effect of situational factors such as visual displays, noise and lighting have on young children's learning is the theme of a provocation provided by *Teachers TV – A positive learning environment* (see Chapter 2).

Evidence suggests that early experiences are generally forgotten (for a discussion of childhood amnesia, see Hamilton, 2014; Bauer, 2013). This is attributed to the overwhelming amount of information young children encounter in their early life. Whilst seminal events may be remembered, holidays, visits to theme parks and so on may be forgotten. In contrast, skills acquired in early childhood such as walking, talking, riding a bike, reading and writing are typically retained. Simply stated, learning acquired through experience involves the acquisition of knowledge and skills (David et al., 2011).

For more than 2,000 years, philosophers, academics and educators have attempted to explain and define human learning. The Greek philosopher Aristotle (384–322 BC) believed that learning develops through repetitive exercises. According to Aristotle, the State must be charged with responsibility for instilling virtue, habits, nature and reason into children and for ensuring that they became citizens of benefit to society. Almost a hundred years later, Socrates (470–399 BC) described learning as a process of remembering. He believed that all knowledge exists within the human soul before birth but, perhaps due to the trauma of birth, the soul forgets all it previously knew. Through a process of questioning and inquiry, termed '*Socratic dialogue*', the soul recovers some aspects of knowledge.

Definition

Learning: the acquisition of knowledge or skill.

In contrast, Locke (1632–1704) argued against the existence of innate ideas (formed before birth), describing the child's mind as a *tabula rasa* or blank slate. Consistent with Aristotelian philosophy, Locke believed that knowledge is acquired through experience, repetition, training and virtue. He emphasized the importance of enjoyable learning and insisted that teaching should begin in early childhood. Locke's assertions were radical for their time but were shared by a number of influential thinkers including, among many others, Pestalozzi (1746–1827), Froebel (1782–1852), Dewey (1859–1952) and Montessori (1870–1952). Whilst each offers a unique insight into children's learning, importantly for our discussion these philosophers and educators have a shared belief in the importance of educating the young child.

Rousseau (1712–78), for example, argued that education should follow the child's natural growth rather than the demands of society. His emphasis on the innate development of human nature became the primary philosophical basis for many alternative movements in education. In the early 1800s, the Swiss humanitarian Pestalozzi opened schools for orphans, based on Rousseau's principles. His work inspired educators in Europe and America. Froebel, a teacher at Pestalozzi's school, later became famous as the founder of the kindergarten concept. Montessori shared Froebel's belief that children should be taught social skills and empathy. While Froebel used creative and imaginative play to achieve his goals, Montessori employed real-world experiences such as cleaning a room, caring for animals, building a toy house or making a garden to develop these skills.

Dewey shared with Montessori and Froebel the notion that education should be child-centred, active and interactive, and that education must involve the child's social world and community. Influenced by the teaching philosophies of the early pioneers in the field of early childhood education, Dewey emphasized the importance of experiential learning and the process of teachers and children learning together. The teachings of the founding fathers and mothers of early childhood education are explored in greater detail in Chapter 3 where their unique contributions are highlighted. Similarly, the topic of experiential learning is given a more thorough analysis in Chapters 5 and 6 where we explore the theories of Piaget (1896–1980) and Vygotsky (1896–1934).

It is, however, theories of learning that form the central foci of this book. The last century witnessed a significant shift away from philosophical propositions to the development of a range of empirical theories of learning; each claims to explain the origins of some aspect of learning. Before considering influential educational theories of learning, in Chapter 2 we believe it is important to define the term *'theory'* and to explore the differences between a theory and a philosophy.

Chapter 4 introduces the theories of Pavlov (1849–1936), Thorndike (1874–1949), Watson (1878–1958) and Skinner (1904–1990). Each explored an aspect of learning underpinned by the principles of stimulus–response. For that reason, they are typically referred to as 'behaviourists'. A branch of psychology, *behaviourism* remained a dominant force in education for more than fifty years. Although it lost prominence in the 1970s, behaviourism continues to have an influence on pedagogical practice in 21st-century classrooms. Behaviourists believe that all behaviour, no matter how complex, can be reduced to a simple *'stimulus–response' association*. They focus on measurable outcomes rather than on introspective processes (imagination, feelings and thoughts etc.).

In the course of his experimental research with dogs, the physiologist Ivan Pavlov noted that dogs salivated when laboratory technicians entered the room. Further research revealed the dogs had made an association between the technicians (neutral stimulus) and food (stimulus) and this caused their drooling response. Termed *classical* or *Pavlovian conditioning*, the theory was developed further by Watson who demonstrated classical conditioning in humans using young boys known as Little Albert and Little Peter.

Skinner extended Watson's stimulus–response theory to explain more complex forms of learning. He believed it was possible to use the principles underpinning animal experimentation with infants and children. He coined the term *operant* or *instrumental conditioning* to explain the influence positive and negative reinforcers have on shaping and maintaining the child's behaviour. Skinner's theory continues to exert a direct and profound influence on education and is particularly evident in the reward and *punishment* systems teachers use to shape and maintain pupil behaviour. Star charts, praise, positive feedback and circle time are examples of popularly used *positive reinforcers* whilst time out is a *negative reinforcer*. The work of the social learning theorist Bandura (b. 1925) is included by some theorists in discussions on behaviourism (Woollard, 2010). Although he employed the experimental methods favoured by behaviourism, Bandura's inclusion of imagery, mental representations and reciprocal determinism (the child influences and is influenced by their environment) marked a radical departure from traditional behaviourist approaches. For that reason, his work is discussed in Chapter 7 alongside Bronfenbrenner's (1917–2005) social learning theory.

Chapter 5 considers the constructivist theory of learning. Though they continue to co-exist, this theory offers a considerable departure from that of behaviourism. Constructivism views learning as an active, constructive process with the child engaged at every stage. Rather than focus on measurement, cognitive theorists use observations and discourse analysis (interviews) to explain the development of internal cognitive processes. The term *cognition* refers to internal mental processes and *cognitive development* to the acquisition of 'knowledge in childhood'. Cognitive constructivism is based on the work of the Swiss biologist and naturalist Jean Piaget. Whilst working with the French psychologist Alfred Binet (the inventor of the first intelligence test), Piaget became curious about the structure of the child's mind. From an analysis of interviews with children of differing ages as they solved problems and his observations of the process, Piaget concluded that older children think in a very different way from younger children. It wasn't simply that older children knew more but that their thought processes had undergone some form of maturational (age-related) change. Piaget continued to study child development for several decades before positing the theory that intellectual development occurs in four distinct stages. Each of these stages is described in detail in this chapter with the strengths and shortcomings of a staged-approach to learning discussed.

Chapter 6 extends the concepts introduced in Chapter 5. Vygotsky, a Russian developmental psychologist, expanded many of the concepts outlined by Piaget to incorporate the child's social environment. He stressed the fundamental role of social interaction in the development of cognition. Vygotsky believed that each child is born with a basic set of unlearned cognitive functions such as memory and attention that facilitate high-level learning. As young children can absorb the rules and *mores* of their culture, Vygotsky believed that learning can precede understanding, whereas Piaget believed that development precedes learning. According to Vygotsky,

> [e]very function in the child's cultural development appears twice: first, on the social level, and later, on the individual level; first, between people (interpsychological) and then inside the child (intrapsychological) (1978, p. 57).

Both Piaget and Vygotsky believed that young children are curious and actively involved in their own learning and in the discovery and development of new understandings/schemas. Whereas Vygotsky placed more emphasis on social contributions to the process of development, Piaget emphasized self-initiated discovery. These points will be considered in greater detail in Chapter 7 where the zone of proximal development, role of *culture*, social factors, language, *peers* and educators are explored in detail.

Chapter 7 examines the social learning theories of Bandura and Bronfenbrenner. As previously discussed (see Chapter 4 above), Bandura's social learning theory has its roots in behaviourism. Whilst sharing the experimental approaches of his contemporaries, Bandura argued that to exclude thinking from any theory of learning would be like reducing 'Shakespeare's literary masterpieces to his prior instruction in the mechanics of writing' (1978, p. 350). Social learning theory advocates that individuals, especially children, imitate or copy modelled behaviour from personally observing others, the environment and the mass media. Reflecting the central tenets of traditional behaviourism, Bandura believed that behaviour can be shaped and maintained by reinforcement. He extended this theory to include two aspects of indirect reinforcement termed *vicarious and self reinforcement*. Vicarious reinforcement or observational learning occurs when a child witnesses the effects of an event and stores it in memory. By way of example, pre-school children refused to wear their seatbelts after watching the children's cartoon character Peppa Pig and her brother George sitting in the back seat of a car without seatbelts. Following complaints from parents, the producers rectified the problem (BBC News, 2010). This example serves to indicate that, consistent with Bandura's theory, the relationship between viewers and television is reciprocal, with each reacting and shaping the other.

Similar themes inform Bronfenbrenner's ecological model of child development. Bronfenbrenner acknowledged the role of media, technology, culture and society on childhood development. Like Bandura, Bronfenbrenner believed that technology has the potential to change and even damage society (Henderson, 1995), and that the child influences and is influenced by their environment. Bronfenbrenner was one of the first psychologists to adopt a holistic perspective of human development. His ecological model of development comprises five interrelated systems each containing the roles, norms and rules that powerfully shape development. Bronfenbrenner recognized that not only is it necessary to understand how the family or school influences human development, but broader influences as well.

Chapter 8 considers Bruner's (b. 1915) discovery learning theory of constructivism. Bruner was influenced by Piaget's ideas about cognitive development in children. During the 1940s, his early work focused on the impact of needs, motivations, expectations (mental sets) and their influence on perception. Like Piaget, he emphasizes action and problem solving in children's learning, but like Vygotsky he underlines the role of social interaction, language and instruction in the development of thinking. To achieve this goal, he devised the concept of *scaffolding*. Whilst the term 'scaffolding' is most closely associated with Bruner, it was coined by Wood et al. (1976) to describe the type of support children need to achieve the zone of development. Though a psychologist by training, Bruner became a prominent figure in education and wrote several influential and highly regarded texts for teachers including *The Process of Education* (1960), *Toward a Theory of Instruction* (1966), *The Relevance of Education* (1971) and *The Culture of Education* (1996). The final section of this chapter includes a detailed review of constructivist and social constructivist theories drawing out similar and disparate threads.

Chapter 9 examines children's learning through the lens of a newly evolving paradigm variously referred to as the 'new social studies of childhood' and the 'new sociology of childhood'. The origins of this theory can be traced to the United Nations Convention on the Rights of the Child (UNCRC, 1989), which was ratified in the UK in 1991. The UNCRC established children's rights to provision, protection and participation and changed the way children were viewed by many social and developmental researchers (Corosa, 2004). In challenging the objectification of children, the UNCRC heralded a well-documented shift away from research being conducted 'on' to research being conducted 'with' children (Porter and Lacey, 2005). Critical of traditional approaches to research on children's learning, proponents of the social studies of childhood reject the empirical methods favoured by behaviourists and critique Piaget's explanation of universal age-related competencies. Advocates of this newly evolving paradigm share the natural methods of enquiry favoured by Piaget and embrace key concepts of the socio-constructivist and ecological theories. This chapter seeks to explore this contemporary theory with reference to more traditional approaches to children's development and learning.

The final chapter of this book offers a departure from theory (Chapter 10). It is written especially for people who work with or care for young children and who would like to enhance children's learning. Consideration is given to the challenges inherent in creating a learning–teaching environment where children play together in creative, investigative and problem-solving ways, where they take ownership of and responsibility for their own learning, and where emotional and imaginative needs are met (Broadbent, 2006, p. 192). In addition, the role of the adult as a facilitator of learning is explored with reference to the theories of Vygotsky, Bronfenbrenner and Bruner. The role of sustained shared thinking in developing children's understanding and critical awareness is also explored. Practical examples from practice pepper and inform this chapter, which seeks to demonstrate the dynamic relationship between theory and practice.

At the end of the book is a Glossary of terms used in the book, which are also italicized on first appearance. The Appendix contains tables in answer to two of the exercises.

Exercise

Before reading further, consider which theorist best explains how children's learning develops.

As you read each of the following chapters, we would ask you to continually review your decision and to consider whether the information provided has changed or strengthened your initial view.

Weblink

'The forgotten childhood: why early memories fade' (Hamilton, 2014) available at: www.npr.org/player/v2/mediaPlayer.html?action=1&t=1&islist=false&id=299189442&m=300617934 (accessed 27.9.14).

RECOMMENDED READING

Fabian, H. and Mould, C. (2009). *Development and Learning for Very Young Children*. London: Sage.

A useful resource, this book concentrates on children in the 0–3 age range. Fabian and Mould cover a breadth of material, including the stages of child development, development and learning, and policy and practice.

Robson, S. (2012). *Developing, Thinking and Understanding in Young Children*, 2nd edn. London: Routledge.

This interesting and challenging text offers an in-depth study of children's thinking and learning. The developing brain and language and communication are discussed through the lens of thinking and learning. Limited to cognitive theory, it offers students an insight into the creative and critical thinking in the developing child.

REFERENCES

Bandura, A. (1978). Perceived effectiveness: an explanatory mechanism of behavioral change. In G. Lindzey, C.S. Hall and R.F. Thompson (Eds) *Psychology*. New York: Worth.

Bauer, P.J. (2013). Event memory: neural, cognitive, and social influences on early development. In M. Legerstee, D.W. Haley and M.H. Bornstein (Eds) *The Infant Mind: Origins of the Social Brain*. New York: Guilford Press. pp. 146–66.

BBC News (2010). Peppa Pig in seatbelt safety row. Available at: http://news.bbc.co.uk/1/hi/8460753.stm (accessed 1.4.15).

Broadbent, P. (2006). Developing an understanding of young children's learning through play: the place of observation, interaction and reflection. *British Journal of Educational Research, 32*, 2, 191–207.

Bruner, J.S. (1960). *The Process of Education*. Cambridge, MA: Harvard University Press.

Bruner, J.S. (1966). *Toward a Theory of Instruction*. Cambridge, MA: Belknapp.

Bruner, J.S. (1971). *The Relevance of Education*. New York: Norton.

Bruner, J.S. (1996). *The Culture of Education*. Cambridge, MA: Harvard University Press.

Corosa, W.A. (2004). *The Sociology of Childhood (Sociology for a New Century Series)*, 2nd edn. Thousand Oaks, CA: Pine Forge Press.

David, T., Goouch, K. and Powell, S. (2011). Play and prescription: the influence of national developments in England. In M. Kernan and E. Singer (Eds) *Peer Relationships in Early Childhood Education and Care*. London: Routledge. pp. 49–60.

DeCasper, A. J. and Fifer, W.P. (1980). Of human bonding: newborns prefer their mothers' voices. *Science, New series, 208, 448,* 1174–1176.

Gray, C. and MacBlain, S. (2012). *Learning theories in childhood.* London. Sage.

Greenough W.T., Black, J.E. and Wallace, C.S. (1987). Experience and brain development. Child Development. *PubMed, 58, 3,* 539–59.

Hamilton, J. (2014). The forgotten childhood: why early memories fade. Available at: www.npr.org/player/v2/mediaPlayer.html?action=1&t=1&islist=false&id=299189442&m=300617934 (accessed 27.9.14).

Henderson, Z.P. (1995). Renewing our social fabric. *Human Ecology, 23, 1,* 16–19.

Hepper, P.G. (1996). Fetal memory: does it exist? What does it do? *ACTA Paediatrica Supplement, 416,* 16–20.

Moon, C., Lagercrantz, J. and Kuhl, P.K. (2012). Language experienced in utero affects vowel perception after birth: a two-country study. *Acta Paediatrica, 102,* 156–60.

Porter, J. and Lacey, P. (2005). *Researching Learning Difficulties: A Guide for Practitioners.* London: Paul Chapman.

Robson, S. (2012). *Developing, Thinking and Understanding in Young Children,* 2nd edn. London and New York: Routledge.

Stiles, J. and Jernigan, T. (2010). The basics of brain development. *Neuropsychology Review, 20, 4,* 327–48. Available at: www.ncbi.nlm.nih.gov/pmc/articles/PMC2989000/ (accessed 1.4.15).

UNCRC (1989). *United Nations Convention on the Rights of the Child.* Available at: www.unicef.org.uk/crc (accessed 1.4.15).

Vygotsky, L.S. (1978). *Mind and Society: The Development of Higher Mental Processes.* Cambridge, MA: Harvard University Press.

Wood, D., Bruner, J.S. and Ross, G. (1976). The role of tutoring in problem solving. *Journal of Child Psychology and Psychiatry, 17, 2,* 81–100.

Woollard, J. (2010). *Psychology for the Classroom: Behaviourism.* Oxon: Routledge.

Want to learn more about this Chapter?
Visit the companion website at **https://study.sagepub.com/grayandmacblain2e** to gain open access to selected SAGE journal articles, author podcasts and weblinks to help further your study.

2

THE DEVELOPMENTAL PROCESSES UNDERPINNING LEARNING: THE ROLE OF THEORY AND PHILOSOPHY

This chapter aims to:

- examine evidence from neuroscience on the developing brain
- define the term 'learning'
- consider differing learning styles
- explore what theory and philosophy tell us about children's learning.

The most successful Early Years providers, whoever they are, are focused on helping children to learn.

(Ofsted, 2014)

THE DEVELOPING BRAIN

As indicated in Chapter 1, learning precedes birth. Brain development begins three weeks after conception. From the 30th week of gestation the neural architecture, sometimes referred to as *wiring* or *hard wired*, that supports the learning process is in place. Moreover, there is now compelling evidence that learning which occurs at the start of the third trimester is remembered up to six months after birth (Moon et al., 2012). Whilst it was previously thought that the brain was complete at birth, it is now known that, in addition to the 100 billion neurons present at birth, through a process of neurogenesis, parts of the brain continue to generate new neurons into adulthood. Other recent evidence suggests that early learning experiences may be forgotten (see Hamilton 2014; Bauer, 2013). Termed *infantile* or *childhood amnesia*, research suggests that young children can accurately recall early events up to the age of seven or eight when it begins to degrade. Bauer (2013) attributes early memory loss to the immaturity of neural pathways in the central cortex of the developing brain that support memory retention and to the genesis of new neural pathways which push out or displace old memories. Events or information learned after the age of seven or eight, she argues, are more likely to be retained across a lifetime (the Reference section includes a link to Hamilton's discussion of Bauer's evidence). Similarly, salient events in the Early Years, such as the death of a parent or a trip to Disneyland, may be recalled across a lifetime. While detail is frequently lost, the distressing or pleasurable sense surrounding the event is often retained. In contrast, as previously stated, skills acquired in early childhood such as walking, talking, riding a bike, reading and writing are typically retained.

Neuroscientists refer to this as 'plasticity'. The benefits of plasticity are evident in the young brain's ability to recover from injury, but it also leaves it susceptible to damage. Traumatic brain injury remains a major cause of death and disability worldwide (Anderson et al., 2005). Whilst there is considerable debate about the extent to which an infant can recover damaged brain function, recent evidence suggests that recovery is facilitated by the delayed maturation of affected cells including astroglia, oligodendroglia and neurons (Salmaso et al., 2014).

Neurons are the functioning core of the brain (see Figure 2.1). A neuron has branches or 'dendrites' emerging from the cell body. These dendrites pick up chemical signals across spaces known as 'synapses'. Some neurons are connected to as many as 15,000 synapses, which are believed to store memories. Dendrites pick up chemical signals across a synapse and the impulse travels the length of the axon. The electrical impulse causes the release of the neurotransmitters, which, in turn, stimulates or inhibits neighbouring dendrites, like an on–off switch.

The increased precision of neuroimaging methods, such as functional magnetic resonance imaging (fMRI), has enabled scientists to identify another type of neuron termed 'mirror neurons', which are implicated in empathy. Research by Lamm and

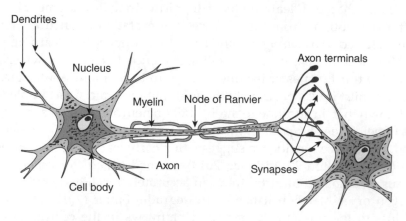

Figure 2.1   The composition of a neuron

Majdandzic (2014) indicates that mirror neurons trigger empathetic responses. For example, seeing another person in pain activates these neurons. Although there is considerable disagreement on the functional role of mirror neurons, they are implicated in imitation, reciprocity, theory of mind, autism and communication (Cook et al., 2014). In a recent study of infant–mother and infant–father interaction at two and four months, Kokkinaki and Vasdekis (2015) found infants significantly more responsive to fathers' playful interactions than mothers'. They attributed the emotional responses displayed by babies to both types of parental interactions to the activity of mirror neurons.

At birth, only the lower portions of the nervous system (the spinal cord and brain stem) are very well developed, whereas the higher regions (the limbic system and cerebral cortex) are relatively primitive (see Figure 2.2). Primitive reflexive responses, essential to life, such as sucking, rooting, grasping, crying and sleeping, are functions of the brain stem and spinal cord. Although all of the neurons in the cortex are produced before birth, they are poorly connected. The formation of the myelin sheath by glial cells speeds the transmission of electrical impulses in the brain. As new connections develop important mental milestones are formed, for example, colour vision and a pincer grasp. At three months the brain has the potential to distinguish several hundred spoken sounds. Over the next few months the brain organizes itself to recognize only the sounds it commonly hears. During early childhood the brain retains its ability (plasticity) to discriminate sounds, making it

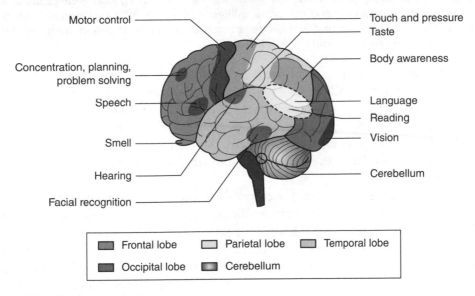

Figure 2.2   The human brain

easier for young children to learn foreign languages. Although older children can still learn a foreign language, greater effort is required. By two years of age, a toddler's cerebral cortex, responsible for higher order functioning, contains well over a hundred trillion synapses. It takes up to 12 years for the brain to become fully organized, with parts of the cortex still to become organized in the later teen years. In essence, infants are born with the cognitive architecture in place to support the learning process but, unlike other primates, higher order functions in humans, including thinking and problem solving, continue to develop over the first 20 years of life.

DEFINITIONS OF LEARNING

Before and after birth environmental factors including a child's living conditions, poverty, ill-health, social and emotional difficulties pose potential threats to the learning process. Shonkoff et al. (2012) traced the antecedents of many adult diseases and developmental disorders to early childhood. Support for the notion that environmental factors can negatively impact the child's development and learning is highlighted in the Early Years Evidence Pack published by the Department for Education, which notes:

> We have found overwhelming evidence that children's life chances are most heavily predi-
> cated on their development in the first five years of life. It is family background, parental
> education, good parenting and the opportunities for learning and development in those
> crucial years that together matter more to children than money, in determining whether
> their potential is realised in adult life. (2011, p. 3)

Experience and the environment are also central to brain development (Robson, 2012). Greenough and colleagues (1987) coined the terms *experience-expectant* and *experience-dependent*. The former refers to the critical role of experience in brain development during the early post-natal stage of life. The latter captures the essential role of learning in neural development. An enriched learning environment is shown to positively affect the complexity and functioning of the developing brain (Stiles and Jernigan, 2010).

It is unsurprising to note that a convincing body of evidence suggests that a positive preschool experience can mediate negative environmental influences. Children's early cognitive outcomes, particularly literacy development, are enhanced by early intervention (Department for Education, 2011; Tickell, 2011; Nutbrown, 2012). Moreover, these early gains are retained across a lifetime. Hence the continued need for quality Early Years provision to support those most at risk of long-term failure. As Nutbrown observes:

Early education and care has the potential to make an important and positive impact on the learning, development and wellbeing of babies and young children, in their daily lives and the longer term. (2012, p. 2)

Nutbrown reminds Early Years professionals and educators that by continuing to develop their own knowledge, skills and understanding of children's learning, they ensure the quality of the provision they provide. Having considered the processes underpinning learning, the role of biological and environmental factors on children's early learning experiences, we include a 'tuning in' exercise we use with our students. Stop for a minute and consider the following questions:

1. What is learning?
2. How do you know when a child has learnt a new skill or acquired new knowledge?

The first author posed the same questions to her final year students and noted some of their responses. Consider how they compare with your thoughts on learning:

'Learning is getting to know new things. I learned to snow board last year. That was a new skill for me, so I suppose it's more than just knowing facts and general knowledge – it includes skills.'

'Sometimes it means gathering more information about something you already know. For example, before I came to university I knew quite a lot about child development from other courses. At university I was given new ideas and a different perspective.'

'Children learn at different rates. Some get things straight away but others take more time. I call it "cooking". You can see the ideas cooking in their little heads then a light bulb moment and you know they understand.'

The following exemplars are students' thoughts on determining whether learning has occurred:

'You could test a child. We set up tasks related to the learning activity we plan and get children to put their knowledge into action. If they can complete the task then we know they have learned.'

'Asking children is a good measure. For example, last week we introduced farm animals and foods they give us. On Monday we put up pictures of animals and the food they give us were underneath, then we had a few rhymes. On Tuesday we had a story about farm animals and food, on Wednesday we did a matching and sorting activity and on Thursday during story time they were asked what does the cow give us? What do we get from pigs? etc. etc. We'll go back over this activity in a few weeks' time as a reminder.'

'Observation, for me that's the only way with young children. It's central to everything we do. How else can I monitor progress?'

The last point made by a mature student sums up the importance of observation in Early Years practice. Testing children below the age of five, though not impossible (see e.g. the work of Gopnick, 2009, 2012; Peterson, Wellman and Slaughter, 2012), can prove challenging. Questioning supposes the child understands the question, can organise their thoughts and then communicate their ideas verbally. The observation technique, introduced by Piaget (1952), offers professionals an opportunity to document a child's learning over time. The role of observation is affirmed in the Statutory Framework for the Early Years Foundation Stage:

> Assessment plays an important part in helping parents, carers and practitioners to recognise children's progress, understand their needs, and to plan activities and support. Ongoing assessment (also known as formative assessment) is an integral part of the learning and development process. It involves practitioners observing children to understand their level of achievement, interests and learning styles, and to then shape learning experiences for each child reflecting those observations. In their interactions with children, practitioners should respond to their own day-to-day observations about children's progress and observations that parents and carers share. (EYFS, 2014, s. 2.2, p. 12)

Definitions of learning

Muro and Jeffrey (2008) define learning as the dynamic interaction between people and the environment in the construction of meaning and identity. Similarly, Piaget (1970) describes learning as an interactive process, incorporating experience and concepts, observations and action as the development of thought takes places through an interaction with the environment. Claxton (1998) offers a broader view of learning which will chime with the experiences of those working with young children. He posits that learning involves imagination, a playful disposition and the ability to learn with and from others (p. 11).

Worthy of note, each of these three definitions highlights the importance of the child's learning environment. As previously indicated, it is now well documented that an impoverished Early Years environment can negatively affect the development of a child's cognitive skills, language development, gross and fine motor skills, school readiness, and academic achievement (Denton and West, 2002; Gershoff, 2003; Rodriguez et al., 2009; Snow et al., 2007; Rodriguez and Tamis-LeMonda, 2011). If a child is hungry, tired, ill, bored, frustrated, under stimulated or over stimulated their learning will be impaired. Environmental factors such as the heat of the room – too warm and the child becomes sleepy, too cold and they find it hard to concentrate – lighting, noise, classrooms packed with displays, can negatively impact the child's ability learning.

The clip below from Teachers TV offers insight into the organization of a fairly typical Early Years setting. Most of us have been in similar settings and you might work in one now. Carefully consider how the organization of this setting might serve to enhance or impede learning. Is it similar or different to your own setting?

Weblink

Teachers TV – A positive learning environment. Available at: www.youtube.com/watch?v=Ku5p-s4B-mrw (accessed 12.4.15).

How might a child with additional needs respond to the organization of this setting?

LEARNING STYLES

Learning is an individual experience. At pains to remind our students about assignment submission deadlines, we put the submission date on module websites, in the module guide and remind students in the assignment preparation lecture. Nevertheless, like most lecturers we are frequently emailed by students who 'just want to check the submission date'. This example suggests that even when a highly educated group are given the same information, some will fail to grasp essential points. It also suggests that individuals process information quite differently.

According to Reiner and Willingham (2010), popular theories concerning learning styles equate to the senses through which they are received; for example, visual, auditory or tactile/kinaesthetic (VAK). Proponents of this notion believe that educators should deliver information in a mode that best suits the learner's preferred learning style (Pashler et al., 2008). It is also claimed that this approach is more egalitarian and can raise achievement by ensuring that information is presented in an accessible mode (Reiner and Willingham, 2010). Learning styles are also linked to Gardner's (1983) theory of multiple intelligences, which highlights individual differences. Indeed, it seems reasonable to suppose that if we have different types of intelligence, then we may also have different learning styles.

In light of these claims, learning styles have proven popular with educators and parents keen to enhance their children's learning experience. An examination of the range of techniques used to support early learning is indicative of the popularity of this approach. In many settings, alongside the white board sit tablet devices, computers, sand and water trays, junk art tables, wall displays, outdoor spaces and creative activities. Using a mixed-method pedagogical approach is thought to reach large numbers of children in the shortest amount of time (Weinberg, 2009).

Given the promise of this approach, it is not surprising that it has spawned more than seventy different models that purport to identify learning styles. An example of one used by the first author with her students is included in Table 2.1. There are no right or wrong answers to the questions, it is simply a test of your learning style.

Exercise

Complete the learning styles test in Table 2.1. Don't ponder too long or over-think the questions as you complete the table. Once completed, simply add the number of ticks in each column and check your score with the answers given in the Appendix (Table A.1). You might find one style is particularly dominant, suggesting you have a preferred approach to learning. If you score highly on two learning styles consider which, if either, you thought would be more dominant. On a few rare occasions, some students score equally across categories – this suggests they have no strong preference.

Are you surprised at the result?

What implications does it have for you as a learner?

What implications does it have for you as an educator?

Table 2.1 Test your learning style (adapted from Rose, 1987)

When you..	?	?	?
Spell	Do you try to see the word?	Do you sound out the word or use a phonetic approach?	Do you write the word down to find if it feels right?
Talk	Do you sparingly listen but dislike listening for too long? Do you favour words such as *see, picture*, and *imagine*?	Do you enjoy listening but are impatient to talk? Do you use words such as *hear, tune*, and *think*?	Do you gesture and use expressive movements? Do you use words such as *feel, touch*, and *hold*?
Concentrate	Do you become distracted by untidiness or movement?	Do you become distracted by sounds or noises?	Do you become distracted by activity around you?
Meet someone again	Do you forget names but remember faces or remember where you met?	Do you forget faces but remember names or remember what you talked about?	Do you remember best what you did together?
Contact people on business	Do you prefer direct, face-to-face, personal meetings?	Do you prefer the telephone?	Do you talk with them while walking or participating in an activity?

When you..	?	?	?
Read	Do you like descriptive scenes or pause to imagine the actions? ✓	Do you enjoy dialog and conversation or hear the characters talk?	Do you prefer action stories or are not a keen reader?
Do something new at work	Do you like to see demonstrations, diagrams, slides, or posters?	Do you prefer verbal instructions or talking about it with someone else? ✓	Do you prefer to jump right in and try it?
Put something together	Do you look at the directions and the picture? ✓		Do you ignore the directions and figure it out as you go along?
Need help with a computer application	Do you seek out pictures or diagrams?	Do you call the help desk, ask a neighbour, or growl at the computer? ✓	Do you keep trying to do it or try it on another computer?

You may be surprised to know that, despite the popularity of learning theories, there is no empirical support for the claim that children learn differently (Reiner and Willingham, 2010). It is, however, generally acknowledged that children have different abilities, and some grasp information more easily than others. Whilst few would argue the importance of including a range of teaching techniques and approaches in education, this is simply a measure of good practice. It is noteworthy that Gardner distanced his theory of multiple intelligences from learning styles. He contends that his theory 'begins from a different point and ends up at a different place from most schemes that emphasize stylistic approaches' (1995, p. 202).

UNPACKING PHILOSOPHY AND THEORY

Exercise

From the list below identify which might be described as: theorists, philosophers, both theorists and philosophers, philanthropists and educators.

Piaget,
Montessori,
Pavlov,
Steiner,
Bruner,

Froebel,
Vygotsky,
Dewey,
the McMillan sisters,

Bronfenbrenner,
Locke,
Rousseau,
Skinner.

List alongside each name the reason for your choice.
Now look at the answers included in the Appendix (Table A.2). Did any surprise you?

The first author includes this exercise in her first lecture with first and final year students on an early childhood studies degree. Typically it provokes a heated debate, with some students perplexed as to why Steiner and Montessori, in particular, are not classified as theorists. Given the lack of information available to students on this topic, this chapter seeks to explore the similarities and differences between these approaches. It will also highlight areas of divergence and the contribution philosophers and theorists make to our understanding of children's learning.

PHILOSOPHY AND LEARNING

Philosophy is, arguably, the oldest academic discipline (Caruana, 2007). The very first philosophers in ancient Greece (Socrates, Plato, Aristotle), China and India (Confucius, Buddha) laid the foundations for what has become Western philosophy. For early societies, the answers to most questions were provided by mythology and religion. The actions of the gods explained the workings of the universe, and provided a framework for human civilisation. Dissatisfied with traditional religious explanations, Thales of Miletus, thought to be the first Greek philosopher, brought groups together to discuss the question 'What is the world made of?' They sought explanations for the Sun, Moon, stars and natural phenomena such as the weather, volcanoes and earthquakes. They also sought to understand how we come to acquire knowledge and how we know what we know (Gopnik et al., 2001).

Despite spanning a 2,500 year history, Gopnik (2009, p. 6) notes that, until recently, philosophers rarely mentioned babies, infants, families, parents, mothers or fathers, and made only four references to children. She argues for a new look at babies, and a new view of babies based on philosophical ideas. According to Gopnik, theory is derived from the scientific approach which is rooted in evolutionary theory. The latter explanation contends that children are born with an innate hardwired system (genes). Consequently, less attention, she argues, has been afforded the impact the environment has on the child's learning or the impact the child has on their environment.

Piaget's staged approach to development offers an example of a theory based on evolutionary principles. Discussed in depth in Chapter 4, he argued that all children follow a prescribed series of stages. Similarly, for many years developmental psychologists sought to determine the universal principles that governed child development. Opponents of this approach believe that the search for universal, culture-free explanations of infancy is based on experimental paradigms that fail to engage with children and lived childhoods (Burman, 2008). Disenchantment with traditional approaches to research on children spawned a new approach that acknowledges the role of children as co-constructors of knowledge and participants in research with a unique perspective on the world. This paradigm affords children a voice in all matters that affect their lives (for a full discussion, see Chapter 9).

Adopting a philosophical approach, Gopnick and her colleagues devised a series of tests which indicated that children as young as 15 months can solve problems, imagine, pretend, show expectation and think about past and future events. Whilst acknowledging that preverbal children can engage in imaginary play, she notes that language offers a powerful vehicle for children to demonstrate imaginary play. Support for her contention comes from our own experiences. The first author has been having pretend tea parties with her granddaughter Isabelle, since Isabelle could walk at 10 months. At 14 months Isabelle was observed pretending to pour tea from a toy teapot into her toy cup and then drinking it whilst saying 'nice tup of tea'. She also shared tea with her favourite doll saying 'baby nice tup of tea.' Isabelle understood this was pretending, no tea was involved, and replicated pretend play repeating the phrases she has come to associate with tea drinking.

Gopneck reports evidence to support her claim that children develop their own theories of how the world is constructed, test their ideas and draw conclusions based on the evidence. She describes them as philosophers, researchers and theorists. She recounts the activities of a 3-year-old boy who demonstrated the impossible. Jumping in the air he showed her that 'you can't just jump in the air and stay there' and how it is impossible to walk through a table (Gopneck, 2009, p. 38). Drawing on her observations and experiments with children, she concluded that:

> [l]earning is a key part of the process, but the human capacity for change goes beyond just learning. Learning is about the way the world changes our mind, but our minds can also change the world. (2009, p. 8)

Definition

Philosophy: an activity and a body of knowledge. It is the process of thinking about and reflecting on what we know, how we know it, what we approve or disapprove and what we wish to happen. It embraces the contribution of human reasoning, insight and intuition. (Thompson, 2010, xii–xiii)

Weblink

Philosophy for beginners. Available at:

www.youtube.com/watch?v=maYsPpxAVrw (accessed 11.4.15).

Crucially philosophy does not seek to answer but to raise questions, to challenge orthodox views and develop new approaches to learning.

UNDERSTANDING THEORY

Theory has been defined as 'a set of interrelated constructs (concepts), definitions and propositions that present a systematic view of phenomena by specifying relations between variables and with the purpose of explaining and predicting the phenomena' (Kerlinger, 1970, p. 9). According to Woollard, a theory is 'an unproven conjecture or hypothesis that gives a tentative insight into a complex situation through to a well-established explanation of that complex situation', (2010, p. 472). Darwin's theory of evolution, Maslow's (1943) hierarchy of needs and Gardner's (1983) theory of multiple intelligence are examples of frequently referenced theories. For Popper, theory is 'the net which we throw out in order to catch the world – to rationalize, explain, and dominate it' (1976, p. 31).

In essence, theory is a potential source of information and discoveries. For example, a scientist develops a hypothesis (a proposition or testable idea) about the relationship between two factors A and B and tests this proposition by logically collecting evidence, analysing the findings, drawing conclusions and providing recommendations. They might conclude that their methods and results are sufficient for them to develop a theory, that their hypothesis was wrong or that more research is necessary before they can make an informed decision. A theory can be complex and intricate, difficult to prove – consider how long it took scientists to confirm the link between smoking and cancer – or it can be simple.

A teacher explains (hypothesises) to her class that tiny alfalpfa seeds grow green shoots when they have water, light and heat. She demonstrates this logical hypothesis by having each child wet a sheet of paper towel, ring it out, fold it in half and sprinkle seeds onto the paper then fold it again and place it into a bag. Each child writes their name on their bag and places it on the window sill. On day four some children see green shoots and by day five all of the children see growth. Using a practical example she demonstrates the link between two variables (the seeds and green shoots) and the factors that affect growth (water, light and heat).

The characteristics of a good theory include predictive and explanatory powers (Cohen et al., 2011). In the example above, the teacher explained the conditions required to support growth and predicted the outcome (green shoots), she tested her theory using a systematic approach. The children observed growth over time and each child had the same results. This latter point is important as replication and *generalization* are among the essential attributes of a good theory. To further explain this point, the Russian scientist Pavlov discovered that the presentation of food caused dogs to salivate. This simple theory can be replicated with all breeds of dogs, in every country in the world. Further generalized, it explains other animal and human behaviour.

In summary, theory is based on an idea that one factor might impact or affect another and is then subject to testing. A range of methods including observation, laboratory experiments, interviews, or questionnaires can be employed to test the theory. Conclusions and recommendations drawn from the findings must meet the criterion that determines the veracity (truth) of the theory.

BLURRING THE EDGES: A THEORY AND A PHILOSOPHY

The distinction between philosophy and theory is frequently blurred. The Reggio Emilia approach, for example, describes itself as an educational philosophy based on the image of the child, and of human beings, as possessing strong potentials for development and as a subject of rights who learns and grows in the relationships with others. (Reggio Children, 2010)

For a further explanation of the Reggio approach to learning, see Malaguzzi (1993). Loris Malaguzzi is variously referred to as a seminal thinker of the 21st century on a par with Piaget and Vygotsky, a pioneer, a philosopher and a theorist. If we accept that a theory is a testable proposition (Cohen et al., 2011) and philosophy is the search for meaning (Vansieleghem and Kennedy, 2011), then Malaguzzi is both a philosopher and a theorist. He developed his approach to preschool and primary education in Italy after the Second World War. In keeping with the systematic approach integral to theory, he describes how he began by making plans, considering options, making cognitive reflections and symbolic representations, and refining communication skills. Sharing a theoretical kinship with Piaget (see Chapter 5), Malaguzzi believed that children are self-learners and co-constructors of knowledge. In keeping with Vygotsky (see Chapter 6), he believes children's learning is supported by interactive experiences constructed with the help of an adult. The teacher's role is complex. They are learners alongside the child while at the same time provoking and stimulating the child's learning. Malaguzzi identified the environment as the third educator. This child-centred philosophy requires the teacher to be alert to the fact that there are many ways in which a child will communicate their thoughts and develop their learning. Malaguzzi famously coined the expression 'A child has a hundred languages'.

The Hundred Languages of Childhood: A child has a hundred languages, but is robbed of ninety-nine. Schools and culture separate the head from the body, they force you to think without a body and to act without a head. Play and work, reality and imagination, science and the fantastic, the inside and the outside, are made into each other's opposites

Loris Malaguzzi, 1993

In keeping with a good theory, the success of the approach is measureable and replicable. There are Reggio Emilia preschools in the UK, Denmark, Sweden and North America, amongst others, and the Loris Malaguzzi International Centre welcomes thousands of visitors each year. More importantly, thousands of children have enjoyed an enriched Early Years experience at Reggio preschools. For more information on the Reggio Emilia Approach see this useful document:

www.educationscotland.gov.uk/Images/ReggioAug06_tcm4-393250.pdf

   Summary

The last two decades have witnessed significant developments in neuroscience that enable us to understand the hidden processes of the brain in ways previously beyond imagination. Compelling evidence reveals that all of the cognitive architecture required to support the learning process is in place by the 30th week of gestation. The process started in week three of gestation continues into early adulthood and shows remarkable adaptability and plasticity. Learning involves the complex interaction of environment, heritability, good health and opportunity. The finding that there is no evidence to support learning styles may disappoint proponents of the approach. Using a variety of strategies to capture the interests of young learners is, however, good practice and to be encouraged. Although there are clear differences between theory and philosophy, at times they appear to overlap. Validity, fidelity, replicability and generalization are features of systematic deductive approaches favoured by theorists. The Socratic dialogue favoured by the early philosophers remains a central tenet of philosophy in the 21st century which seeks to understand, challenge orthodoxies and, in the final analysis, to raise more questions. This reminds us of the complexity of the topics covered in each chapter of this book. Unlike the sciences, education is a messy subject. Today's lesson plan might have to be abandoned when a child kicks off or we may find the learning activities we spent so much time preparing fail to capture the interest of our children. Theory and philosophy offer guidance and insight into new approaches to teaching and learning.

Weblink

Hamilton, J. (2014). The forgotten childhood: why early memories fade. Available at: www.npr.org/player/v2/mediaPlayer.html?action=1&t=1&islist=false&id=299189442&m=300617934 (accessed 27.9.14).

This podcast reports an interview with Bauer, who explored memory development and loss in young children. It reports evidence from children of salient memory retention and highlights the age when and reasons why children's memory of early events degrades.

RECOMMENDED READING

Robson, S. (2012). *Developing, Thinking and Understanding in Young Children*, 2nd edn. London and New York: Routledge.

This interesting and challenging text offers an in-depth study of children's thinking and learning. The developing brain and language and communication are discussed through the lens of thinking and learning. Limited to cognitive theory, it offers students an insight into the creative and critical thinking in the developing child.

Rodriguez, E.T. and Tamis-LeMonda, C.S. (2011). Trajectories of the home learning environment across the first 5 years: associations with children's vocabulary and literacy skills at prekindergarten. *Child Development, 82, 4*, 1058–75. Available at: https://steinhardt.nyu.edu/scmsAdmin/uploads/006/861/Rodriguez,%20E.,%20%26%20Tamis-LeMonda,%20C.,%20Child%20Dev,%20 2011.pdf (accessed 11.4.15).

Available for download, this article reports the development of a large sample of children from low-income families (1,852) at 15, 25, 37 and 63 months. Environment was found to have a significant impact on the development of a range of skills including language, cognitive and fine and gross motor skills. Readiness for school and overall achievement are also negatively affected by an impoverished environment. Although the authors do not explore social and emotional development, you might like to consider the impact underachievement has on a young child's self-esteem.

REFERENCES

Anderson, V., Catroppa, C., Morse, S., Haritou, F. and Rosenfeld, J. (2005). Functional plasticity or vulnerability after early brain injury? *Pediatrics, 116*, 1374–82.

Bauer, P.J. (2013). Event memory: neural, cognitive, and social influences on early development. In M. Legerstee, D.W. Haley and M.H. Bornstein (Eds.), *The Infant Mind: Origins of the Social Brain*. New York, NY: Guilford Press. pp. 146–66.

Burman, E. (2008). *Deconstructing Developmental Psychology*, 2nd edn. London: Taylor & Francis.

Caruana, R. (2007). The drama of being: Levinas and the history of philosophy. *Continental Philosophy Review, 40,* 251–273.

Claxton, G. (1998). *Hare Brain, Tortoise Mind: Why Intelligence Increases When You Think Less.* London: Fourth Estate.

Cohen, L., Manion, L. and Morrison, K. (2011). *Research Methods in Education,* 7th edn. London: Routledge.

Cook, R., Bird, G., Catmur, C., Press, C. and Heyes, C. (2014) Mirror neurons: from origin to function. *Behavioural and Brain Sciences, 37,* 177–92.

Denton, K. and West, J. (2002). *Children's Reading and Mathematics Achievement in Kindergarten and First Grade.* Washington, DC: National Center for Education Statistics.

Department for Education (2011). *Early Years Evidence Pack.* Available at: www.gov.uk/government/publications/early-years-evidence-pack (accessed 1.4.15).

EYFS *Statutory framework for the early years foundation stage.* (2014). Setting the standards for learning, development and care for children from birth to five. Reference: DFE-00337-2014.

Gardner, H. (1983). *Frames of Mind: The Theory of Multiple Intelligences.* New York: Basic Books.

Gardner, H. (1995). Reflections on multiple intelligences: myths and messages. *Phi Delta Kappan, 77,* 200–209.

Gershoff, E. (2003). *Living at the Edge: Low Income and the Development of America's Kindergarteners.* New York: National Center for Children in Poverty.

Gopnick, A. (2009). *The Philosophical Baby: What Children's Minds Tell Us about Truth, Love and the Meaning of Life.* London: Bodley Head.

Gopnik, A. (2012). Scientific thinking in young children. Theoretical advances, empirical research and policy implications. *Science, 28, 337,* 1623–1627.

Gopnick, A., Meltzoff, A. and Kuhl, P. (2001). *How Babies Think: The Science of Childhood.* London: Phoenix.

Greenough, W.T., Black, J.E. and Wallace, C.S. (1987). Experience and brain development. Child Development. *PubMed, 58, 3,* 539–59.

Hamilton, J. (2014). The forgotten childhood: why early memories fade. Available at: www.npr.org/player/v2/mediaPlayer.html?action=1&t=1&islist=false&id=299189442&m=300617934 (accessed 27.9.14).

Kerlinger, F.N. (1970). *Foundations of Behavioural Research,* 3rd edn. New York: Holt, Reinhart & Winston.

Kokkinaki, T. and Vasdekis, V.G.S. (2015). Comparing emotional coordination in early spontaneous mother–infant and father–infant interactions. *European Journal of Developmental Psychology, 12, 1,* 69–84.

Lamm, C. and Majdandzic, J. (2014). The role of shared neural activations, mirror neurons, and morality in empathy – a critical comment. Available at: www.sciencedirect.com/science/article/pii/S0168010214002314 (accessed 20.10.14).

Malaguzzi, L. (1993). For an education based on relationships (trans. L. Gandini). *Young Children, November,* 9–12. Available at: https://reggioalliance.org/downloads/malaguzziyoungchildren.pdf (accessed 12.4.15).

Maslow, A.H. (1943). A theory of human motivation. *Psychological Review, 50, 4,* 370–96.

Moon, C., Lagercrantz, J. and Kuhl, P.K. (2012). Language experienced in utero affects vowel perception after birth: a two-country study. *Acta Paediatrica, 102*, 156–60.

Muro, M., and Jeffrey, P. (2008). A critical review of the theory and application of social learning in participatory natural resource management. *Journal of Environmental Planning and Management, 51*, 325–44.

Nutbrown, C. (2012). Foundations for quality: The independent review of early education and childcare qualifications. Final Report. London: Department for Education. Available at: www.gov.uk/government/uploads/system/uploads/attachment_data/file/175463/Nutbrown-Review.pdf (accessed 11.4.15).

Ofsted (2014). Raising standards improving lives: The report of Her Majesty's Chief Inspector of Education, Children's Services and Skills Early Years. Available at: http://www.gov.uk/government/uploads/system/uploads/attachment_data/file/386504/Ofsted_Early_Years_Annual_Report_201213.pdf (accessed 06.07.2015).

Pashler, H., McDaniel, M., Rohrer, D. and Bjork, R. (2008). Learning styles. Concepts and Evidence. *Psychological science in the public interest, 9, 3*, 105–119.

Peterson, C.C., Wellman, H.M. and Slaughter, V. (2012). The mind behind the message: advancing theory of mind scales for typically developing children, and those with deafness, autism, or Apergers Syndrome. *Child Development, 83, 2*, 469–485.

Piaget, J.P. (1952). *The Origins of Intelligence in Children*. New York: International Universities Press.

Piaget, J.P. (1970). *Science of Education and the Psychology of the Child*. New York: Orion.

Popper, K. (1976). *Logik der Forschung*, 6th edn. Tübingen: Mohr.

Reggio Children (2010). The Reggio Emilia approach. Available at: www.reggiochildren.it/identita/reggio-emilia-approach/?lang=en (accessed 12.4.15).

Reiner, C. and Willingham, D. (2010). The myth of learning styles. *Change, The magazine of higher learning,* September–October.

Robson, S. (2012). *Developing, Thinking and Understanding in Young Children*, 2nd edn. London and New York: Routledge.

Rodriguez, E.T. and Tamis-LeMonda, C.S. (2011). Trajectories of the home learning environment across the first 5 years: associations with children's vocabulary and literacy skills at prekindergarten. *Child Development, 82, 4*, 1058–75. Available at: https://steinhardt.nyu.edu/scmsAdmin/uploads/006/861/Rodriguez,%20E.,%20%26%20Tamis-LeMonda,%20C.,%20Child%20Dev,%202011.pdf (accessed 11.4.15).

Rodriguez, E.T., Tamis-LeMonda, C.S., Spellmann, M.E., Pan, B.A., Raikes, H., Lugo-Gil, J. and Luze, G. (2009). The formative role of home literacy experiences across the first three years of life in children from low-income families. *Journal of Applied Developmental Psychology, 30*, 677–694.

Rose, C. (1987). Accelerated learning. Available at: http://www.upb.pitt.edu/uploadedFiles/Learning%20Styles%20Inventory.pdf (accessed 21.04.15).

Salmaso, N., Jablonsja, B., Scafadi, J., Vaccarion, F.M. and Gallo, V. (2014). Neurobiology of premature brain injury. *Nature Neuroscience, 17*, 341–346.

Shonkoff, J.P., Garner, A.S., Siegel, B.S., Dobbins, M.I., Earls, M.F., McGuinn, L., Pascoe, J. and Wood, D.L. (2012). The lifelong effects of early childhood adversity and toxic stress. *Pediatrics, 129, 1, 1*, e232–e246.

Snow, C.E., Porche, M.V., Tabors, P.O and Harris, S.R. (2007). *Is Literacy Enough? Pathways to Academic Success for Adolescents*. Baltimore, MD: Brookes.

Stiles, J. and Jernigan, T. (2010). The basics of brain development. *Neuropsychology Review, 20, 4,* 327–48.

Tickell, C. (2011). *The Early Years: Foundations for Life, Health and Learning*. London: DfE. Available at: www.gov.uk/government/uploads/system/uploads/attachment_data/file/180919/DFE-00177-2011.pdf (accessed 11.4.15).

Thompson, M. (2010). *Understand Philosophy*. London: Teach Yourself.

Vansieleghem, N. and Kennedy, D. (2011). What is philosophy *for* children, what is philosophy *with* children – after Matthew Lipman? *Journal of Philosophy of Education, Special Issue: Philosophy for Children in Transition: Problems and Prospects, 45, 2,* 171–82.

Weinberg, D. (2009). Using learning styles for more effective teaching. The Association of Pet Dog Trainers, Lexington, KY. *The APDT Chronicle of the Dog,* November/December 2009. Available at: www.mydoghasclass.com/docs/resource-list/Weinberg_ND09.pdf (accessed 11.4.15).

Woollard, J. (2010). *Psychology for the Classroom: Behaviourism*. Oxford: Routledge.

Want to learn more about this Chapter?
Visit the companion website at **https://study.sagepub.com/grayandmacblain2e** to gain open access to selected SAGE journal articles, author podcasts and weblinks to help further your study.

3

THE FOUNDING FATHERS AND PHILOSOPHIES OF LEARNING

This chapter aims to:

- explore the work of key philosophers and theorists who have influenced thinking and practice in the field of Early Years education and practice
- examine the work of these philosophers and theorists within the social and historical contexts in which they developed their ideas.

Our understanding of how children think and how they experience the worlds in which they live is limited. For this reason, we need to engage with different and creative ways of seeking to capture, and then understand and explain their learning (Hunter and Walsh, 2014; Long et al., 2012; Marsh and Bishop, 2014; Walsh et al., 2011). How, for example, do we begin to understand the thoughts expressed below by the philosopher Jean-Paul Sartre who lost his father when he was still only a very young child:

> Jean-Baptiste's death was the great event of my life: it returned my mother to her chains and it gave me my freedom … Dying is not everything: you have to die in time. Later on, I felt guilty; a sensitive orphan blames himself: his parents, offended by the sight of him, have retired to their flats in the sky. But I was delighted: my unhappy condition imposed respect and established my importance; I numbered my mourning among my virtues. (1967, p. 15)

How can a child be 'delighted' following his father's death, how can bereavement 'impose respect' and how can mourning be considered a virtue? Why, over time, did Jean-Paul's feelings and emotions turn from feelings of freedom and self-importance to feelings of guilt?

How we view childhood and the manner in which young children are best educated and supported in their development will change radically even in the next few decades (MacBlain, 2014). Much of our current thinking is informed by what has been written in the past and is shaped daily by the ever-shifting world in which we live (MacBlain et al., 2015; Zwozdiak-Myers, 2007). Indeed, it has been suggested that it is only in the last fifty years or so that we have really begun to properly understand childhood and child development in any meaningful and measured way (Corsaro, 2014). There is still so much that we do not know and so much we still need to learn. For this reason, it is essential that all of us who work with children, and who study their development, maintain a strong sense of critical reflection and openness in how we view child development and education as well as our own professional practice.

Whilst we are guided by the thinking and the theories and philosophies of those notable individuals who have written about children over the centuries, we are also influenced by the events which structure our own lives and perceptions, and perhaps most importantly by the ever-shifting and rapidly changing shape of the world around us. Our understanding, therefore, and our interpretations of how children's lives become structured by their experiences and by the types of play they engage in are fundamental. Equally important are the manner in which they use their imaginations and come to internalize ideas about love and morality, both of which are central to their learning and to their social and emotional development (Colverd and Hodgkin, 2011; Gopnick, 2009; Wood, 2013). Much of what we do, think and practise has its roots in the work of those philosophers and thinkers who, in many ways, have altered the course of education and learning not only in the UK but across the globe. Indeed, it is largely because of their ideas and their own unique developed practice that we now work with children in the way we do. In order to properly understand these key figures and their views, however, it is important to say something of the events that shaped their own lives, in particular their early lives and the world they were born into.

JOHN LOCKE (1632–1704)

John Locke is considered by many to be one of England's most enlightened thinkers. Locke was born into a world where 'wife beating' was considered to be the legal right of a husband, where a woman's entire belongings became the property of her husband following marriage, and where women and children were expected by society to be unwavering in their obedience to their husbands and fathers. King Charles I was still relatively new to the throne of England, having begun his rule as monarch in 1629. In fact, John Locke was to live through the beheading of King Charles, the Civil War in England, Cromwell's Protectorate from 1654 to 1658, the Restoration of King Charles II in 1659, the reigns of King James II and then William and Mary and, finally, the reign of Queen Anne.

Locke published *Some Thoughts Concerning Education* in 1693, in which he set out his philosophy of education. His views on education were radical for the time and though he wrote about these nearly 400 years ago, they continue to influence the way we think about the education and rearing of children today. Locke was a truly influential thinker and he belongs to that group of English philosophers known as the *empiricists* who believed that our knowledge and understanding of the world comes about through 'sensory experience'.

This view lies very much at the heart of what we now know as the 'sciences', at the root of which lies the concept of 'empirical thinking' whereby we observe, acquire and quantify data. Closely linked to this view was Locke's strongly held belief that individuals should use their own reason to explore what is true and what is not, as opposed to simply accepting what they are told by those in authority. He further rejected the place of superstition in the thinking of individuals.

Locke held the view that when individuals are born they begin life as a 'blank slate' (often referred to as *tabula rasa*) upon which is written their life experiences gained through the senses. This was, Locke believed, the very essence of learning and the basis for the acquisition of knowledge. In more recent years, particularly during the post-war years, this empirical view that we could understand experience through the observation and measurement of behaviours, which are in response to external sensory stimuli, grew in strength, especially within the field of psychology, and came to underpin that branch of psychology known as the 'behaviourist tradition'. Not only did this philosophy of empiricism offer a theory, it also offered psychology and methodology, at the core of which was the observation and recording of behaviours (Gross, 1992; Smith et al., 2011). This is quite different from the nativist view, which saw individuals as inheriting abilities. Here, we can see quite clearly the link between philosophy and theory.

Exercise

What benefits can Early Years practitioners gain from observing and recording the behaviours of young children and how reliable can their interpretations of these observations be?

Locke saw the purpose of education as that of instilling within individuals a strong sense of virtue: 'I place virtue as the first and most necessary of those endowments that belong to a man or a gentleman' (2001, p. 148). Locke also placed great emphasis upon the importance of learning how to learn. Here, it is possible to see just how far ahead of his time he was, as in recent decades the emphasis that has been placed upon learning how to learn and upon learning styles has grown dramatically. In addition to this emphasis upon employing thinking in a different and more structural manner, Locke also placed considerable emphasis upon the importance of language and communication, and perhaps most interestingly, given the nature of society at the time, the idea that learning should be enjoyable. In many respects, we can argue that John Locke laid down the building blocks for future thinking around the importance of play and the development of language. In doing so, he prepared the way for others to address the importance of education and learning in young children.

JEAN-JACQUES ROUSSEAU (1712–78)

Born in Geneva in 1712, it is worth considering that perhaps one of the most defining moments of Jean-Jacques Rousseau's life was the death of his mother some nine days after giving birth to him. This must have had a great influence upon Rousseau and upon his views regarding early childhood and parenting. Later, at the age of 10, Rousseau's father moved away and left Jean-Jacques to be reared by relatives. Shortly after leaving, his father remarried and the young Rousseau saw very little of him from that time on. This was clearly a second major loss experienced by the young Rousseau. Such events in the life of any young child will be central to the way in which they go about constructing the world in which they live. It can be suggested that much of Rousseau's childhood would have been unhappy due to the death of his mother and the subsequent loss of his father. It should also be recognized that Rousseau was born into a world where the French revolution had not yet taken place and it was less than fifty years earlier, in 1665, that the Great Plague had hit London, leaving behind it such incredible devastation and grief.

At the very core of Rousseau's philosophy of education is the view that all human beings are born 'good'. Rousseau believed, as many of his time did, that individuals inherit much of what would contribute to their potential make-up. Whilst he held the view that individuals inherit the propensity to be good, he also saw the societies within which individuals grow up as being agents of potential perversion. Such a view can still be found today, with individuals in some quarters emphasizing the adverse impact on children of such factors as elements of the media, materialism and an exaggerated notion of rights without responsibilities. Rousseau chose to develop his ideas about life and education through the publication of his book *Emile* (1911), in which he introduced the reader to the character of a young boy. In the book, Emile begins to be introduced to lessons in morality whilst in infanthood. These lessons are then extended through adolescence and into adulthood whilst all the time being overseen by a tutor who, Rousseau proposed, crucially offers direction and guidance.

Rousseau saw education as the means by which the natural make-up of individuals could be developed to not only improve them but also to improve society through the manner in which individuals engage with one another. For Rousseau, the importance of developing the character of individuals was a fundamental goal of those education processes that took place in schools. This should not, he felt, be overshadowed by an emphasis upon the giving and receiving of information as characterized by so many schools at the time. Here, we can draw similarities with the recent emphasis that governments in the UK have placed upon citizenship, and the expectations made upon Early Years practitioners and teachers to develop positive values within the children they manage.

For Rousseau, the role of tutor was of the upmost importance and required the shaping of those environments within which the young person is introduced to learning. In this way, Rousseau suggested that growing children acquire increased awareness of the world around them, but more particularly, they increase their understanding of such essentials as humility, honesty and dishonesty, and respect for themselves and for others. Rousseau saw the primary function of education as being *'l'art de former des homes'* or the art of forming men. Interestingly, Rousseau saw the role of the tutor as being that of guiding the child in such a way that the child learns the difference between right and wrong, not as a result of being punished, as was common at the time, but as a result of understanding the consequences of their actions. Here, again, we can see strong similarities with the thinking of modern educationalists in the UK who, in the 1970s and 1980s, argued for the banning of all physical punishment in schools and the promotion amongst growing children of self-awareness and the feelings of others. Such a view is the norm now in all pre-school, primary and post-primary education. At the time that Rousseau lived, however, it was very much not the case. Indeed, it was generally accepted by those living at that time that all individuals, though essentially 'good', were in fact born into the world with impulses, drives and needs, which lay beneath their 'goodness' and which could, if not harnessed, lead to, amongst other things, 'wickedness'. Rousseau, therefore, saw a primary function of the tutor, or teacher, as being that of channelling these impulses and drives, and giving some form of positive expression to them.

Rousseau is recognized as being one of the first proponents of developmental education. Indeed, he considered that individuals progress through a number of stages, the first being that of birth to around 12 years of age. It was during this stage, Rousseau believed, that the child was influenced and directed in their thinking and actions, and by their emotions and impulses. The next stage takes the child to 16 when, Rousseau considered, reason begins to take over from emotions. After the age of 16, the child moves through to adulthood.

Rousseau's views can be considered as revolutionary for the time and we see his notion of stages being echoed in the work of more recent theorists such as Jean Piaget and Eric Erikson. Rousseau's philosophies have also much in common with, amongst others, those of Maria Montessori and John Dewey who will be referred to later. It is useful at this point to now turn to the work of one further key figure who was born towards the end of Rousseau's life and whose influence upon the way we work with young children has lasted for over 150 years, and is even currently experiencing something of a revival (Miller and Pound, 2011, p. 64).

FRIEDRICH FROEBEL (1782–1852)

Froebel (also spelled Fröbel) was born in 1782 in Oberweißach in what is now Germany, and experienced the death of his mother some nine months after his birth. This loss affected him deeply and must certainly have had an impact on the way he perceived childhood. In the years following his birth, he received little comfort and it was not until 1792 when he was some 10 years of age that he experienced a more caring environment when he went to live with an uncle who was a caring and affectionate man. In 1818, he married Wilhelmine who then died in 1839 leaving no children. Friedrich remarried some years later, to Louise in 1851. As a young man, Froebel was impulsive and after trying a number of jobs he joined a school in Frankfurt as a teacher under the direction of Anton Gruner who had organized his school along the principles set out by Johann Pestalozzi, a Swiss educator and reformer who advocated progressive methods in teaching. It was whilst working at this school that Froebel realized his desire to be a teacher, and in 1816 he opened his own school. In 1826, he published *On the Education of Man*, which set out his philosophy and the methods he had used in his own school. In 1831, he was invited by the Swiss government to become involved in the training of teachers working with young children. Later, in 1837, he opened a school for very young children, which he renamed, after some time, '*kindergarten*'.

Froebel was one of the most influential thinkers of his time and his philosophy of education continues to influence practice today. Froebel viewed play as central to the education of children and their future development and though most, if not all, practitioners working with young children today would see this as a given, it was not always the case. Froebel believed passionately in the importance of children expressing themselves through their own individual play as well as through play with others. This view, however, stood in marked contrast to much of the practice of the time when many young children found themselves in schools being unhappily 'drilled' and regularly 'chastised' by teachers. Froebel, it can be suggested, liberated the notion of play and made it central to the education of young children. Some thirty years ago, Tizard and Hughes commented that:

> [t]he value of learning through play was first put forward by the German educationalist Friedrich Froebel ... The kindergarten and nursery school movement which developed from his writings freed young children from the tyranny of sitting in rows chanting and writing ABC. (1984, p. 4)

Now consider, for example, the opening lines of Charles Dickens's novel *Hard Times,* first published in 1854, two years after Froebel's death, where the fictional headmaster of a school in the north of England is setting out his own philosophy of education:

> Now, what I want is, Facts. Teach these boys and girls nothing but Facts. Facts alone are wanted in life. Plant nothing else, and root out everything else. You can only form the minds of reasoning animals upon Facts: nothing else will ever be of service to them. This is the principle on which I bring up my own children, and this is the principle on which I bring up these children. Stick to Facts, Sir! (p. 1)

Though the headmaster and school were fictional, Dickens was, nevertheless, attempting to draw to public attention, and to policy and decision makers, the scandalous nature of much of the teaching and learning that took place in schools at this time. Years later, the renowned academic, philosopher and theologian C.S. Lewis (author of the *Chronicles of Narnia*) was also able to speak in less than positive terms about how dreadful aspects of his own early education were. Lewis's biographer A.N. Wilson has since written:

> C.S. Lewis remained obsessed by Wynyard [Lewis' preparatory school] for the rest of his life. Although he spent only eighteen months as a pupil there, he devoted nearly a tenth of his autobiography to describing it, in the most lurid terms, as a 'concentration camp'. (1991, p. 23)

Unlike many educators and thinkers of his time, Froebel held the view that individuals were born creative and, through their industry and active belief in God, developed as good members of society. In this way, he argued, they came to better understand the world in which they lived. It was because of his belief in the importance of play that Froebel set about creating specialized educational 'materials' to be used by children in their early education. Indeed, one of the many legacies left by Froebel to educators were these 'materials' or 'gifts' as he, himself, called them. These 'gifts' included, for example, shapes such as spheres and blocks and were purposefully used to assist in the process of stimulating the thinking and learning of young children (it is possible to view some of these 'gifts' in the Froebel College at Roehampton University). Froebel believed that being active was very important for children. He referred to the activities he developed for children as 'occupations'. Froebel also recognized and understood the value of music in the education of young children and the value of singing to accompany play. His beliefs are now taken as accepted by many practitioners working with young children.

JOHN DEWEY (1859–1952)

What is remarkable about John Dewey is the span of history through which he lived. Born in America some two years before the outbreak of the American Civil War, and in the same year as the infamous American outlaw Billy the Kid and the French artist Seurat, and the first publication of Charles Dickens's novel *A Tale of Two Cities*, his life ended seven years after the end of the Second World War and just eight years before the 'swinging sixties' exploded with the music of Elvis Presley, the Beatles and Bob Dylan. Dewey was born into a world where Queen Victoria ruled the British Empire, where British veterans were coming to terms with their recent experiences of war in the Crimea and the Charge of the Light Brigade, and the British nation was applauding the work of Florence Nightingale. In a sense, he bridged the gap between the old and the modern. Dewey grew up and lived in an America where there were extreme racial tensions in parts of the country and where children in some states were not accorded the same civil and human rights as others because of their colour.

It is important to consider the work of John Dewey in greater depth because of the controversial nature of his ideas and because of the significant influence he has had on educational practice in the past 50 years, and which continues even today. Perhaps a good starting point for considering the influence that John Dewey has had on the education system can be found in the words of the American philosopher Nell Noddings (2005), cited in Pring:

> not only has he [Dewey] been hailed as the savior of American education by those who welcome greater involvement of students in their own planning and activity [but also] he has been called 'worse than Hitler' by some who felt that he infected schools with epistemological and moral relativism and substituted socialization for true education. (2007, p. 3)

Pring also cites, as part of his own experience in relation to the influence of Dewey, the following incident:

Indeed, when I came to Oxford in 1989, I was seated at dinner next to Lord Keith Joseph, who had been Secretary of State for Education under Prime Minister Margaret Thatcher. He accused me of being responsible for all the problems in our schools – because I had introduced teachers to John Dewey. (2007, p. 3)

It must be recognized at the outset that Dewey was writing at a time when much of the learning and teaching that took place in schools was of a very formal nature. Pre-school education was ill-understood and much of Early Years practice that we now take for granted simply did not exist. It should also be remembered that as Dewey was growing up, and reflecting upon his own experiences of education and how children could be educated, that society across the emerging industrialized world was extraordinarily varied. In contrast to the experiences of his early life in the USA, there persisted across the Atlantic in Victorian England, for example, an infamous practice known as 'baby farming'.

Due to there being no reliable means of contraception at the time, many young women in Victorian England, often from 'good' families, found themselves giving birth to children outside of wedlock. Such births resulted most frequently in a great deal of social stigma. Any form of abortion, which at the time was illegal, had its dangers and all too frequently resulted in death. Mothers or fathers who abandoned their offspring at this time were also subject to severe punishment by the law. Because of the harsh penalties meted out by Victorian courts, many of these mothers 'farmed' out their young children to other families for what was then a sizeable sum of money, usually around £10–£20. There were no regular adoption services during this period and the practice of 'farming' out children became widely practised. Some of the women who took on these children were quite unscrupulous and many of these children became lost to their parents. Amongst these 'baby farmers' were some women who maltreated the children placed in their care, with some even murdering them and a small number being identified as serial killers. 'Baby farmers' who were caught murdering their children faced the death penalty and were hanged. One such case was that of Selina Wedge, who was hanged on 15 August 1878 at Bodmin in the county of Cornwall following the murder of her illegitimate son. At the time of Selina Wedge's execution, Dewey would have been around 19 years of age, Montessori about 8 years of age, and Steiner about 17 years of age.

Dewey and education

Dewey has become associated in the minds of many with the notion of *child-centered education*. At the heart of Dewey's philosophy of education lies the importance of understanding children's experiences (MacBlain, 2014). It should be noted, however, that a common misunderstanding of Dewey's philosophy is that he supported free, student-led education; on the contrary, he believed strongly that the education of children required clear structure. Dewey also believed that children needed support and direction in structuring their own learning in order to gain the maximum benefit. Like many philosophers and theorists before and after him, Dewey was an exponent of the view that educators must acknowledge the uniqueness of each individual child. This uniqueness, Dewey believed, was formed genetically as well as experientially. Arguably, Dewey was ahead of his time in that he believed that each child engaged with the curriculum offered by their schools in qualitatively different ways. Because of this, he argued that the curriculum should take account of and allow for these differences. Dewey was also an exponent of the view that education should be seen as having a wider social purpose: that of preparing children to become effective members of their society and to be valued by their societies. Indeed, Dewey saw education and democracy as being intrinsically linked.

Exercise

To what extent should Early Years practitioners engage in preparing young children to be 'good' citizens in the future, and to what extent should they be expected to 'teach' behaviour?

Central to Dewey's philosophy of education were his views drawn from his Laboratory School where he could subject his ideas and theoretical position to scrutiny and analysis (Dewey started Laboratory Schools in 1896 in Chicago, with children being admitted from nursery to the 12th grade). Pring offers the following:

> [B]ehind Dewey's experimental school was a particular view of the normal young learner: someone who is curious and interested, but whose curiosity and interests had been sapped by modes of learning which took no account of that *interest* in learning. (2007, p. 16)

Dewey espoused two important notions. First, schools should be seen as communities in themselves, and second, educators cannot alter the past experiences of children. This also applies to those working in Early Years settings. Dewey argued that educators must deal with the present and the future. By engaging in the process of understanding the past experiences of their pupils, they can, however, be more informed and more cognizant of how to effect change over what the pupil will learn and in what way it is directly relevant to each pupil. Pring offers a summary of Dewey's views:

First, the school should be an extension of the home and the community ... Second ... the school should value manual and practical activity ... Third, the interests of young people were to be treated as of importance in their own right, not simply as something that can be harnessed to the aims of the teacher for the purpose of motivating them to do things that they are not really interested in ... Fourth ... their (*school subjects*) value lies in their usefulness ... Fifth, a young person whose interests are taken seriously and whose teacher seeks to develop those interests ... will be disciplined by the pursuit of those interests – making the regime of externally imposed discipline irrelevant. (2007, pp. 15–17)

Taking Dewey's views into account, then, it can be argued that we all learn from what we do. In the case of young children, their experiences are of great immediate value in that they will affect future experiences and learning. For Dewey, however, experiences have no attached value in themselves. Rather, it is what each individual draws from the experience that is important, and no two individuals will encounter an experience in exactly the same way. What will be beneficial for one person might be devastating for another. We now turn to a figure who has, some would argue, dominated a great deal of our thinking and practice in the area of Early Years.

Weblink

Readers should take time to view the following excellent YouTube video link entitled *Nursery School* (1953), which offers insights into the nature of nursery education back in the 1950s. Available at: www.youtube.com/watch?v=lx3DtrPWpmo (accessed 11.4.15).

Readers may wish to consider some of the issues relating to differences in expectations of boys and girls at the time.

MARIA MONTESSORI (1870–1952)

Maria Montessori is a name that has universal meaning, and she is recognized as being a hugely creative and influential figure in the world of Early Years education. Born in 1870 in Italy, she was the first of her gender to become a medical doctor. Maria was also a single parent. At the age of 13 she attended a single-sex school for boys with the plan of becoming an engineer. Maria was deeply interested in the needs of children with learning difficulties, what we now refer to as 'special educational needs'. Maria had considerable success with these children who at the time were considered uneducable. She was appointed Director of the Scuola Ortofrenica, which was one of a number of institutions in Italy that looked after those with mental health problems.

Montessori viewed the course of development in young children as being guided by directives that are already located within the child's nature (Feez, 2010). The Montessori teacher, therefore, places great emphasis upon the environment in which the child learns. In a sense, the teacher becomes the guardian of that environment and, by altering it, the teacher enables the child to develop at their natural pace, thus allowing their creativity to flourish and their learning to be supported.

Montessori introduced the notion of the *Casa dei Bambini,* or Children's House, in which the teacher created an environment that offered stimulation and where children were free to develop their learning in a natural and individualized way. Montessori strongly advocated the importance of young children learning through their senses. She also considered it fundamental to the education process that children should take responsibility for their own learning. To assist them in this, Montessori took the initiative of designing the furniture within her Children's House so that it was of a suitable size for the children, a factor we nowadays take for granted.

At the heart of the Montessori Method lies the notion of 'Planes', or stages, that children pass through on their learning journey. It is during the first 'Plane' that the child experiences significant levels of change in the areas of physical, social and emotional development. Here, the infant starts to take their first steps, use their first words and engage with others. By the time they are ready to move to the next Plane, they can run, jump and climb, and engage in conversation with others using complex and sophisticated language structures and vocabulary. They are beginning to understand the feelings of others and adapt their own behaviours and actions in accordance with these. In addition, they are learning to interact with those around them, make friendships and adapt to the complexities of social interaction outside of their families. It is during this first Plane that children also develop their abilities in such important areas as memory, information processing, and expressive and receptive language, and it is during this Plane that adults working with young children typically observe the greatest steps in learning taking place. Within the first Plane, Montessori identified what she termed 11 'sensitive' periods: movement; language; small objects; order; music; grace and courtesy; refinement of the senses; writing fascination; reading; spatial relationships; and mathematics. These will be discussed more fully in Chapter 9.

One interesting element of Montessori's original thinking, however, is her lack of enthusiasm for pretend and imaginative play, which, given her emphasis upon child-centred education and early development, may appear surprising. In fact, Montessori saw limited value in this type of play, preferring, instead, to place greater emphasis upon the value of practical activities: 'She preferred to encourage children actually to serve meals, for example, and to clear up around the house themselves, rather than play at mealtimes in a "play house"' (Smith et al., 2011, p. 230).

Exercise

At the heart of the Montessori method lies the notion of 'Planes', or stages. How useful is it to think of children's development in terms of stages?

Having looked at key elements underpinning the ideas of Maria Montessori, we now turn to those of Rudolf Steiner who, like Montessori, has left an enormous legacy, which continues to guide the thinking and practice of many practitioners working with young children today.

Weblink

Readers should take time to view the YouTube video link *Early Childhood Education, Froebel and Montessori*, which offers an interesting account of the works and ideas of Friedrich Froebel and Maria Montessori. Available at: www.youtube.com/watch?v=OLcKTB_aAFs (accessed 11.4.15).

RUDOLF STEINER (1861–1925)

Rudolf Steiner was born in what is now part of Croatia and was then part of the Austro-Hungarian Empire. He was born in February 1861, two years after the birth of John Dewey, and died in 1925. Steiner was accomplished in many areas; he was a very competent linguist, mathematician, architect, scientist and classical scholar. Throughout his life, Steiner remained true to his convictions that a fundamental aim of education was to develop the potential of children. It is clear that Steiner's philosophy and his activities and efforts in the field of education have had a major impact upon practitioners, writers and academics today.

There are currently over 1,000 Steiner schools and over 2,000 Early Years establishments across the world. Though the original philosophy remains constant, many Steiner schools throughout the world have evolved in different ways, which, in itself, reflects the highly creative and scholarly approach originally adopted by Steiner himself. Steiner founded his first school in the city of Stuttgart following an invitation to do so from a leading industrialist Emil Molt, owner of the Waldorf-Astoria cigarette factory. The purpose of opening the school was to educate the children of those who worked in the factory, hence the legacy by which some Steiner schools are still referred to as *Steiner Waldorf* schools. This school was built upon progressive views of education and was a huge success. Steiner involved himself in all aspects of the organization of this school and even engaged in the training of the teachers.

Steiner believed that the function of education was to respond to the changing needs of children, and not only their physical needs but, more importantly, their cognitive and emotional needs (Goddard Blythe, 2008, cited in Miller and Pound, 2011). Steiner schools do not have a head teacher and teachers share the responsibilities.

Key points that underpin the Steiner philosophy are as follows. In the first years of a child's education and up to age 7, there is significant emphasis placed upon play, art and drawing, upon the natural world of the child, and upon links between art and science. Prior to age 7, children are not formally taught to read, the idea being that children will learn to read more effectively if they have developed emotionally and socially. Children are introduced to reading and writing as well as mathematics later than children in other schools. The belief is that children, when older, will be more mature and will acquire formal literacy and numeracy more easily and with less potential stress. Interestingly, the Steiner philosophy holds that children should be taught to write before being taught to read. Once again, it is worth drawing comparisons between this philosophy and current practice in the UK, which advocates the learning of phonics by children when they first enter school at around the age of 5.

Children are encouraged to sing each day and to learn to play musical instruments. They are also introduced to the idea of making their own lesson books, which they write and illustrate. Assessment of children is carried out mainly through observation by the teacher, who focuses upon emotional and social aspects as well as academic progress. The child, where possible, keeps the same teacher until the secondary stage, thereby building upon the importance of relationships and the teacher's knowledge of the child's emotional and social development.

Teachers working in Steiner settings use a 'narrative' approach to learning, which places particular emphasis upon listening and involves young children in the internal representation of characters and the development of imagination. Having been introduced to material in the form of a story on a given day, for example, the children are required to revisit the content on the following day and retell it, the aim being to improve spoken language and memory. When these processes of listening and recalling are worked through, the children can then write these down. Again, it is worth considering how valuable this process can be in our modern society when many children come to school with poor listening skills, delayed language and poor vocabulary (Palmer, 2014; Zwozdiak-Myers, 2007).

In part, Steiner's emphasis upon the individuality of education came about because of his own extensive work with individual children. It is interesting to make comparisons with current practice in the majority of developed countries whereby the needs of individual children, especially those with learning difficulties, have become central to many teaching programmes and practice. It is also interesting to make comparisons with the nature of the curricula currently offered in state schools in the UK and the degree of emphasis (or not) that is placed upon creativity and independent learning.

RACHEL MCMILLAN (1859–1917) AND MARGARET MCMILLAN (1860–1931)

Rachel McMillan was born on 25 March 1859 in New York, USA. Her sister Margaret was born on 20 July 1860. Rachel and Margaret's parents had emigrated from Scotland some years before in 1840. Sadly, their father James died, along with their sister Elizabeth, in 1865 when Margaret was aged just 5. Their mother then returned to Scotland, taking her two daughters with her. Some years later in 1877, their mother also died, leaving the two girls without any parents; Margaret was only 17. Following the death of their grandmother in 1888, Rachel moved to London to be closer to Margaret. Much of London at this time was characterized by poverty, poor sanitation and a need for social reform. In fact, it was during the year that Rachel moved to London that the infamous murderer Jack the Ripper became linked to five murders. It was in 1899 that school attendance became compulsory and it was into this London that both sisters threw themselves with zeal, enthusiasm and a strong vision of how young children should be educated.

Following a sustained campaign, the McMillan sisters achieved the successful introduction of free school meals for children, following the passing of the Provision of School Meals Act in 1906. The two sisters were also responsible for introducing regular medical inspections of school-aged children with the first clinic being opened in 1908. It must be remembered that at this time there was exceptional poverty in England, and especially in the cities. London at this time contained many slum areas where infant mortality was extremely high and the standard of living extremely low. In 1841, for example, Londoners could, on average, expect to live until the age of 35. Seventy years later, in 1911, they could, on average, expect to live until they were 50 (Hall, 1998, p. 695). Many houses had little sanitation and families were crowded into tiny areas within houses, often sharing only single rooms. Most individuals of the time who died did so because of infectious diseases, with many very young babies dying due to diarrhoea caused by disease-carrying flies. It is estimated (Horn, 1997) that in the first half of the nineteenth century around 30,000 homeless children frequented the streets of London, often impoverished, undernourished and sleeping rough. In the previous decades, between 1831 and 1866, some 140,000 individuals died from cholera.

Like Montessori and others, the McMillan sisters believed that the first years of a child's life were extremely important for future development. In fact, they founded what is now known as the *Nursery School Movement*. In many respects, they can be viewed as social reformers. They also placed great emphasis upon the importance of open-air learning, which could be seen as a precursor to the current emphasis placed by many Early Years practitioners upon playing out doors and, more recently, 'Forest Schools'. It should be remembered, however, that when the McMillan sisters encouraged outdoor learning, they were working largely with children from very poor and disadvantaged backgrounds. Nowadays, it is considered wholly appropriate for children to play outside. In fact, playing outside is viewed by most Early Years practitioners to be an important part of the child's curriculum. In past decades, however, this was not always the case as playing outside was often seen as merely a 'break' from within-class activities.

In 1904, Margaret published *Education through the Imagination*, in which she argued against the commonly held notion of the time that imagination was of little use to children in their learning. She argued, in fact, that imagination was very important and should be a key element in the education of children and their learning. Moreover, she considered it to be an important element for the betterment of society. This is, of course, a view widely held by many today. The McMillan sisters also involved the young children in their nurseries in caring for animals and plants as a way of instilling within them the values of caring for themselves and for others. Margaret was influential in the training of teachers and, some years after the death of her sister, she founded the Rachel McMillan College in 1930 because she strongly believed in the importance of proper training for those working in nurseries.

 ## Summary

This chapter has examined a range of philosophies that have influenced the way in which we view young children and their social, emotional and cognitive abilities and potential. Particular consideration was given to the historical context within which each philosophy was founded and the nature of society at the time. Whilst not all philosophers agree with each other, they nevertheless all offer insights into how we think about children and their development. They set the scene for us to explore and to question ourselves and others about what are effective and meaningful ways of working with young children. This is now more important than ever as the world in which we live is changing more quickly than ever before.

RECOMMENDED READING

Feez, S. (2010). *Montessori and Early Childhood*. London: Sage.

A detailed and readable text, which offers a comprehensive account of Montessori's contribution to our understanding of children's development.

Johnson, J. (2010). *Positive and Trusting Relationships with Children in Early Years Settings*. Exeter: Learning Matters.

A comprehensive, readable and visual text offering the student and practitioner a great deal of relevant knowledge.

Whitebread, D. (2012). *Developmental Psychology and Early Childhood Education*. London: Sage.

A comprehensive and accessible text, which offers readers substantial insights into the application of psychology in young children's learning and development.

REFERENCES

Colverd, S. and Hodgkin, B. (2011). *Developing Emotional Intelligence in the Primary School*. London: Routledge.

Corsaro, W. (2014). *The Sociology of Childhood*, 4th edn. London: Sage.

Dickens, C. (1854). *Hard Times*. London: Wordsworth.

Feez, S. (2010). *Montessori and Early Childhood*. London: Sage.

Froebel, F. (1826). *On the Education of Man*. Leipzig: Weinbach.

Goddard Blythe, S. (2008). *What Babies and Children Really Need*. Stroud: Hawthorn Press.

Gopnick, A. (2009). *The Philosophical Baby: What Children's Minds Tell Us about Truth, Love and the Meaning of Life*. London: The Bodley Head.

Gross, R. (1992). *Psychology: The Science of Mind and Behaviour*. London: Hodder & Stoughton.

Hall, P. (1998). *Cities in Civilization*. London: Weidenfeld & Nicolson.

Horn, P. (1997). *The Victorian Town Child*. Stroud: Sutton.

Hunter, T. and Walsh, G. (2014). From policy to practice? The reality of play in primary school classes in Northern Ireland. *International Journal of Early Years Education, 22, 1*, 19–36.

Locke, J. (2001 [1693]). *Some Thoughts Concerning Education*. New York: Harvard Classics. Available at: www.bartleby.com/37/1/ (accessed 11/4/15).

Long, L., McPhillips, T., Shevlin, M. and Smith, R. (2012). Utilising creative methodologies to elicit the views of young learners with additional needs in literacy. *Support for Learning, 27, 1*, 1–9.

MacBlain, S.F. (2014). *How Children Learn*. London: Sage.

MacBlain, S.F., Long, L. and Dunn, J. (2015). *Dyslexia, Literacy and Inclusion: Child-centred Perspectives*. London: Sage.

Marsh, J. and Bishop, J. (2014). "We're playing Jeremy Kyle"! Television talk shows in the playground. *Discourse: Studies in the Cultural Politics of Education, 35, 1,* 16–30.

McMillan, M. (1904). *Education through the Imagination.* London: Swann Sonnenschein.

Miller, L. and Pound, L. (2011). *Theories and Approaches to Learning in the Early Years.* London: Sage.

Palmer, S. (2014). *Toxic Childhood,* 2nd edn. London: Orion.

Pring, R. (2007). *John Dewey: A Philosopher of Education for Our Time?* London: Continuum.

Rousseau, J.J. (1911). *Emile.* London: Dent.

Sartre, J.P. (1967). *Words.* Harmondsworth: Penguin.

Smith, K.S., Cowie, H. and Blades, M. (2011). *Understanding Children's Development,* 5th edn. Oxford: Blackwell.

Tizard, B. and Hughes, M. (1984). *Young Children Learning: Talking and Thinking at Home and at School.* London: Fontana.

Walsh, G., Sproule, L. McGuinness, C. and Trew, K. (2011). Playful structure: a novel image of Early Years pedagogy for primary school classrooms. *Early Years, 31, 2,* 107–9.

Wilson, A.N. (1991). *C.S. Lewis: A Biography.* London: Flamingo.

Wood, E. (2013). *Play, Learning and the Early Childhood Curriculum,* 3rd edn. London: Sage.

Zwozdiak-Myers, P. (ed.) (2007). *Childhood and Youth Studies.* Exeter: Learning Matters.

Want to learn more about this Chapter?
Visit the companion website at **https://study.sagepub.com/grayandmacblain2e** to gain open access to selected SAGE journal articles, author podcasts and weblinks to help further your study.

4

CLASSICAL AND OPERANT CONDITIONING: THE EARLY YEARS EXPERIENCE

This chapter aims to:

- familiarize students with classical and operant conditioning learning theories
- illustrate these theories using practical examples
- highlight similarities and differences between early learning theories.

This chapter examines a number of influential learning theories developed within the behaviourist paradigm (also termed *behaviourism*) between the 1900s and 1950s. Terms used in this chapter may be unfamiliar to you, largely due to the paucity of textbooks within the social studies of childhood/early childhood studies stable offering a detailed discussion of the principles of behaviourism. Yet aspects of these theories continue to inform classroom practice. For example, you may have worked in settings that regularly employ a range of strategies to shape and maintain appropriate behaviour in young children and other strategies to discourage inappropriate behaviour. These strategies may include verbal praise, positive body language (smiling, nodding, thumbs up), visual timetables, star charts, timers, class behaviour charts and/or smiley-face stickers. You may also have heard practitioners talk about the need for children to learn that actions have consequences and will certainly have been alerted to the setting's behaviour management policy and your role in implementing it in a consistent way. The notion that actions have consequences is directly informed by behaviourism. Similarly, the requirement for Early Years providers to have a behaviour management policy (DfE, 2011) that promotes and encourages good behaviour reflects the central tenets of the behaviourist approach. In essence, the influence of the behaviourist approach continues to inform educational practice. Behaviourists share with John Locke (1632–1704) the belief that, at birth, the human mind is a blank slate (*tablua rasa*) and that behaviour is shaped and maintained by environmental cues. Though each theory offers a different interpretation of learning, they are predicated on the following assumptions:

- behaviour is the result of stimulus–response
- all behaviour is learnt from the environment
- external behaviour can be objectively measured
- all theory should be supported by testable data
- mental concepts (thinking, feelings and emotions) are irrelevant in trying to predict and control human behaviour
- there is no free will; this radical assumption is believed, to a greater or lesser extent, by individual theorists within the behaviourist family. Those who take this stance argue there is no difference in the way humans and animals learn. Consequently, the outcome of experiments originally conducted on animals are assumed to explain human behaviour.

The chapter begins with the work of Pavlov. Similar to other scientists (e.g. Wilhelm Roentgen's discovery of X-rays in 1895 and Marie Curie's work on radioactivity in 1898), Pavlov's learning theory was based on a serendipitous (unexpected but fortunate) finding that provided the platform for more complex and sophisticated theories of learning. Although his work is presented first, he was not a behaviourist. It was the American psychologist John Watson who founded and popularized behaviourism, and applied Pavlov's principles to his research with children.

Classical and operant conditioning are frequently confused. To support your learning, text boxes are included to highlight the key features of each theory, practical examples are offered, exercises are available and a comparative table (see Table 4.2 at the end of the chapter) is provided to highlight the similarities and differences of the presented theories.

IVAN PAVLOV AND CLASSICAL CONDITIONING

Ivan Pavlov (1849–1936)

A Russian physiologist, Pavlov was born on 14 September 1849 in the village of Ryazan. His father was a priest. Pavlov was the oldest of eleven children, six of whom died during childhood. He married and had three sons and a daughter. His life's work focused on identifying the link between digestion and salivation using dogs. His efforts were rewarded when he was awarded the Nobel Prize in Physiology or Medicine (1904) for his work on the underlying mechanisms in the digestive system in mammals. Quite by chance, Pavlov noticed that the dogs salivated when no food was presented. This led him to develop a theory of conditioned reflexes (explained in the body of this chapter). Pavlov's theory, termed *classical conditioning*, offered the first testable and verifiable account of how some forms of learning take place.

His theory has had a major influence on the fields of psychology and education.

Pavlov conducted a series of laboratory experiments into the relationship between salivation and digestion in dogs. The research involved cutting the dog's salivary glands and re-attaching them to the outside of the dog's cheek, where they were fixed to test tubes. Using this technique, Pavlov was able to accurately measure dog salivation before, during and after digestion. During his experiments, he noticed that the dogs drooled when a laboratory assistant entered the room. Observing the dogs' behaviour over time, Pavlov concluded that the dogs' drooling was their response to their expectation of being fed. Even when there was no food brought for the dogs, the mere sight of the laboratory assistants was enough to make the dogs drool. Pavlov termed this 'associated learning', meaning the dogs had built up an association between the laboratory assistant and food. Fascinated by this form of learning, Pavlov found that he could train the dogs to drool to the sound of a bell.

Stimulus (food)

↕

Response (drool)

Figure 4.1 illustrates how Pavlov described the process and gave each aspect a different term.

1   When the dog is given food it salivates/drools.

Drooling when food is given was termed an *unconditioned response* (UCR), while the food is an *unconditioned stimulus* (UCS).

2   A bell is presented and rung immediately before food arrives – initially, the dog does not drool. The bell is a *conditioned stimulus* (CS).

3   After a number of pairings of the bell and food, the dog drools in anticipation of food on every hearing of the bell. Pavlov termed this a *conditioned response* (CR).

Even when Pavlov manipulated the bell's ring tone to a higher or lower pitch, the sound made the dog drool. Pavlov called this *generalization*. He also noted that, when a bell is rung without food, the dog's drooling response eventually weakens and seems to disappear. Pavlov termed this reaction *extinction*. Importantly, he noticed that the dog's response had not gone but was *latent* and could be quickly relearnt – he labelled this *spontaneous recovery*. This is an important point and one you will notice in practice.

Figure 4.1   Classical conditioning

> **Example**
>
> Pavlov's research demonstrated that one pairing is sufficient to condition a response, by way of example:
>
> > Noah loves chips and would eat them at every meal. He has a tummy bug and is sick immediately after eating. Noah subsequently refuses to eat chips. He has formed an association between eating chips and being sick.
>
> **Points to keep in mind**: Here, as in Pavlov's experiment, there was no intention to shape or change Noah's behaviour. Instead, one pairing of two unrelated events was sufficient to form an association that may last a lifetime. Also note that *no reward or punishment* was necessary to shape Noah's behaviour.

Pavlov concluded that once learned, associations are difficult to erase. The notion that learned associations can be dormant but reappear when a trigger is reintroduced has implications for those trying to overcome *phobias* and drug, alcohol and gambling addictions, or those learning healthy eating habits. Although Pavlov's experiments were confined to the laboratory, as we will see in the examples included in this chapter and in the section detailing Watson's work with phobias, classical conditioning offers a robust explanation for some forms of learning.

Extinction

Spontaneous recovery

Learning is not erased but suppressed. The examples included above indicate how a positive or negative learned response can be changed but can reappear.

> **Example: Classical conditioning in action**
>
> 1. Strapped in his buggy, Karl is shocked and upset when a large dog reaches down and licks his face. Based on this one encounter, Karl may cry every time he sees a large dog and generalize his fear to all dogs. Although the initial incident is forgotten, from childhood Karl has been frightened of dogs.

2. A teacher uses a bell to signal quiet time. When the bell rings, the children fold their arms on their desk and rest their head on their hands. Over time, picking up the bell is sufficient for the children to fold their arms and rest their heads. An association has been made between the bell and quiet time.

3. Abbey (aged 18 months) is shopping with her mummy. She screams when she hears a loud clap of thunder. Eventually Abbey's reaction to thunder disappears. Some time later, caught in a violent thunderstorm with her mummy, 3-year-old Abbey becomes hysterical and remains terrified of thunder throughout her life.

WATSON AND BEHAVIOURISM

John B. Watson (1878–1958)

An American psychologist, Watson was born on 9 January 1878 in South Carolina. After a scandalous divorce, Watson married his student, Rosalie Rayner. Inspired by the work of Pavlov, Watson applied the principles of classical conditioning to children. He founded a new school of thinking, *behaviourism*, in America in 1913. For more than 50 years, classical conditioning had a major influence on teaching and learning, until the late 1960s when it was challenged by Piaget's discovery learning theory. It continues nonetheless to exert a considerable impact on pedagogy and practice in 21st-century classrooms.

According to Rotfeld, 'psychologists "invented" Behaviourism itself as a basis for theoretical explanations, prediction, and testing' (2007, p. 376). From its inception, the term 'behaviourism' provided a direction for social science research that '... would allow control and measurement of all relevant variables by ignoring human thought or cognition' (p. 376).

Extending Pavlov's theory to humans, Watson was intrigued by the notion that he could condition a fear response to an innocuous object, such as a rabbit, or remove an existing fear response. The following case studies offer insight into his work with children.

Little Albert (1920)

Although there are varying accounts of the experiments conducted on Little Albert, it is generally agreed that his mother was a wet nurse in a children's hospital. When Albert was approximately nine months old, Watson and his student Rayner tested the baby's reaction

(Continued)

(Continued)

to a range of objects including a white rat, a dog, masks with and without hair, cotton wool and a hammer. They concluded that Albert was a healthy and stolid little boy whose only fear was the noise produced when a steel bar was struck by a hammer, creating a loud bang. At approximately 11 months, Albert was introduced to a white rat. To induce fear, Watson crept up behind the baby and hit the bar with the hammer. This process was repeated seven times until the baby cried when shown a white rat. His fear generalized to the extent that Albert cried when shown a range of soft white objects including cotton wool, a Santa Claus mask and Watson's white hair.

Little Albert's mother reportedly left the hospital before Watson could remove Albert's fears and, until quite recently, little was known about his whereabouts. Beck et al. (2009) spent seven years tracking Little Albert and concluded that 'Little Albert' was a pseudonym used to protect the identity of a boy named Douglas Merritte who died at the age of six from hydrocephalus. Their finding raised serious questions about the fidelity of research based on a child with a known neurological disorder. Psychologists continue to review and debate the footage of the experiment. Some are convinced that the toddler at the centre of the experiment had a disorder; others argue this conclusion is flawed. They claim that the boy involved in the experiment was not Douglas Merritte but Albert Barger, a typically developing child who was born in the same hospital (Bartlett, 2014).

Irrespective of their belief about which child was involved in this experiment, psychologists agree that Watson succeeded in inducing a fear response in a child who was previously unafraid.

In an equally famous reversal of the first experiment, under the supervision of Watson, his student Mary Cover Jones (1924) aimed to remove the fears of a young child called Little Peter.

Little Peter (1924)

An orphan, Peter was aged 2 years and 10 months when Jones and Watson began to study him. He was afraid of a white rat, and this fear extended to a rabbit, a fur coat, a feather, cotton wool and so on – but not to wooden blocks and similar toys. A rabbit was placed in a wire cage in the room where Little Peter ate lunch. Each day, the rabbit in the cage was brought a little nearer to Peter, who eventually ate his lunch whilst nursing the rabbit on his lap.

Although it was never clear how Peter acquired his phobia, this experiment provided the first evidence that fears could be treated. Wolpe (1958) later termed this approach *systematic desensitization*. He believed that phobias were anxiety responses that had become classically conditioned.

> **Definition**
>
> **Systematic desensitization:** this works on the principle that an individual cannot experience two opposing emotional responses at the same time. Teaching an individual to employ relaxation strategies in fearful situations creates a counter-conditioning process which can reduce anxiety and inhibit the fear response (Danial et al., 2013). Although anxiety is frequently associated with adults, Przeworski (2013) points out that as many as 20 per cent of school-aged children experience a form of anxiety that may negatively impact their learning. She provides a range of age-appropriate relaxation techniques that can be used by parents and practitioners to deal with a variety of fears.

Based on the success of his experiments, Watson famously declared:

> Give me a dozen healthy infants, well-formed, and my own specified world to bring them up in and I'll guarantee to take any one at random and train him to become any type of specialist I might select – doctor, lawyer, artist, merchant-chief and, yes, even beggar-man and thief, regardless of his talents, penchants, tendencies, abilities, vocations and the race of his ancestors. (1928, p. 82)

> **Exercise**
>
> Consider the ethical implications of replicating Watson's experiments with young children in the 21st century. Do you think there is ever a time when this type of research might be justified? The EECERA (2014) guidelines for researchers working with young children may inform your answer.

Undoubtedly, classical conditioning theory does explain some aspects of learning. You may have noticed the similarities between Watson's theory and Locke's 17th-century philosophy of learning. Locke described the child's mind at birth as a blank slate (*tabula rasa*). Locke and Watson appear to share the notion that the child's outcome – whether they become a beggar or a king – is totally determined by life experience. In essence, both view the learner as a passive rather than an active participant in the learning process. Watson's theory was a major influence in education. Throughout the 1940s, 1950s and into the 1960s, education was target- rather than process-driven. As noted in the CBI *First Steps* report (2012), governments continuously use this approach to measure success through a narrow matrix. The report concludes that, rather than enhance achievement, this has led to an acceptance of mediocrity. Nonetheless, measurable outcomes continue to impress and a parent may proudly tell you that their toddler can count up to 10, 20 or even 100. Though impressive, practitioners understand that this is repetition without understanding and that few children of this age have a grasp of skills such as one-to-one correspondence. An unlikely defence for this approach comes from Vygotsky (1978), who believed that learning precedes understanding. In essence, introducing young children to the language of numbers and letters provides a springboard for the development of literacy and numeracy.

LEARNING THROUGH TRIAL AND ERROR

Edward Thorndike (1874–1949)

An American psychologist, Thorndike was born on 31 August 1874 and was one of the first pioneers of *active learning*, a theory proposing that children should be encouraged to learn by themselves rather than rely on teachers for instruction. Unlike the other theorists discussed in this chapter, Thorndike was a teacher educator, not a scientist. He believed that trial and error constitutes the most basic form of learning. According to the *law of effect*, connections between actions and outcomes are strengthened in the presence of a reward. Thorndike famously identified the *halo effect* (1920); according to this theory, an attractive child will be viewed as more intelligent, pleasant and kind than a less attractive child.

Although he accepted the principles of classical conditioning, Thorndike believed that the majority of learning was acquired through trial and error. He believed that when the outcome is positive, a connection (habit) is formed and the behaviour is repeated. Originally pioneered by Watson, Thorndike adapted the puzzle box experiment to test the laws of learning. He placed a hungry cat in a box in clear view of a fish. The cat's task was to escape from the box and get the fish. Each time the cat escaped, it was returned to the box. At first, trial and error secured the cat's release. Over time, the escapes became faster as the cat made a connection between its paw movements and the door lever.

Weblink

For a simulation of Thorndike's puzzle box, see www.youtube.com/watch?v=kzNIV0mTROU (accessed 11.4.15).

Thorndike termed the process, which started with random acts and then became quite deliberate, the 'law of effect'. He believed that acts which produce negative consequences weaken and disappear, whereas acts which produce pleasurable outcomes are strengthened and maintained.

Exercise

Trial and error undoubtedly explains an aspect of learned behaviour. Consider the following example, wherein Malachi learns by trial and error.

Weblink

'Malachi learning by trial and error': www.youtube.com/watch?v=ogrCJBmqv0k (accessed 11.4.15).

Note in this short clip the number of attempts Malachi makes at climbing the fence and attempts at playing with items in the playground before he abandons the exercise.

Consider the similarities and differences between Malachi's behaviour and the mouse Brightcheta on the wheel:

www.youtube.com/watch?v=D7cS97jZJMQ (accessed 11.4.15).

From these examples, would you agree with the behaviourists that animal and human learning follows a similar path? Consider the reasons that informed your answer.

Given the complexity and perverseness of human nature, the notion that behaviour producing negative consequences always weakens and disappears may be simplistic. Consider roller-coaster rides such as Vanish (Japan), Millennium Force (Ohio), Oblivion (England) and the Tower of Terror II (Australia), which induce stomach-churning terror. Yet people travel the world in search of the ultimate thrill.

Moreover, if, as Thorndike suggests, all inappropriate behaviour was reversible more than half a century ago, behavioural units in schools, young-offender centres and prisons would be unnecessary. Similar to Pavlov and Watson, in Thorndike's research the impact of psychological (what I think/understand), social (environmental) and emotional (how I feel) factors were ignored in favour of overt behaviour.

BEHAVIOUR HAS CONSEQUENCES

B.F. Skinner (1904–1990)

An American psychologist, Skinner was born on 20 March 1904 in Pennsylvania and was eventually married with two daughters. Skinner's research was heavily influenced by the work of Thorndike and Watson. He disagreed with the tenets of classical conditioning, which portrayed the learner as a passive recipient of knowledge. He agreed with Thorndike's theory that individuals are not passive but active learners whose behaviour is shaped and maintained by rewards or punishments (consequences). His techniques continue to inform child behaviour programmes (such as star charts) and interventions for children with *autism*, elective mutism and problem behaviour.

Similar to Watson, Skinner believed that the mind and mental processes are 'metaphors and fictions', and that 'behaviour' is a function of the 'biology' of the organism (as cited by Gregory, 1987). Weegar and Pacis (2012, p. 5) describe Skinner as a 'Behaviourist in the strictest sense' who shared Watson's belief that everything human beings do is controlled by their experience. According to this notion, the 'mind' (not the brain) has nothing to do with how people behave.

According to Skinner, learning is not the passive process described by classical conditioning theory but an active process. Although he initially assumed that humans respond to triggers within the environment, he later amended his theory to recognize the role of previous experience in the individual's response to the environment.

Example

Tim (aged 16 months) lifts up a sausage and blows on it, all the time saying 'hot, hot, hot'. Having previously burned his tongue, he is taking no chances and holds the sausage out to his mummy so that she can also blow.

Definition

Operant conditioning: (also referred to as 'instrumental conditioning') theory states that learning occurs when behaviour is either rewarded or punished. Through operant conditioning, an association is made between a behaviour and its consequences.

Operant conditioning is more active, less rigid and more unpredictable than classical conditioning. Skinner concurred with Thorndike's belief that pleasant responses can strengthen a behavioural response and unpleasant responses can weaken and diminish behaviour. Skinner described the learning process as: first, positive reinforcement (such as praise, smiles, pats on the back, stars etc.) strengthens behaviour; second, negative reinforcers or punishers (such as the naughty step and time out) can discourage certain behaviours (see Figure 4.2).

Figure 4.2   Positive and negative re-enforcers

Another important aspect of Skinner's work concerned the frequency of reinforcement. For example, if a child is praised every time they say 'thank you', the praise soon loses value. Rarely praised, the child may feel undervalued and refuse to say 'thank you'. In both cases, the behaviour weakens over time and disappears. Findings from his experiments with animals led Skinner to identify four *reinforcement schedules*. As illustrated in Table 4.1, using 'please' as an example, once behaviour is established, rewards given on an intermittent/variable schedule have the greatest effect. Whilst continuous reinforcement might be useful at the start of the process, intermittent or variable reinforcement appears to have a longer-lasting effect on behaviour.

Table 4.1   Reinforcement schedules and likely outcomes of behaviour: Saying 'please'

Reinforcement	Pattern of Praise	Likelihood of Repetition
Continuous	Given at each utterance	Low / moderate
Fixed ratio	At fixed interval *(e.g. every 4th or 6th time)*	Low / moderate
Fixed interval	Given if said within fixed period of time *(e.g. within 10 mins.)*	Low / moderate
Intermittent / Variable	Follows no set pattern *(e.g. 3rd, 8th & 11th times)*	Moderate / high

ENHANCING MOTIVATION

Introducing reinforcers as a reward must be managed carefully by practitioners who aim to increase children's intrinsic motivation (i.e. sense of enjoyment or mastery of a task) and to reduce children's extrinsic motivation (reliance on external rewards). Evidence suggests that the insensitive application of external rewards can undermine intrinsic motivation. By way of example, research suggests that helping behaviour is an innate trait that appears in and around a child's first birthday (Hepach et al., 2012). By 18 months the trait is well established and young children can be seen attempting to comfort their distressed peers or helping an adult to tidy up. Perversely, children aged 20 months given a reward for self-initiated helping behaviours are less likely to repeat the same actions in the future. To test this theory, Warneken and Tomasello (2008) had an adult sit at a desk and drop a pen in front of a 20-month-old child and then attempt to find it. Children in group A received a small reward every time they offered to help, group B received a verbal reward (thank you) and group C received no reward. Repeated at a later stage, only groups B and C offered help. The researchers concluded that the introduction of a tangible reward for innately motivated tasks is particularly negative for young children when a task is interesting (Warneken and Tomasello, 2008).

In essence, extrinsic motivators such as verbal praise, stickers, and/or additional play time offer useful short-term rewards and can be used to initiate behaviour, but once established they should be withdrawn to enhance children's motivation, self-esteem and self-efficacy. The inappropriate use of rewards can undermine a child's intrinsic motivation.

Exercise

Jacob started nursery school in September and settled well. His teacher describes him as a delightful child. At home Jacob is increasingly demanding and clingy. He cries and appears distressed when his mother plays with his baby brother Seth. Jacob's nursery teacher thinks he may be jealous and is trying to divert his mum's attention away from Seth. She suggests a star chart to reward Jacob's good behaviour. She also believes the reward period should be short to ensure Jacob understands that the reward is linked to positive behaviour. Three days of stars are rewarded by a trip to the park with mummy; Seth stays at home with granny. Jacob's behaviour shows rapid improvement.

- What tips would you offer Jacob's mum to help strengthen and maintain his good behaviour?
- Can you think of any examples from your practice to support her efforts?

Behaviourism, education and the 21st century

Wheldall (2012) claims that recent years have witnessed a resurgence of interest in behaviourist approaches in the classroom. He attributes this renewed interest to the fact that teachers now understand that behaviourism is about good teaching 'systematised into a clear and coherent framework ... based on positive, non-aversive approaches' (p. 1). Behaviourists believe that some associations are learned more easily than others and that learning involves small incremental steps. In developing his theory, Skinner concluded that classroom teaching required a knowledgeable teacher with a clearly articulated lesson plan and a mode of delivery with material presented using a staged approach. This, he claimed, would enable a teacher to reinforce correct answers and to shape children's learning. Instruction, then, becomes a process of transmission or delivery (Wonu et al., 2010).

To enhance the teaching and learning experience, he proposed an alternative teaching technique called *programmed learning/instruction* and also a teaching machine that could present programmed material, termed *computer-assisted learning* (CAL). Using a simple teaching package, he rewarded right answers with, for example, a star or 'well done' on screen, whilst a wrong answer received a 'try again'. Although CAL failed to gather support in the 1950s, by the 1990s the principles of operant conditioning were informing a number of therapeutic approaches used with, amongst others, disaffected children – children for whom school holds no point (Davies, 2008) – and children with autism (Silver and Oakes, 2001).

For more than 60 years *applied behavioural analysis* (ABA) has been a treatment of choice for behavioural problems associated with autistic spectrum disorders, brain injury and other neurological disorders (Axelrod et al., 2012). Although there is no direct link between behaviourism and special needs, ABA was developed by Lovaas (1987) with the aim of systematically reinforcing appropriate forms of behaviour in children with autism. The programme involves teaching linguistic, cognitive, social and self-help skills across all settings and breaking down these skills into small tasks which are taught in a highly structured and hierarchical manner. There is a focus on rewarding, or reinforcing, desired behaviours and ignoring, re-directing or otherwise discouraging inappropriate behaviours. Lovaas recommends introducing a child with autism to an ABA programme before they reach 5 years of age. A modified version of ABA in the form of play therapy for children aged 3 years and under, was also devised by Lovaas. Despite an impressive record accrued over 50 years, Fennell and Dillenburger (2014) note that researchers and autism experts remain reluctant to use behaviour-analysis interventions. Nevertheless, proponents argue that ABA has proven particularly effective in the treatment of young children with autism, and has served to reduce stereotypical and disruptive behaviours before they become established (Axelrod et al., 2012).

Many schools employ an inducement scheme in the form of tokens to reward school attendance, good time-keeping, neatness and good work. Pupils can exchange the tokens for prizes such as cinema tickets. As the pupil's behaviour improves, rewards are slowly replaced by verbal praise and eventually good grades.

Exercises

1. Review your setting's behaviour management policy. Identify the positive reinforcers used in the setting to shape and maintain appropriate behaviour. What negative reinforcers are used to discourage inappropriate behaviour?
2. Identify the similarities and differences between classical and operant conditioning.
3. Identify examples of both learning theories. Which, if either, best explains learning?

 ## Summary

This chapter sought to familiarize students with two key learning theories: classical and operant conditioning (see Table 4.2). Pavlov's serendipitous discovery – that his experimental dogs had made an association between the laboratory assistants and food, causing them to drool – provided the first systematic, testable evidence about how learning is acquired. Watson applied Pavlov's principles of classical conditioning to humans and found it was possible to create or remove fears and phobias. The principles of systematic desensitization continue to be widely used. Whereas Pavlov and Watson viewed the learner as a passive recipient of information, Skinner believed that learning is an active process. In Skinner's theory of operant conditioning, behaviour is believed to be shaped and maintained by its consequences. It is less predictable and more varied than classically conditioned responses, as it is under the control of the individual. Similar to Thorndike, Skinner believed that negative rewards weaken negative behaviour and positive rewards strengthen positive behaviour. He later amended his theory to include experiential learning. See Table 4.3 for a summary of behaviourism timelines and biographies.

The principles of operant conditioning are practised on an almost daily basis in classrooms throughout the developed world. Star charts are frequently used to encourage good behaviour, whereas time out, withdrawal from an interesting activity and behaviour charts are used to discourage naughty or inappropriate behaviour. These principles have also been applied in work with children with autism and elective mutism. On the one hand, proponents of behaviourism point out that for more than sixty years it has had a major influence on the content and delivery of education in the Western world. It also provided a platform for other theorists to develop their own hypotheses of learning. Critics, on the other hand, note how behaviourists failed to consider the complexity of human thought, motivation and intention, or the social context of learning. For example, the perversity of human behaviour – willingly taking a roller-coaster ride even when it makes you sick – cannot be explained by behaviourism. The impact that covert processes such as thinking, intentions, motivation and understanding exert on learning are explored in the following chapters.

Table 4.2 Classical and operant conditioning: similarities and differences

	Classical	Operant
Believe that learning is based on associations (*stimulus-response*)	✓	✓
Explain aspects of learning	✓	✓
Employ experimental, laboratory-based methods	✓	✓
Consider the role of creative or insightful problem-solving in learning	-	-
Consider the impact that intentions, beliefs or experiences have on learning	-	-
Learner is perceived as passive in the learning process (*e.g. learning happens* to *rather than* with *the learner*)	✓	-
Learning is based on an association between behaviour and its consequences (*e.g. a child will work hard for a reward and try to avoid punishments*)	-	✓
Learner is thought to be an active participant in the learning process. Learning is voluntary (*e.g. if the task is too difficult, the child will stop even when a reward is offered*)	-	✓

Table 4.3 Behaviourism timelines and biographies

	Biography	Research
Classical conditioning	**Ivan Pavlov (1849–1936)** A Russian physiologist, Pavlov was born on 14 September 1849 in the village of Ryazan.	His work on dog salivation led him to develop a theory of conditioned reflexes. Pavlov's theory, termed classical conditioning, has had a major influence on the field of psychology.
Classical conditioning (Behaviourism)	**John B. Watson (1878–1958)** An American psychologist, Watson was born on 9 January 1878 in South Carolina.	Inspired by the work of Pavlov, Watson applied the principles of classical conditioning to children. He founded a new school of thinking, 'Behaviourism', in 1913. Learning develops in response to external stimuli – thoughts and emotions do not inform behaviour. It is primitive and reflexive.

(Continued)

Table 4.3   (Continued)

	Biography	Research
Law of Effect	**Edward Thorndike (1874–1949)** An American psychologist, Thorndike was born on 31 August 1874.	Thorndike was one of the first pioneers of active learning. He believed that trial and error learning constitutes the most basic form of learning.
Operant conditioning	**B.F. Skinner (1904–1990)** An American psychologist, Skinner was born on 20 March 1904 in Pennsylvania.	Skinner was influenced by the work of Thorndike. He agreed that individuals are not passive but active learners whose behaviour is shaped and maintained by rewards or punishments (their consequences). Complex thought does not inform learning. Rewards/positive reinforcers lead to good behaviour and punishment/negative reinforcers eliminate unacceptable behaviour.

RECOMMENDED READING

Gross, R.D. (2010). *Psychology: The Science of Mind and Behaviour*, 6th edn. London: Hodder Education.

In its sixth reprint, this is a core text that offers students a thorough introduction to classical and operant conditioning. Primarily written for psychology students, the language is straightforward and examples are provided to ensure understanding.

Open access articles which should prove of interest include:

Strain, P.S., McConnell, S.R., Carta, J.J., Fowler, S.A., Neisworth, J.T. and Wolery, M. (1992). Behaviourism and early intervention. *Topics in Early Childhood Special Education, 12, 1,* 121–41. Available at: http://tec.sagepub.com/content/12/1/121.full.pdf+html (accessed 11.4.15).

This article explores the application of Behaviourist techniques by early childhood special educators. Mounting a robust defence of behaviourism, the authors unpack the strengths of the approach for practitioners. Given many aspects of the approach continue to inform policy and practice, this paper offers some useful insights.

Sunberg, M.L. and Michael, J. (2000). The benefits of Skinner's analysis of verbal behavior for children with autism. *Behavior modification, 25, 5,* 698–724. Available at: http://bmo.sagepub.com/content/25/5/698.full.pdf+html (accessed 11.4.15).

Given the continuing significance of Skinner's work to the field of Autism, researchers exploring aspects of this disorder will find the historical detail included in this article a good starting point for their literature review.

REFERENCES

Axelrod, S., McElrath, K.K. and Wine, B. (2012). Applied behavior analysis: autism and beyond. *Behavioral Interventions, 27, 1,* 1–15.

Bartlett, T. (2014). The search for psychology's lost boy. *The Psychologist, 24,* 392–395.

Beck, H.P., Levinson, S. and Irons, G. (2009). Finding little Albert: a journey to John B. Watson's infant laboratory. *American Psychologist, 64, 7,* 605–614.

CBI (2012). *First Steps: A New Approach for Our Schools.* London: Confederation of British Industry.

Danial, J.T., Lin, C.E. and Wood, J.J. (2013). Desensitization. *Encyclopedia of Autism Spectrum Disorders,* 869–75. New York: Springer. DOI 10.1007/978-1-4419.

Davies, M. (2008). Disaffected school children would be better off at work. *Independent,* 13 November

DfE Guidance (2011). *Behaviour and Discipline in Schools* (DfE Website – www.education.gov.uk)

EECERA (2014). *Ethical Code for Early Childhood Researchers.* Birmingham: EECERA. Available at: www.eecera.org/documents/pdf/organisation/EECERA-Ethical-Code.pdf (accessed 11.4.15).

EYFS Statutory framework for the early years foundation stage. (2014). Setting the standards for learning, development and care for children from birth to five Reference: DFE-00337-2014.

Fennell, B. and Dillenburger, K. (2014). The evidence base for behavioural interventions for autism. *International Research in Education, 2, 2.*

Gregory, R.L. (1987). *The Oxford Companion to the Mind.* Oxford: Oxford University Press.

Hepach, R., Vaish, A. and Tomasello, M. (2012). A new look at children's prosocial motivation. *Infancy, 18, 1,* 67–90.

Jones, M.C. (1924). A laboratory study of fear: the case of Peter. *Pedagogical Seminary, 31,* 308–315.

Lovaas, O. I. (1987). Behavioral treatment and normal educational and intellectual functioning in young autistic children. *Journal of Consulting and Clinical Psychology, 55,* 3–9.

Przeworski, A. (2013). 'Don't worry, mom': coping with anxiety in families. *Psychology Today.* Available at: www.psychologytoday.com/blog/dont-worry-mom/201302/12-tips-reduce-your-childs-stress-and-anxiety (accessed 4.12.14).

Rotfeld, H.H. (2007). Theory, data, interpretations, and more theory. *The Journal of Consumer Affairs, 41, 2,* 376–80.

Silver, M. and Oakes, P. (2001). Evaluation of a new computer intervention to teach people with autism or Asperger syndrome to recognize and predict emotions in others. *Autism, 5,* 299–316.

Thorndike, E.L. (1920). A constant error in psychological ratings. *Journal of Applied Psychology, 4,* 467–77.

Vygotsky, L.S. (1978). *Mind and Society: The Development of Higher Mental Processes.* Cambridge, MA: Harvard University Press.

Warneken, F. and Tomasello, T. (2008). Extrinsic rewards undermine altruistic tendencies in 20-month-olds. *Developmental Psychology, 44, 6,* 1785–8.

Watson, J.B. (1928). *Psychological Care of Infant and Child.* New York: Norton.

Weegar, M.A. and Pacis, D. (2012). A comparison of two theories of learning: behaviorism and constructivism as applied to face-to-face and online learning. *E-Leader Manila.* Available at: www.g-casa.com/conferences/manila/papers/Weegar.pdf (accessed 11.4.15).

Wheldall, K. (ed.) (2012). *The Behaviourist in the Classroom*. Oxford: Routledge.

Wolpe, J. (1958). *Psychotherapy by Reciprocal Inhibition*. Stanford, CA: Stanford University Press.

Wonu, N., Umanah, E.U. and Didi, K.D. (2010). The effectiveness of computer assisted instruction (CAI) in the teaching of statistical measures of location (SML) at senior secondary (ssc3) level. *Journal of Vocational Education & Technology, 7, 1 and 2*, 25–45.

Want to learn more about this Chapter?
Visit the companion website at **https://study.sagepub.com/grayandmacblain2e** to gain open access to selected SAGE journal articles, author podcasts and weblinks to help further your study.

5 PIAGET, LEARNING AND COGNITIVE CONSTRUCTIVISM

This chapter aims to:

- familiarize students with Piaget's theory of cognitive development
- illustrate this theory using practical examples
- highlight the strengths and weaknesses of Piaget's theory.

JEAN PIAGET (1896–1980)

Jean Piaget was a Swiss scientist, born in Neuchâtel, Switzerland on 9 August 1896. A precocious and brilliant child, he wrote his first paper, regarding an albino sparrow, at the age of 11. He continued to write and study throughout his life, producing more than 100 papers and books. Having studied the natural sciences at university, in later life Piaget developed an interest in psychoanalysis and intelligence testing. His research in developmental psychology and genetic epistemology had one unique goal: to understand how knowledge grows. Piaget is best known for his research on children's cognitive development, which drew heavily on observational studies of his infant children. He is credited with providing the first evidence that children's and adults' thinking are qualitatively different.

For almost fifty years, behaviourism – the school of thought that embraces classical and operant conditioning theories, discussed in Chapter 4 – remained a dominant force in education. Classroom teaching was based on *rote* and *drill* (involving the repetition of times tables, spellings etc.) in the belief that this would promote learning. Using these approaches, teachers could test children's memory for facts such as the letters of the alphabet, colours, spelling and multiplication tables. Critical of the behaviourist approach, Piaget argued it merely encouraged the repetition of 'meaningless strings' and 'circus tricks' but failed to promote understanding (Piaget 1952). He favoured discovery learning through practical activities.

Example

Consider Jack, who (at 3 years and 2 months) is learning his colours at nursery. Every day the teacher sets up a row of coloured blocks and has Jack repeat the colours with her before she asks him to point to the red or yellow block. Despite doing very well on this task, observations of Jack show he has not learned his colours. Playing with his friend Sam, Jack holds up a car and asks, 'Is that the blue one or the green one?' His friend considers and then tells him, 'It's blue. My daddy has a blue car so I know it's blue.' The teacher realizes that Jack has merely repeated the words without connecting the colours with their name. In the following weeks, Jack's teacher introduces a number of games and activities aimed at reinforcing children's knowledge of colour. She links stories with colour and introduces a colour table which changes each week. Within a short time, Jack is observed talking confidently about colours.

In 1954, Piaget published *The Construction of Reality in the Child*. In this book, Piaget described the child as a lone scientist who creates his or her own sense of the world. According to Piaget, knowledge is constructed by the knower based on mental activity. His theory termed *constructivism* (a theory of knowledge positing that humans generate knowledge and meaning from an interaction between their experiences and their ideas) provided the first major challenge to behaviourism. The popularity of this theory grew from the fact that it offered one of the first theories about the emergence and development of children's thinking.

It is interesting to consider how a scientist with an interest in the natural world came to be known as 'the giant of the nursery' (Elkind, 1972). A promising student, Piaget found himself working for Theodore Simon, the co-author of one of the world's first intelligence tests. Working in Binet's laboratory on the standardization of test items, Piaget found the types of errors children made on test items more interesting than correct responses. He was convinced that errors were age-related rather than random and believed they offered an insight into how children think and learn. This work led him to conclude that children's thinking is radically different from adult thinking and that younger children think differently from older children. These claims were considered revolutionary in their time. Many of Piaget's contemporaries refused to accept this notion and disputed his claims that infants' thinking evolves and changes with age and experience. Ignoring the controversy, over a 50-year period Piaget continued to refine and develop his theory. In the course of his investigations, he drew on the work of James Mark Baldwin (1861–1934), one of the first psychologists with an interest in the cognitive development of infants and children. The terms *accommodation* and *adaptation*, frequently attributed to Piaget, were originally coined by Baldwin.

Definitions

Assimilation: according to Piaget, 'assimilation is the integration of external elements into evolving or completed structures' (1970, p. 706). By this he means that new information is added into existing schemas or categories. Assimilation is an active and selective process.

Accommodation: changing or adapting an existing schema, concept or idea to embrace new knowledge. Piaget believed that children learn by adaptation, which includes assimilation and accommodation.

Scheme/schema: Piaget used the term 'scheme', most often referred to as a 'schema', to describe the basic unit of intelligent behaviour. It is an active process which sorts information into simple categories. Schemas are not fixed but evolve and develop with experience.

Equilibration: the child finding balance between external (environmental) and internal thinking processes. Disequilibrium is the result of a mismatch between the two.

Weblink

A further explanation of these concepts, with simple examples included, is available at: www.youtube.com/watch?v=3-A9SgbAK5I

This video offers illustrations of schemas using drawings to explain how each is constructed, how information is assimilated into an existing schema, disequilibrium when new information conflicts with their existing knowledge, and finally accommodation.

Piaget eschewed the experimental laboratory methods favoured by the behaviourists. Instead, he observed the development of children (using his own three children as a starting point) in their natural environment and recorded the slightest change in their actions. He also listened carefully to the explanations children gave as they completed a series of tasks. Piaget believed that children's thinking begins before they have the language to express their thoughts. Early thinking is more primitive and underdeveloped than later thinking and takes the form of schemes, which encapsulate a number of schemas. For example, a baby aged between 4 and 8 months may have a scheme for shaking which incorporates a rattle schema and a shaky toy schema. Sutherland explains Piaget's theory using the following analogy: 'just as a child's body's growth determines what size and shape of clothes he needs, so a child's thinking determines the language he needs' (1992, p. 33). Language, in Piaget's view, is merely a tool used to develop and enhance thinking. He believed that early speech is an expression of the child's needs and desires, and he termed it

4. Formal operational (11–15 years)

3. Concrete operational (7–11 years)

2. Pre-operational (2–7 years)

1. Sensorimotor (0–2 years)

Figure 5.1 Piaget's stages of cognitive development

autistic. Autistic speech is replaced by egocentric speech. The latter verbalizes the child's actions and movements; for example, 'I am going to sit on the big chair with mummy'. As the child becomes more aware of social expectations, egocentric speech begins to fade and speech is internalized. Placing less importance on the development of speech than on cognitive development, Piaget interpreted this as evidence that the child was becoming less egocentric.

Two important trends underlie Piaget's theory of cognitive development. First, he believed that the child is powerfully and actively engaged in the learning process. Second, cognitive development follows a series of stages and substages. The stages and substages in Piaget's theory are invariant, meaning that each child must progress through each stage and substage in turn. They cannot skip a stage, nor can they return to an earlier stage. If you imagine a child on a ladder (see Figure 5.1), they start at the first rung and must move onto the next and the next until they have reached the top of the ladder; there is no stepping-off point. Picture a queue (knowledge and experience) building up behind the child; there is no going back. It is therefore unsurprising that this aspect of his theory has been roundly criticized. Also disputed is Piaget's claim that, irrespective of their culture or race, all children follow the same developmental pathway. The term 'universal' is frequently used to sum this view.

THE SENSORIMOTOR STAGE (0–2 YEARS)

The first stage of cognitive growth is termed the 'sensorimotor stage'. It derives its name from the early knowledge that babies gain through their senses by sucking, shaking, grasping and observing. Piaget believed that newborns are incapable of thinking; instead, they engage in reflexive activity. Most of these primitive reflexes are thought to be innate and include sucking and rooting reflexes. Using detailed observations of his own children, Piaget noted that, even in the first month of life, basic reflexes are modified by experience. For example, a young baby will continually turn its cheek until it locates the teat of a bottle. Within a few weeks, the baby's movements are less random and more deliberate, enabling it to locate the teat quickly. The sensorimotor stage is divided into six substages:

1. **Reflexive (0–1 month)**

   This is the most basic stage of development and is marked by simple reflexive activity such as grasping and sucking. Many of these reflexes are thought to be innate and essential to the baby's survival.

2. **Primary circular (1–4 months)**

   Activities in this stage are centred on the baby's own body. They are called 'primary' because they are the first motor habits to appear and 'circular' because pleasurable activities tend to be repeated. This stage marks the emergence of relatively primitive schemas.

3. **Secondary circular (4–8 months)**

   Activities in this phase are also repeated for pleasure. In contrast to the previous stage, the baby begins to notice interesting things happening in the environment. For example, having accidentally kicked the cot mobile, the baby watches it swing backwards and forwards. Although the baby may repeat this action several times, Piaget believed this was not intentional behaviour but discovered by chance.

4. **Coordination of secondary schemes (8–12 months)**

   Intentional and planned behaviour begins to appear as the baby begins to manipulate the environment. For example, the baby reaches for its bottle, puts it into its mouth and takes a drink. In linking these lifting and grasping movements, the baby begins to coordinate previously unrelated movements to achieve a goal. Object permanence begins to appear during this stage, meaning an infant understands that the toy hidden under the blanket has not disappeared but can be uncovered.

5. **Tertiary circular (12–18 months)**

   Rather than repeat actions to create the same effect, infants begin to experiment to create their own effects. For example, having knocked over her baby cup, Nitta watches as the milk spills. Lifting the cup, she holds it upside down and then begins to shake it to make the milk pour out. This stage heralds the emergence of curiosity.

6. **The beginning of representational thought (18–24 months)**

   This stage marks a significant shift in intellectual development. Problem solving begins to emerge through a combination of signs, symbols and mental imagery. Sitting in her car seat after a day at nursery, 2-year-old Lydia is observed opening and closing her fingers and moving them up and down as she mimes 'Incy Wincy Spider' climbing up the spout.

The description of the sensorimotor stage provided by Piaget explains how, in two short years, an infant will progress from primitive reflexive movements such as grasping and sucking to become an experimental problem solver. The model fails, however, to explain the reason behind the transition from the sensorimotor to the pre-operational stage, described below.

Exercise

Examine the six substages of the sensorimotor stage. Consider why Piaget argued that each stage must be completed before an infant could progress to the next and that no stage could be missed. Do you agree with this theory? Gather evidence to support your point of view.

THE PRE-OPERATIONAL STAGE (2–7 YEARS)

According to Piaget, an infant's thinking continues to develop throughout the pre-operational stage. As language develops, schemes become much more common. This stage of Piaget's theory has been criticized for focusing on the limitations of a young child's thinking rather than on their progress (Meadows, 1993). The pre-operational stage has two substages: the preconceptual phase (2–4 years) and the intuitive stage (4–7 years).

Preconceptual phase (2–4 years)

During this phase, toddlers increasingly engage in imaginative and symbolic play. Symbols can be images or words that stand for something else, as reported in Piaget's observation of his infant daughter Jacqueline at play:

> At 21 months Jacqueline saw a shell and said 'cup'. After saying this she picked it up and pretended to drink … The next day, seeing the same shell, she said 'glass', then 'cup', then 'hat' and finally 'boat in the water'. Three days later she took an empty box and moved it to and fro saying 'motycar'. (Piaget, 1962, p. 124)

Observations of toddlers show they can now engage in make-believe play and imitate behaviour during this phase: Clip-clopping in high heels, Piers pretends to be a mummy going to the shops, while Jenna pretends she is a doctor looking after a sick child. For Piaget, play – particularly imaginative play – is an essential aspect of cognitive development. Thinking during this stage is, however, limited by a number of factors including *egocentrism*, animism, *rigidity of thought* and transductive reasoning. Each is examined in turn below.

Figure 5.2   The 'three mountain scene'

Definition

Egocentrism: the child's inability to understand the world from another's point of view. For example, during a game of hide and seek, Isabelle (2 years old) covers her eyes with her hands. She shouts *"I's over here"*. When Isabelle can't see others, she believes they can't see her. Piaget demonstrated this theory using the 'three mountain scene' experiment depicted in Figure 5.2. (Piaget and Inhelder, 1956)

In this experiment, a child is first shown a cardboard mountain scene from a number of angles. A doll is placed opposite the child, who is then asked to describe what the doll can see. The child can select the doll's viewpoint from a set of pictures. Throughout these experiments, young children consistently selected the picture that reflected their own view of the mountain scene. Based on evidence from a range of similar experiments with young children, Piaget concluded that during the pre-operational stage the young child has no sense of empathy (the ability to understand and identify with the feelings, thinking and motives of another).

In contrast to Piaget's claims, a compelling body of research says that helping behaviour (an aspect of empathy) is an innate trait, which appears in and around a child's first birthday (Hepach et al., 2013a). By 18 months of age children show empathy for a distressed peer by patting and trying to soothe them. Although overt distress is sufficient to elicit a sympathetic response, the researchers found that 3-year-olds were more responsive when they thought crying was justified or were unaware of the cause of an individual's distress. They were much less responsive when they considered the behaviour to be unjustified (Hepach et al., 2013b). In essence, from an early age children show empathy for others but their response is tempered by the context and whether they judge the response to be justified.

> **Exercise**
>
> Drawing on your placement experience, can you think of a time when you saw a young child show empathetic behaviour towards another child or to an adult? How does this experience relate to Piaget's theory of egocentrism?

Animism

According to Piaget, egocentrism pervades all aspects of the young child's thinking and is responsible for *animistic thinking*, which ascribes feelings to objects. For example, every night, Isabelle (aged 2 years and 2 months) takes her babies to bed. She kisses each one in turn, saying 'night night, sleep tight'. She has a special cot blanket for her dolls to keep them 'toasty, cosy' at night.

Piaget's claim that the pre-operational child is egocentric has been more heavily criticized than his other claims. His greatest opponent was Vygotsky (1986), followed by Donaldson (1978) and others.

Hughes (1978) tested Piaget's theory using a cross-shaped screen with a toy policeman positioned to the right of the child. To the left, a doll was hidden from the policeman but visible to the child. After training, nearly all of the children aged between 3½ and 5 years of age could correctly say when the policeman could and could not see the doll. Contrary to Piaget's assertion, Hughes concluded that children of this age can take on another's perspective.

Donaldson (1978) was particularly critical of the questions Piaget asked children. She argued that they were phrased in such a way that they would catch children out rather than help them. Support for this notion comes from a more recent study into animism, which showed that children have no difficulty understanding the difference between living things and objects when the word 'alive' is replaced with less ambiguous terms such as 'breathing' (Leddon et al., 2008). Leddon et al. concluded that the word 'alive' was masking children's understanding of the very concept under investigation.

Rigidity of thought and transductive reasoning

During the pre-operational stage, thinking is further limited by rigidity of thought and *transductive reasoning*. Rigidity of thought is the child's inability to reverse sequences and their inability to adjust to changes in appearance. For example, Deven is playing in the water tray. He watches Anya pour water from the red beaker into the blue beaker and back into the red beaker. When their teacher asks them which beaker has more water, both point to the red one. Their conviction is based on the fact that the red beaker is taller than the blue one. Children in the pre-operational stage have difficulty adjusting to changes in appearance. Using evidence from an experiment with pre-school children, Schaffer (2004, p. 176) illustrates this point. Pre-school children were shown a dog and asked to identify the animal. They correctly said it was a dog. While the children watched, a cat mask was placed over the dog's face. Asked to name the animal, most said it was a cat. Interestingly, each time the mask was removed and replaced, the children shifted from cat to dog.

Example

Aged 3 years and 2 months, Deven is very distressed when he sees that his daddy, Sanja, has shaved off his beard. Deven shouts that he wants his 'real daddy'. Sanja explains that he is his 'real daddy' but Deven refuses to be consoled and asks Sanja to put his beard 'back on'.

Transductive reasoning occurs when a toddler makes inferences about relationships where there are none. For example:

- Carey has a baby in her tummy. Her tummy is very big and fat. Therefore, Melvin has a baby in his tummy because he has a big fat tummy.
- Joe's ball is round and the Sun is round so Joe concludes that the Sun is a ball.

Transductive thinking begins to disappear at around the age of four (Lefrancois, 1995) but thinking in the latter part of the pre-operational stage remains intuitive rather than logical. Intuitive thought is based on perceptual attributes such as size and shape.

The intuitive phase (4–7 years)

This substage is only a slight advancement on preconceptual thinking. Children are getting better at seeing the whole scene rather than focusing on aspects of the scene. Piaget termed this ability 'decentring'. However, the child's thinking is limited by their inability to transfer their attention from the whole to the part and then back to the whole. In the example on the next page, Orla begins by centring her attention on the whole group (paper plates) before focusing on a subgroup (colour).

Example

Four-year-old Orla is organizing plates into sets according to colour. Asked what she is doing, she explains that she is sorting paper plates into a yellow pile and a blue pile. Asked if there are more blue plates than yellow ones, Orla correctly points out that there are more blue ones. Asked 'are there more blue plates or paper plates?' Orla replies 'blue ones'. Having centred her attention on sorting by colour, Orla finds it difficult to transfer her attention back to the whole group – paper plates.

Piaget also believed that pre-operational children's understanding of *conservation* tasks is limited by their inability to move their focus beyond visual cues such as size and shape. In the conservation tasks (illustrated in Figure 5.3) a child is shown two beakers of water and agrees that they contain the same amount of water. When one beaker of water is poured into a shorter but wider beaker, the pre-operational child argues that they are not the same and the taller beaker holds more water.

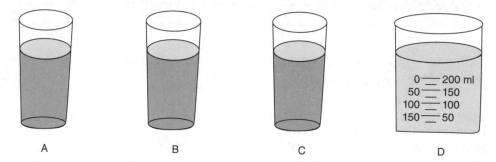

Figure 5.3   A water conservation task

Weblink

Examples of how visual cues can influence a child's reasoning in a conservation task can be seen on the video link 'A typical child on Piaget's conservation tasks', available at: www.youtube.com/watch?v=gnArvcWaH6l (accessed 11.4.15).

Definition

Conservation: the principle that quantities remain constant regardless of changes to their appearance.

Piaget believed that the ability to recognize conservation marked the end of the pre-operational stage and the beginning of concrete operations. Children in the latter phase of the pre-operational stage ask endless questions and understand the difference between reality and fantasy. Critics argue that the end of Piaget's pre-operational stage is mainly defined by what children cannot do rather than by what they can do (Sutherland, 1992).

THE CONCRETE OPERATIONAL STAGE (7–11 YEARS)

The main difference between the pre-operational stage and the concrete operational stage is that children can now use logical rules to solve problems. According to Piaget, operational rules evolve gradually and sequentially as simple skills are consolidated, combined and reorganized into increasingly complex structures. Children are now able to reverse their thoughts when solving problems. This makes thinking more flexible and effective, though it is constrained by the child's need to have a concrete representation of mental thoughts. For example, Josh (aged 7) is adding 6 + 9. First, he uses his fingers to count to 6 and then to add 9. He does this several times but keeps losing track of the numbers. Next, he uses a set of counters to help him and quickly works out that 6 + 9 = 15.

'Seriation' and 'transitivity' are other hallmarks of the concrete operational stage. Seriation involves ordering objects or concepts according to a particular feature such as height, weight or speed. Closely related to seriation, transitivity is the ability to work out relationships, such as if Sean is younger than Jamie but older than Ashley, who is older than Ahmed, who is the oldest?

As previously mentioned, pre-operational children appear to have some difficulty in grasping the concept of conservation. While children are able to understand some forms of conservation, others prove more difficult. The water conservation task illustrated in Figure 5.3 involves the conservation of liquids and is understood by children of 6 and 7 years old. However, the conservation of weight is not seen until the age of 9, while the conservation of volume is not understood until the age of 11 (Piaget, 1969). For example, test your understanding of weight by considering: 'Which is heavier – a ton of lead or a ton of feathers?'

Understanding the conservation of volume involves recognizing that five ice cubes in a glass displace the same volume of water as one large ice cube of equal size and weight to the five. Acknowledging that some forms of conservation seem to be more easily understood than others, Piaget coined the term *horizontal décalage* (see Figure 5.4) to explain developmental inconsistencies in children's learning.

Figure 5.4   An illustration of horizontal décalage

Definition

Horizontal décalage: there are varying interpretations of the meaning of horizontal décalage; however, it can be understood as a term used to describe inconsistent performance on tasks involving similar mental operations. For example, a child might easily understand that there are 10 sweets in a line but not understand that there is the same number in a different configuration.

THE FORMAL OPERATIONAL STAGE (11–15 YEARS)

Having completed the first three stages, at approximately 11 years of age a child progresses to the formal operational stage, which is the highest level of thinking. Piaget believed that the transition from the concrete to the formal operational stage takes place gradually over several years. Again, he failed to explain the reasons for this progression or why some children were more delayed or advanced than others.

This stage differs from the concrete operational stage in several ways. Thinking is:

- more flexible: There is less need for concrete props.
- more symbolic: For example, in maths, understanding that a symbol can stand for a number becomes important in answering questions such as 'What is Y in the sum $3 \times X = Y$, if $X = 4$?' The answer is 12.
- no longer constrained by personal experience or even reality. Children can begin to think about what they would like to do in the future. They can imagine what it would be like to have special powers or to live in a parallel universe.

- logical and deductive. This enables the child to deduce what might happen if two elements are added together. For example, when direct heat is added to a magnesium strip, the magnesium burns and gives off a bright white light. A child will test theories in a more flexible and reflexive manner, noting the operations that do and do not work.

According to Sutherland (1992), Piaget failed to fully describe this last stage of development. Instead, it was left to *neo-Piagetians* (a group of researchers who sought to develop and refine Piaget's theory) such as Peel (1971) and Flavell (1963, 1977) to interpret his messages. Flavell, for example, described formal operations as a general orientation towards problem solving. Piaget never identified a stage past the formal operations, but several neo-Piagetians proffered a post-formal stage of operations to address some of the shortcomings of Piaget's theory (see Fischer, 1980). Perhaps due to the fact that a considerable number of adults never achieve the level of formal operational thinking described by Piaget, post-formal theories have failed to gain popularity. Given that the tasks used to measure formal operations focus on mathematics and science, critics point out that adults from societies that place less emphasis on these subjects will fail on tasks used to identify them as post-operational thinkers (Dasen and Heron, 1992). Similarly, adolescents taught in schools that focus on the arts or sports will do less well than budding scientists on these tasks. In later years, Piaget (1972) attributed these differences to the importance individuals placed on the tasks and argued that most people will solve at least one task. Nevertheless, Claxton (1998) remained highly critical of Piaget's emphasis on logical deductive thinking. He argued that this devalued other forms of thinking, such as intuitive (an aspect of the pre-operational stage) and creative thinking.

SCHEMA FORMATION

Although there is some debate as to who first introduced the term 'schema', in his early work Piaget employed the word to describe 'general cognitive structures in children under the age of five' (Athey 2003 [1990], p. 35). It was in his later work that Piaget drew a distinction between the terms *schema* and *scheme*. The former term was used to denote figurative thought and the latter operational thought. Figurative thought involves innate processes such as perception, memory and imagery. Piaget's concern was not, however, with these abilities but with their effect on problem solving and operational thinking (Chapman, 1999). He believed that schemas precede schemes and are the mental plans that inform action. Schemas are strongly visual. They help us to form impressions and identify inconsistencies in the environment. Look at the letters in Figure 5.5; do you notice anything different in the example?

Figure 5.5   An illustration of schematic bias

Although Piaget believed schemas are essential sources of information, they have the potential to bias our interpretation of facts and situations. Josh, for example, enjoys dressing up and likes the compliments he receives about his choice of dress. When he insists on wearing his sister's summer dress to nursery, he finds the reaction very different. Several of the boys laugh, point and call him a girl. The girls seem equally appalled that a boy is wearing a dress. Young children form a gender schema around the age of 18 months. At this age, they understand that they are a boy or girl and over the next year understand that their gender is fixed. Their gender schemas are primitive at this stage and hold stereotypical information about what it means to be a boy or girl, including appropriate clothing. Consequently, any breach of this code will be noted and cause a reaction.

For Piaget, schemas are concepts that evolve and develop through two complementary systems – *accommodation* and *assimilation* – using perception and memory to facilitate learning. *Equilibration* is achieved when internal and external events or information are in balance.

The example in Figure 5.6 draws on Lydia's (aged 4 years and 5 months) experience during a visit to the zoo. Watching the penguins, she described them as 'funny fish'. She was quite upset when told that penguins are birds. Pointing out that they don't fly but do swim, she concluded that penguins are fish. With help from her auntie, she searched the computer for evidence to support her notion that penguins are fish. Together, they discussed the fact that turkeys can't fly either and agreed that turkeys are birds, whereas swans and ducks swim and they are birds. A close-up picture of a penguin revealed its feathers and showed penguins sitting on nests to protect their eggs. The weight of evidence convinced Lydia, who achieved a stage of equilibration by assimilating and accommodating this new information into her bird schema.

Tracking and gazing are the first schemas to develop. At first, they are separate but become coordinated over time. Amir (aged 3 months) was observed on many occasions tracking the movements of the mobile hanging above his cot. Excited by

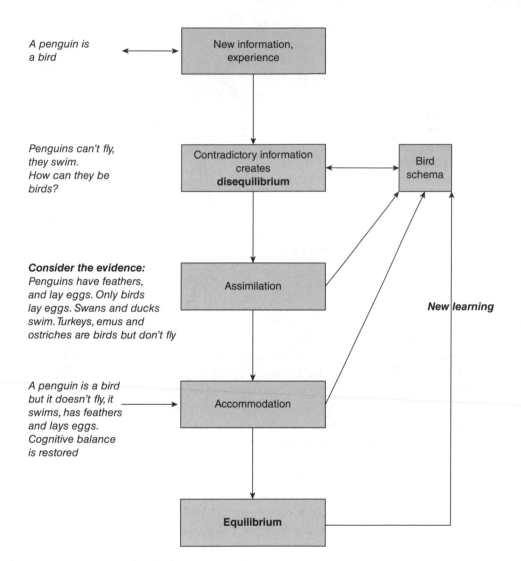

Figure 5.6   An example of schema formation

the movement, he kicks out and accidentally touches the mobile making it swing backwards and forwards. This excites him more. Over time, Amir's movements become more purposeful and his kicking deliberate. His actions were initially informed by his tracking and gazing schemas.

Athey (2003 [1990]) identifies a number of schemas which denote specific behaviours. They include:

- dynamic vertical
- dynamic back and forth/side to side
- dynamic circular
- going over and under
- going round a boundary
- enveloping and containing space
- going through a boundary.

Many of these actions can be observed in children during the latter part of the sensorimotor stage or in the pre-operational stage. According to Hunt (1961), experience and an enriched environment are essential for the child to test and develop a repertoire of schemas.

Opportunities for the development of the dynamic vertical schema include activities involving height. Dylan (aged 1 year and 10 months) jumps off the bottom stair. He repeats this activity a number of times, shouting 'up, down'. Dylan is gaining a rudimentary understanding of height, which will continue to develop.

The children in a playgroup session develop their understanding of tall and small when the staff draw around each child. They cut out each child's silhouette and then arrange them around the walls in order of height. Emma (aged 4 years and 3 months) is the tallest girl and Tanya (aged 3 years and 3 months) the smallest; George (aged 4 years and 8 months) is the tallest boy and Marc (aged 3 years) the smallest. Each child can compare their height with others in the class.

The dynamic back and forth/side to side can be seen in the play of Jack (aged 16 months). He toddles backwards and forwards between his play box and his nanny, each time bringing another wooden block. When nanny has all the blocks, Jack fetches stuffed toys. Although underdeveloped, these actions form the rudiments of a schema that will continue to develop over time.

Exercise

Using evidence from practice, identify examples of each of the following schemas:

- a dynamic circular
- going over and under
- going round a boundary.

Given the opportunity, children will test out their ideas about space, capacity and volume, as illustrated in the examples below.

> **Examples**
>
> 1. Jenny (aged 3 years and 2 months) is playing with a toy bus. She fills the bus with toy people until there are no more seats left. She places the last two toy people beside the bus. Asked what she is doing, Jenny explains that the bus is full and there are no more seats so the people will have to wait for the next bus.
> 2. Kyle (aged 3 years and 8 months) is playing at the water tray. He fills the bucket with water and then pours it into a smaller bucket, watching as the water pours over the side. He repeats this action several times before filling the big bucket from the smaller bucket. He points to the bucket and tells his key worker 'there's still room. See the little bucket gets full but the big bucket it's got more room for water.' Kyle understands, though he doesn't have the vocabulary to explain, that the big bucket has greater capacity and holds a larger volume of water than the small bucket.

Highlighting the value of schema theory to Early Years practitioners, Nutbrown observes that:

> What a schema is called is a way of labelling children's consistent patterns of action, and schemas are useful as an observational tool. They provide another way of looking at children, by giving focus to observational details which might otherwise become a list of disconnected events without much indication of learning or possible action to follow. Identifying a child's activities in terms of different schemas is only the first part in the process; the next step is to use detailed observations of children to decide how best to extend their learning. (2011, 25)

CRITICISMS OF PIAGET'S THEORY

Before examining further criticism of Piaget's theory, it is useful to keep in mind his contribution to our understanding of the developing child. He was the first theorist to attempt to explain the internal process of thinking. He offered researchers a range of new tools to examine the pre-verbal child's development including observations, detailed note-taking and child-centred experiments. He placed the child at the centre of his studies and, in order to gain insight into their thinking, listened carefully to the answers they gave. Piaget was interested in process and how a child arrived at their final answer. In offering a model of how children's thinking develops, he advanced the growth of a new area of study, namely 'child development'.

Nevertheless, a number of criticisms have been levelled at Piaget's theory, particularly his claim that cognitive development happens in discrete stages. This theory has been widely disputed. In later years, Piaget (1970) modified the step-wise approach originally proposed in favour of a 'spiral' process of change. Using this analogy, Piaget described the process of intellectual development as an upward, expanding spiral in which children constantly reconstruct previously learned ideas. Despite these revisions, Piaget failed to explain why a child is driven to progress from one cognitive stage to another. Similarly, opponents argue that Piaget's claims regarding the role of equilibrium in children's learning lacks clarity and is impossible to either prove or disprove (Sutherland, 1992).

The methods used by Piaget to investigate children's thinking have been the subject of considerable criticism (Erneling, 2014). Meadows (1993), for example, argued that the language used in Piaget's experiments was too complicated for young children. She claimed that the wording was deliberate and chosen to 'catch children out' rather than to help them find the correct answer. Consequently, Piaget may have underestimated the child's ability to complete the task. Susan Isaacs was an early critic of Piaget's ideas, arguing that he tended to portray children in a negative light, emphasizing what they *could not* do rather than what they *could do* (Isaacs, 1930). In contrast, Duveen (2000) contends that the child's response was merely a starting point for Piaget to explore the child's understanding using a discursive approach. Faithfully recording every aspect of the child's think-ing enabled Piaget to determine which elements of the problem caused them most difficulty. Another area of criticism concerns the small sample size employed in Piaget's research studies. The sample for Piaget's infancy research comprised his own three children. Although later childhood samples were larger, Piaget failed to record the exact numbers involved in his observations and tasks. Without a descriptive account of the children involved in his studies, Piaget has been accused of generalizing the results he gathered from samples of white, middle-class children with university-educated parents to children from other cultures and classes (Calloway 2001).

Piaget's assertion that learning can never be accelerated has also been refuted. Meadows (1993) found it was possible to teach pre-school children to perform con-crete operational tasks successfully three to four years ahead of time. Cognitive acceleration programmes such as those described by Shayer and Adey (2002) offer further evidence that it is possible to develop children's thinking. They had 5-year-old children participate in an activity with a teacher who asked them to sort a collection of dinosaurs into a T. Rex pile and a blue pile. Cognitive conflict arises when a child has to decide where to place the blue T. Rex. Using similarly challenging tasks, Shayer and Adey found it was possible to develop the child's cognitive ability. In a more recent study, Huntsinger et al. (2011) found differences in the creativity and drawing ability of Chinese and American children. Whereas Chinese parents believe that the essentials of drawing should be taught, American mothers believe it is an innate quality which will emerge naturally. Huntsinger et al. took samples of the children's drawings at 5, 7 and 9 years of age and found that at each age the Chinese children were more skilled at drawing and more creative than their American counterparts. Given the evidence base, it is unsurprising to note that countries in the developed world continue to fund early-intervention programmes aimed at raising the educational standards of children, particularly those from disadvantaged areas.

Other than providing the child with a stimulating learning environment, Piaget's theory places little emphasis on the role of the teacher. By contrast, theorists such as Vygotsky (1978) and Bruner (1986) believe that teachers play a pivotal role in the development of the child's thinking and learning. Similarly, Vygotsky and Bruner take issue with Piaget's failure to consider the effect of culture and environment on the child's cognitive development. Consider, for example, an experiment conducted in a Mexican village where the native children made pottery to earn a living. When these children were tested using clay for conservation of mass, their answers were found to be significantly more advanced than those of their Western counterparts (Price-Williams et al., 1969).

A final criticism concerns his proposition that learning involves schemas. Since this notion is purely hypothetical, it cannot be tested so is beyond refutation or verification. Similarly, the claims that information is assimilated and accommodated into existing schemas is argued to be vague and under-developed (Sutherland, 1992).

Exercise

Can you give an example of a young child who appears highly motivated to learn, a child who shows some motivation to learn and a child who appears to lack any motivation to learn? What might Piaget suggest to increase each child's motivation?

PIAGET IN THE EARLY YEARS SETTING

By the 1960s, enthusiasm for the 'chalk and talk' approach favoured by behaviourists was fading fast as Piaget's theory of discovery learning gathered momentum. Children were no longer taught by rote and drill but allowed to discover facts for themselves with the help of a teacher who facilitated their learning. The physical environment changed as desks were organized into small groups rather than in rows facing the front of the classroom and children sat at child-sized furniture rather than at adult-sized desks. Whilst Piaget believed that teaching must be age-appropriate, in later years he accepted that some children progress at different developmental rates.

Rather than focus on accelerating the child's learning, he encouraged teachers to examine the processes children use to arrive at their answers. By using this approach, a teacher could identify the child's stage of 'readiness' to learn. The concept of 'readiness' has generated a considerable amount of discussion in educational circles (Smidt, 2009). Given the notion that learning should be child-centred and tailored to meet the child's stage of readiness to learn, it is unsurprising to note that nursery teachers are the best customers of Piagetian messages (Sutherland, 1992). The similarities between Piaget's theory and the messages of Montessori (1972 [1949]), Froebel (1782–1852) and Dewey (1959) proved particularly popular with Early Years professionals. This was particularly true of their shared view that children learn best through practical activities, and that the role of the adult is to foster the child's inner drive, not impair it by imposing too many restrictions and obstacles in the child's environment. Both Dewey and Piaget believed that a child-centred teacher is a guide and an arranger of the environment, rather than an instructor. All of these theorists believed that teachers should provide the materials and activities that enable the young child to progress from discovery to discovery.

Another feature of Piaget's theory that proved popular with teachers was his emphasis on the role of peer interaction in the child's cognitive development. Corsaro (1992) defined the term 'peers' as a group of children who spend time together on a daily basis. Collaborative working on tasks which generate controversy, Piaget believed, enriches the child's communication skills and fosters intellectual development. His thoughts on the value of peer interaction are summed up in the following five points:

1. Children value the activities preferred by their peers.
2. Peers can role-model new concepts and skills.
3. A more able peer can explain an activity in simple terms to a learner.
4. The more able peer learns from verbalizing the problem.
5. Both the learner and peer gain a greater insight into the problem through their shared learning experience.

In the mid-1970s, a group of researchers explored the benefits of cooperative learning using a variety of concrete tasks which bore some similarity to Piaget's three-mountain task. The children, aged between 5 and 7 years, first completed a task alone. One week later, half of the group again completed the task alone, while the other half completed it with a peer. Doise et al. (1975) found that children who worked alone operated within the pre-operational stage, whereas those engaged in a shared learning experience tended to perform at the higher concrete operational stage. However, Piaget believed that a child's learning should not be accelerated. Instead, he advised teachers to engage children in stimulating tasks appropriate to their stage of development.

Although the popularity of Piaget's theory waned in the late 1970s, he retains a strong presence in Early Years settings. For example, practitioners continue to ask open-ended questions that foster and develop the child's thinking. They observe children and focus on the process rather than on the output of learning. Rather than lead the child, practitioners continue to support and facilitate the child's learning. The Statutory framework for the early years foundation stage (EYFS, 2014) mentions play twelve times and is heavily focused on the child's social, emotional, physical and cognitive development, as previously proposed by Piaget.

Examples of Piaget's theory in action

1. Noting that it is snowing outside, a Year 1 teacher encourages the children to put on their outdoor clothes and together they go out into the snow. One group of children can be seen lifting the snow and throwing it, then squeezing it through their fingers before working it into snowballs to throw. Another group built a snowman, adding a nose, mouth, eyes, hat and scarf. The cold drives the children inside where they continue to talk about the snow and to draw pictures of snowflakes. The following day, some of the children are distressed to see that the snowman has begun to melt. The teacher takes them outside to gather snow in jars. Some children place their jars on their desks where they can watch it. Others place it on the heaters and a few place their jars in the freezer. Later, the children are fascinated to see that the snow in the jars on the heater and on their desks has melted into water but the snow in the freezer still looks like snow. Kelly asks the teacher if she can make the melted water into snow again. Rather than answer, the teacher encourages Kelly to place her jar in the freezer. At the end of the day, they check the jar and Kelly and her friends see that the water has frozen and is now ice. The teacher asks Kelly what has happened and Kelly explains that she had 'snow first, then water and now ice'. She thinks about it and then decides that she has had 'lots of things but it's all water.'

2. The following example was provided by an Early Childhood studies student during a class discussion:

    After a particularly dry summer and autumn the children (5 to 6 years old) were excited by an unexpected torrential downpour. The sky had darkened and the noise of the rain thundered on the window distracting the children from the set task. Rather than compete for their attention, the teacher pulled up the blinds and encouraged the children to go to the window and to watch the rain. The children then searched the class library for books about weather and rain and asked *where rain is stored? and what causes it to fall out of the sky?* (condensation and precipitation). Finally they considered where it goes (evaporation) and how the process can start all over again, and they drew pictures to show the rain cycle. Harnessing the children's excitement and curiosity, the teacher used this naturally occurring event as an opportunity to support the children's development of new knowledge.

Summary

Piaget described the child as a lone scientist who learns through practical experience. He viewed learning as a journey of discovery and was more interested in the process than the outcome. He was one of the first researchers to base his research on detailed observations of children, to use a diary to note small changes in infant development and to use interviews with older children to determine what they were thinking. Using this evidence, he devised a theory that children's thinking follows a step-wise three-stage approach, which he argued was invariant and universal. Each of the three stages outlined by Piaget must be completed before the child can progress to the final stage of formal operations. For Piaget, schemas are concepts that evolve and develop through two complementary systems: accommodation and assimilation. Equilibrium is achieved when internal and external events or information are in balance. As children attempt to reduce the mental conflict caused by tension between what they know (their internal mental state) and external information, they develop and enhance their thinking. His theory fuelled interest in child development and led others to develop alternative theories. The concepts of equilibration and egocentrism have been the subject of considerable criticism. Similarly, Piaget's theory failed to consider the influence that individual differences, culture, environment, gender or motivation exert on the child's cognitive development. Whereas Piaget had no access to Vygotsky's work, Vygotsky was deeply influenced by Piaget's theory and proposed a theory which took account of the child's environment and culture. Vygotsky's theory is discussed in detail in Chapter 6. Table 5.1 presents the strengths and weaknesses of Piaget's theory, and Table 5.2 compares the similarities and differences.

Table 5.1   Strengths and weaknesses of Piaget's theory

Strengths	Weaknesses
Adopts a child-centred approach. Children are viewed as active and powerful participants in the learning process.	
Posits a theory of cognitive development.	The theory is argued to be inflexible, rigid and to underestimate young children's ability.
	The theory fails to acknowledge the importance of culture, the child's environment, race, gender and motivation in the child's ability to learn.
	Terms such as equilibration lack clarity and are impossible to either prove or disprove.
Employs qualitative approaches including observations, listening to children as they complete tasks and interviewing children.	Lacks detail. Information concerning the participant groups is missing.
	The sample employed in observations was too small for the generalizations made by Piaget.
	Opponents claim that the questions posed in tasks are designed to 'catch children out'.

Strengths	Weaknesses
Is devised around a range of experimental tasks.	The tasks are argued to be complex and unfamiliar to the children.
	Wood (1998) pointed out that the vocabulary used in the tasks was too advanced for young children and caused them to fail.
	Egocentrism: Research suggests that children are considerably less egocentric than Piaget believed (Donaldson 1978).
Focuses on process rather than product.	
Recognizes the central importance of play.	
Highlights the importance of the child's 'readiness' to learn.	This suggests there is little an adult can do to enhance children's thinking.
	It assumes that readiness can be identified.
	As Duckworth (1987, 31) notes, in waiting for readiness a teacher is 'either too early and they [children] can't learn it, or too late and they already know it'.
	The concept of readiness ignores culture, race, gender and social and emotional differences.
Identifies the importance of peer interaction and collaborative learning.	
Affords the teacher a minimal role.	It gives the teacher a secondary role.
	It assumes that all children are capable of discovery learning without assistance or direction.
	Piaget tended to portray children in a negative light, focusing on what they couldn't do rather than on what they could do.

Table 5.2   Piaget and behaviourism: similarities and differences

Similarities	Differences
Theory: Pavlov, Watson, Skinner and Piaget posited ground-breaking theories of learning.	**Theory:** Piaget offered the first detailed explanation of the processes involved in children's acquisition of learning.
Evidence base: They provided empirical evidence to support their learning theory.	**Education:** Piaget described children as lone scientists who are actively involved in their own learning. He viewed teachers as facilitators rather than instructors of learning. In contrast, Behaviourists promoted a didactic 'chalk and talk' approach to learning.
Child participants: Watson, Skinner and Piaget studied children's learning.	
Active participants: Skinner and Piaget believed that children were active participants in the learning process.	

(Continued)

Table 5.2 (Continued)

Similarities	Differences
Research: The theories posited by Pavlov, Watson, Skinner and Piaget fuelled interest in the development of learning. Research continues to examine the processes involved in the transmission and acquisition of learning.	**Process vs product**: Piaget was more interested in process than product.
Unpopularity: Behaviourism, like Piaget, lost favour, though it remains an influential theory.	
Qualitative methods: Whereas Behaviourists favour quantitative experimental methods, Piaget employed a qualitative approach to study child development. The methods included observations, interviews and listening to children as they completed tasks.	

 RECOMMENDED READING

Duveen, G. (2000). Piaget ethnographer. Symposium: Qualitative methods. *Social science information, 39,* 79–97. Available at: http://ssi.sagepub.com/content/39/1/79.full.pdf+html (accessed 11.4.15).

While Piaget's theory has been extensively critiqued, less attention is afforded his contribution to qualitative research. In this paper, Duveen explores Piaget's contribution to the interpretative approach.

Erneling, C. (2014). The importance of Jean Piaget. *Philosophy of the Social Sciences, 44, 4,* 522–35. Available at: http://pos.sagepub.com/content/44/4/522.full.pdf+html (accessed 11.4.15).

Published by SAGE, this open access article offers a robust critique of *The Cambridge Companion to Piaget* published in 2009, edited by Müller, Carpendale and Smith. Erneling argues the authors have misinterpreted Piaget's theory and draws on a substantial evidence base to support her claims. This thought-provoking article will extend your understanding of Piaget's theory.

Nutbrown, C. (2011). *Threads of Thinking: Schemas and Young Children's Learning,* 4th edn. London: Sage.

A favourite amongst early childhood students, Nutbrown offers excellent insight.

REFERENCES

Athey, C. (2003). *Extending Thought in Young Children: A Parent–Teacher Partnership.* London: Paul Chapman.

Bruner, J.S. (1986). *Achial Minds, Possible Worlds.* Cambridge: Harvard University Press.

Calloway, W.R. (2001). *Jean Piaget: A Most Outrageous Deception*. New York: NOVA.

Chapman, M. (1999). Constructivism and the problem of reality. *Journal of Applied Psychology, 20,* 31–43.

Claxton, G. (1998). *Hare Brain, Tortoise Mind: Why Intelligence Increases When You Think Less*. London: Fourth Estate.

Corsaro, W.A. (1992). Interpretative reproduction in children's peer cultures. *Social Psychology Quarterly, 55,* 160–77.

Dasen, P.R. and Heron, A. (1992). Cross-cultural tests of Piaget's Theory. In L. Smith (Ed.) *Jean Piaget: Critical Assessments*. London: Routledge.

Dewey, J. (1959). *School and Society*. Chicago, IL: University of Chicago Press.

Doise, W., Mugny, G. and Perret-Clermont, A.N. (1975). Social interaction and the development of cognitive operations. *European Journal of Social Psychology, 5, 3,* 367–83.

Donaldson, M. (1978). *Children's Minds*. Glasgow: Fontana.

Duckworth, E. (1987). *The Having of Wonderful Ideas and Other Essays on Teaching and Learning*. New York: Teachers College Press.

Duveen, G. (2000). Piaget ethnographer. Symposium: Qualitative methods. *Social science information, 39,* 79–97. Available at: http://ssi.sagepub.com/content/39/1/79.full.pdf+html (accessed 11.4.15).

Elkind, D. (1972). Giant in the nursery – Jean Piaget. In R.F. Biehler (Ed.) *Psychology Applied to Teaching: Selected Reading*. Boston, MA: Houghton Mifflin.

Erneling, C. (2014). The importance of Jean Piaget. *Philosophy of the Social Sciences, 44, 4,* 522–35. Available at: http://pos.sagepub.com/content/44/4/522.full.pdf+html (accessed 11.4.15).

EYFS Statutory framework for the early years foundation stage (2014). Setting the standards for learning, development and care for children from birth to five Reference: DFE-00337-2014.

Fischer, K.W. (1980). A theory of cognitive development: the control and construction of hierarchical skills. *Psychological Review, 8, 2,* 477–531.

Flavell, J.H. (1963). *The Developmental Psychology of Jean Piaget*. New York: Van Nostrand.

Flavell, J.H. (1977). *Cognitive Development*. Englewood Cliffs, NJ: Prentice Hall.

Hepach, R., Vaish, A. and Tomasello, M. (2013a). A new look at children's prosocial motivation. *Infancy, 18, 1,* 67–90.

Hepach, R., Vaish, A. and Tomasello, M. (2013b). Young children sympathise less in response to unjustified emotional distress. *Developmental Psychology, 49, 6,* 1132–8.

Hughes, M. (1978). Selecting pictures of another person's view. *British Journal of Educational Psychology, 1,* 207–219.

Hunt, J.M. (1961). *Intelligence and Experience*. New York: Ronald Press.

Huntsinger, C., Jose, P.E., Kreig, D.B. and Luo, Z. (2011). Cultural differences in Chinese American and European American children's drawing skills over time. *Early Childhood Research Quarterly, 26, 1,* 134–45.

Isaacs, S. (1930). *Intellectual Growth in Young Children*. London: Routledge & Kegan Paul.

Leddon, E.M., Waxman, S.R, and Medin, D.L. (2008). Unmasking 'alive': children's appreciation of a concept linking all living things. *Journal of Cognition and Development, 9, 14,* 461–73.

Lefrancois, G. (1995). *Theories of Human Learning*, 3rd edn. Pacific, CA: Brooks/Cole.

Meadows, M. (1993). *The Young Child as Thinker: The Cognitive Development and Acquisition of Cognition in Childhood*. London: Routledge.

Montessori, M. (1972 [1949]). *Education and Peace*. Chicago, MA: Regnery.

Müller, U., Carpendale, J.I.M. and Smith, L. (2009). *The Cambridge Companion to Piaget*. Cambridge: Cambridge University Press.

Nutbrown, C. (2011). *Threads of Thinking: Schema and Young Children's Learning,* 4th edn. London: Sage.

Peel, E.A. (1971). *The Nature of Adolescent Judgment*. London: Staples.

Piaget, J.P. (1952). *The Origins of Intelligence in Children*. New York: International Universities Press.

Piaget, J.P. (1954). *The Construction of Reality in the Child*. London: Routledge & Kegan Paul.

Piaget, J.P. (1962). *Play, Dreams and Imitation in Childhood*. New York: Norton.

Piaget, J.P. (1969). *Intellectual Operations and their Development*. New York: Basic Books.

Piaget, J.P. (1970). *Science of Education and the Psychology of the Child*. New York: Orion.

Piaget, J.P. (1972). *To Understand is to Invent*. New York: Viking.

Piaget, J.P. and Inhelder, B. (1956). *The Child's Conception of Space*. London: Routledge.

Price-Williams, D., Gordon, W. and Ramirez, M. (1969). Skill and conservation: a study of pottery-making children. *Developmental Psychology, 1,* 769.

Schaffer, H.R. (2004). *Introducing Child Psychology*. Oxford: Blackwell.

Shayer, M. and Adey, P. (Eds.) (2002). *Learning and Intelligence: Cognitive Acceleration Across the Curriculum from 5 to 15 Years*. Buckingham: Open University Press.

Smidt, S. (2009). *Introducing Vygotsky: A Guide for Practitioners and Students in Early Years Education*. Routledge: London.

Sutherland, P. (1992). *Cognitive Development Today: Piaget and his Critics*. London: Paul Chapman.

Vygotsky, L.S. (1978). *Mind in Society: The Development of Higher Psychological Processes*. Cambridge: Harvard University Press.

Vygotsky, L.S. (1986). *Thought and Language,* 2nd edn. Oxford: Blackwell.

Wood, D. (1998). *How Children Think and Learn,* 2nd edn. Oxford: Blackwell.

Want to learn more about this Chapter?
Visit the companion website at **https://study.sagepub.com/grayandmacblain2e** to gain open access to selected SAGE journal articles, author podcasts and weblinks to help further your study.

6 VYGOTSKY: LEARNING IN A SOCIAL MATRIX

This chapter aims to:

• familiarize students with Vygotsky's theory of social constructivism
• illustrate this theory using practical examples
• highlight the strengths and weaknesses of Vygotsky's theory.

LEV SEMYONOVICH VYGOTSKY (1896–1934)

Lev Vygotsky was born into a traditional Jewish family in Orsha, Russia (now Belarus) on 17 November 1896, the same year as Piaget. He began his studies in medicine at Moscow University at a time when Jews suffered considerable discrimination. He transferred to law school before again changing course to study literature, art and philosophy at Shanavsky University in Moscow. After completing his dissertation on *The Psychology of Art*, he became a junior psychologist at the Psychological Institute of Moscow University. He later taught psychology at a local teacher training college where he formed a research 'troika' (threesome) group with Alexander Luria and Alexei Leontiev. During his short lifetime, Vygotsky wrote more than 180 papers; some are only now being translated. Similar to Piaget, Vygotsky's focus was on child development. He is, however, credited with developing an approach that connects social and mental processes and describes cognitive development as an essentially social process. Vygotsky married and had two daughters. His daughter and granddaughter continue to develop his work.

Theories of the mind

At their height in the late 1920s, Vygotsky's theories about the mind were among the most influential in Russia. Such was the popularity of his work that it attracted the attention of the Communist government, who denounced it on the grounds that it was little more than bourgeois idealism that referenced the Western theorists Freud and Piaget. Vygotsky's work was subsequently banned by Stalin and confined to a single central library in Moscow, accessible only by special permission from the secret police. There it remained undiscovered by Western scholars until the 1960s. Vygotsky's popularity soared and waned again in the 1970s, only to emerge as a *tour de force* in the mid-1980s. Indeed, such was his renewed popularity that Toulmin (1978) described Vygotsky as 'the Mozart of Psychology'. You will notice that, although he is long dead, references to Vygotsky's work are cited as 1956, 1962, 1971, 1978, 1987–98. These books and papers are recent translations of Vygotsky's original papers. Both Meadows (1993) and Daniels (2005) note that many of these translations are peppered with inaccuracies and misinterpretations, and are truncated (abbreviated) to exclude all mention of Marxist philosophy. This is an important omission, since Marxism serves to contextualize and explain the influences that determined Vygotsky's views.

Mindful of these points, the information presented in this chapter is drawn from a large body of credible sources that seek to faithfully report Vygotsky's theory (including Daniels 2005; Meadows 1993; Schaffer, 2004 and Sutherland, 1992).

VYGOTSKY AND SOCIAL CONSTRUCTIVISM

According to *social constructivist* theory, it is important to consider the quality and nature of the child's environment, their age, culture and life experiences before drawing any conclusions about their development.

Definition

Constructivism: an approach to teaching and learning based on the premise that cognition is the result of mental construction.

Vygotsky believed that all aspects of a person's learning have a history based on real-life experience, much of it acquired before a child ever starts formal education. In keeping with his theoretical perspective, Vygotsky never proposed a theory of child development. Schaffer notes that:

the only statement he made about age was to suggest that children up to two years are influenced primarily by biological forces and that the socio-cultural influences which form the focus of his writings do not come into play until after that age – an assertion clearly not supported by more recent work. (2004, p. 201)

Similarly, his interest was never in the child as an individual but, reflecting his Marxist ideology, in the child as a member of their cultural context. According to Vygotsky, development is not an individual process but the result of an aggregate of social relations embodied within the individual. In order to understand the path and nature of child development, Vygotsky believed that it is essential to examine the social context in which children develop (Flewitt and Ang, 2015). He pointed out that children do not develop in isolation but in a social matrix. This social matrix is formed by the interconnection of social relationships and interactions between themselves and other children (Corsaro, 1992). Through these relationships and interactions, children collaborate towards a shared goal. Vygotsky's theory on the process of child development is summed up in the following comment:

> In the process of development, children begin to use the same forms of behaviour in relation to themselves and others initially used in relation to them. Children master the social forms of behaviour and transfer these forms to themselves ... It is through others that we develop into ourselves and ... this is true not only with regard to the individual but with regard to the history of every function. (Wertsch 1981, p. 164)

Like Piaget, he believed that infants are born with the basic building blocks of cognition: these include visual recognition, memory, attention and speed of processing. This enables the child to develop *higher-order thinking* skills such as problem solving, reasoning, planning and remembering (Rose et al. 2003). The child also has an innate ability to learn through instruction, a characteristic complemented by the adult's willingness to help and instruct. Thus, the cultural norms (accepted practices) of a society begin at the external level and, through experience and mediated learning, become internalized as thought.

> Every function in the child's cultural development appears twice: first, on the social level, and later on the individual level; first, between people (interpsychological), and then inside the child (intrapsychological). This applies equally to voluntary attention, to logical memory, and to the formation of concepts. All the higher functions originate as actual relations between human individuals. (Vygotsky, 1978, p. 57)

Exercise

Consider the above quote carefully. What does Vygotsky mean when he claims that learning involves two levels: a social and an individual level?

CULTURE AND SOCIETY

As previously suggested, Vygotsky's life and views were shaped by the social and political forces which revolutionized Russia. Vygotsky was particularly interested in supporting children with special educational needs and sought to explain the social and educational inequalities of the time. Similar to his contemporary Piaget, he believed that children are active constructors of their own knowledge and skills. In contrast to Piaget, however, he believed that child development is the result of interactions between the child and their social environment.

Example

Julie, aged 3 years and 2 months, is pretending to be a contestant on *Britain's Got Talent*. She is frustrated because she cannot work the toy microphone. She shakes it and bangs it before throwing it down. Clare (a playgroup assistant) picks it up and asks 'has it got batteries?' Turning it over in her hands, she points out that 'it's not switched on'. Passing the microphone back to Julie, Clare shows her how to switch it on and then encourages Julie to have a go. Clare further extends Julie's play by inviting Issac and Branden, who have been watching this exchange, to be judges with her on the *Britain's Got Talent* panel while Julie sings.

Both Piaget and Vygotsky would agree that the collaborative interaction taking place in the above scenario is extending Julie's knowledge of how a microphone works. As a social interactionist, Vygotsky would also note the shared cultural experience which underpins this interaction. Here, no explanation of this popular talent show is required; everyone involved is familiar with the programme and understands the roles involved. Reflecting Vygotsky's belief that children are not solitary constructors of their knowledge but members of their prevailing culture, he observes how social interaction can involve parents, siblings, peers, teachers and significant objects such as books or favourite toys. Each, he argued, provides the *cultural tools* necessary to develop the child's thinking.

Definitions

Social constructivism: this emphasizes the importance of culture and context in understanding what occurs in society and constructing knowledge based on this understanding (Pagram and McMahon, 1997).

> **Culture:** a complex concept; put simply, it involves the socially transmitted behaviour patterns, arts and beliefs passed from one generation to another.
>
> **Cultural tools:** the products of human cultural and historical activity.

Whilst cultural tools such as nursery rhymes, fairy stories, folklore, music and art become so familiar as to be invisible, Vygotsky was keen to acknowledge their role in the development of thinking. His views on the importance of cultural tools are best summed up in the following quote from Pea, who notes that:

> these tools literally carry intelligence in them, in that they represent some individual's or some community's decision that the means thus offered would be reified, made stable as quasi permanent, for the use of others. (1993, p. 52)

Consider the following examples.

Examples

1. Dylan (aged one 1 year and 10 months) is observed lifting his daddy's mobile phone and holding it to his ear, shouting 'hello, hello'. Later, he points the phone at the television; pressing several buttons, he tries to change channels.
2. Every morning, Anelisa (aged 3 years) and her sister Miriam (aged 5 years and 2 months) fetch drinking water from the stream (2 miles away) using plastic containers left by relief workers. The containers are light, have handles and are easy for the girls to carry.
3. Saturday is library day and Lita (aged 5 years and 6 months) is excited. She is hoping to borrow the book recommended by her friend Raine, *The Princess Mouse: A Tale of Finland* (Shepard, 2008). While Lita searches the shelves, her mummy watches from the coffee shop and chats to her friends. Lita can't read and doesn't start her formal education until she is 7 years old, but she enjoys meeting friends at the library.

In brief, cultural tools influence our perception, understanding and experience of the world. For Vygotsky, *lower-order thinking* involves unconscious biological functions such as memory, attention and intelligence. These processes are not value-free and are influenced by our feelings and emotions. Since lower-order functions are linked by biological, social, affective and cultural factors, Vygotsky termed them 'psychobiological functions'. In contrast, higher-order functions involve conscious deliberate intentions and actions, for example, problem solving

Lower-order thinking   *Higher-order thinking*

Thoughts ⎫ Attention   Mediated social   Problem solving
Feelings ⎬ Memory   collaborative activity   Logical reasoning
Values   ⎭ Intelligence   Abstract thinking

Figure 6.1   Bridging lower- and higher-order thinking

and logical reasoning. Mediated, social, collaborative activity can be thought of as the bridge that brings a child from lower-order (concrete) thinking to higher-order (abstract) thinking (see Figure 6.1).

In the latter part of this chapter we consider Vygotsky's notion that children make sense of the world through language and as they read. At this point we examine Vygotsky's theory on the role of language skills, which he viewed as essential in the development of concept formation.

> **Exercise**
>
> Look at Figure 6.1. Consider how thoughts, feelings and values might affect a child's attention, memory and intelligence. Would these factors have any impact on a child's ability to problem-solve, think logically, reason or think abstractly?

DEVELOPING LANGUAGE AND THOUGHT

Language is another cultural tool which Vygotsky believed mediates thinking and learning. He described it as 'a powerful and strong tool' in children's interactions. As children listen and respond to each other's ideas and contributions, they develop and enhance their own understanding. For Vygotsky, language plays a central role in the development of cognition:

> The structure of speech is not simply the mirror image of the structure of thought. It cannot, therefore, be placed on thought like clothes off a rack. Speech does not merely serve as the expression of developed thought. Thought is restructured as it is transformed into speech. It is not expressed but completed in the word. Therefore, precisely because of the contrasting directions of movements, the development of the internal and external aspects of speech forms a new unity. (Vygotsky 1987–98, cited in Holzman 2006, p. 115)

Although this aspect of his work was incomplete, Vygotsky attempted to chart the developmental course of language. He believed that language carries meaning and sense and must be interpreted by the child. Through these interpretations, the child contributes to society and society to the child. It is the interactive reciprocal nature of these relationships that underpins *social constructivism*. Vygotsky's theory comprises four stages, starting with the pre-verbal stage and progressing to the internalization of speech as thinking. It is important to remember that, unlike Piaget, Vygotsky was offering a general theory, not advocating a fixed and universal staged approach.

1. **Primitive stage**: Children under 2 years of age use vocal activity as a means of emotional expression and for social engagement. Non-verbal gesturing is not unusual during this stage as behaviour becomes increasingly purposeful and goal-directed. At the primitive stage, thought and language are separate. Pointing and staring are not uncommon during this stage and are easily interpreted by a sensitive caretaker who uses language to reinforce non-linguistic communications. Bruner (1986) saw gesture and non-verbal cues as having an enormous impact on the later development of language.

   Josh (aged 18 months) wants his bottle. Babbling, he points to the bottle on the work top and stares at it until his mum notices, interprets and rewards his actions. Giving him the bottle, she confirms 'you want your bottle'.

2. **Practical intelligence**: During this stage, the child's language uses syntactic (rules of speech) and logical forms. These forms of speech are linked to the child's practical problem-solving activities but are not linked in a systematic way (Meadows, 1993, p. 245).

   Maisie (aged 3 years and 2 months) has lost a piece of her jigsaw puzzle. She searches the table, then under the table, then in her pockets. Kerry, her key worker, asks if she is looking for the piece sitting on top of the nearly-completed jigsaw. Maisie laughs and slots it into place. Maisie has some understanding of logical actions but at this stage her search tends to be unsystematic and a little haphazard.

3. **External symbolic stage**: Thinking aloud is common during this stage, with language used to help with internal problem solving. The transition between external social speech and internal private speech is marked by egocentric speech – also termed 'thinking aloud'. Thinking aloud enables the child to self-regulate and plan their activities. Although Vygotsky believed that social speech precedes egocentric speech, he agreed that speech does not always require an audience.

   Katrina (aged 6 years and 4 months) is observed quietly counting on her fingers as she completes an exercise in class. She seeks the teacher's attention only to check her work.

4. **Internalization of symbolic tools**: Between 7 and 8 years of age, children internalize thinking and egocentric speech begins to disappear. Problem-solving continues to be guided by speech

but the voice is internal (thinking). This stage leads to greater cognitive independence, flexibility and freedom. Thought continues to be framed by internalized individual, cultural and societal norms.

Aarav (7 years old) is having a birthday party. His excitement intensifies as each friend arrives with a beautifully wrapped gift. His delight is not simply the present, though that signifies the importance of the event, but his friends' recognition that today is his special day. Aarav has internalized the cultural practices and expectations associated with birthday parties.

Unlike Piaget, Vygotsky did not advocate a staged, unidirectional approach to development. On the one hand, he believed that development is progressive and tends to follow an incremental pathway. On the other, he acknowledged that a child may move backwards or forwards between the stages outlined above as their thoughts mature. Problem novelty or difficulty can cause a child to regress to an earlier stage, whereas experience will progress development. It was the flexibility of his theoretical approach to how language development informs thinking that led Sutherland (1992) to conclude that Vygotsky's theory was decades ahead of its time.

PLAY, CREATIVITY AND THOUGHT

Vygotsky believed that imaginary play is a precursor to abstract thinking. Through play children exercise their understanding of objects, develop relationships, mimic adult behaviour and adopt fantasy roles. Vygotsky (1987–98, p. 28) described play as 'self-education'. Vygotsky's notion of the development of play parallels the work of Piaget. Both believed that infants as young as 12 months are capable of object substitution (using one object to substitute for another) but that it mainly occurs in the second year and, for Vygotsky, is initiated by adults. As with other social and cultural behaviours, play is mediated through the nursery rhymes, songs, stories and fables that denote the child's culture.

According to Vygotsky, children's play is not merely a process of repetition. While it begins in social interactions with adults, the child soon displays independent, pretend and creative play. During this latter phase, the child is beginning to develop autonomy and takes charge of their play experience. They become more confident and adventurous, and develop rules that they may share with their peers but which may exclude adults. Wood (2011), for example, observed children's play in a nursery playground over a period of time. Concerns had been raised regarding the children's failure to use the climbing equipment in the playground. In the course of her observations, Wood found that the children had invented their own game, which excluded the Troggs (what the children called the adults in the setting). The game had set rules with punishments included for violations. The children would sneak into the playhouse to hide from the Troggs but peep up every so often to see if they had been caught. If caught, the children imposed their own punishment – hopping through a set of tyres. The climbing frame was considered to be 'out of bounds' because it was visible to the adults in the setting.

Vygotsky would explain this behaviour as imaginative play predicated on a shared understanding of the rules. Vygotsky believed that imaginative play begins at the social level; then through the medium of language it becomes internalized as thought. By early adolescence, social and environmental props are no longer required to support fantasy and imaginative thought. Interestingly, today's children and adults are less likely to abandon props and increasingly engage in fantasy play through the medium of computer games.

Vygotsky's theory of imaginative play is extended by Marilyn Fleer (2014), who offers a brief explanation of how Vygotsky's conception of play is a central design principle for supporting creativity when using digital tools.

Weblink

Fleer, M. (2014) 'Vygotsky's conception of play in context of slowmation'. Available at: www.youtube.com/watch?v=dY3EH7YQhww (accessed 11.4.15).

THE ZONE OF PROXIMAL DEVELOPMENT: WALKING A HEAD TALLER

The *zone of proximal development* (ZPD) is one of the most extensively referenced and least understood aspects of Vygotsky's work (Palinscar 1998). Although it appears in only a few of the many thousands of pages Vygotsky wrote during his short lifetime, students tend to focus on this aspect of his work to the exclusion of others (Tudge, 1992). Murphy (2012) described the ZPD as a work in progress and notes that the term was initially used as an index for intellectual potential and later as an educational concept focusing on the conditions necessary to establish a ZPD. Vygotsky defined the ZPD as:

> those functions which have yet to mature but are in the process of maturing … 'buds' or 'flowers' of development rather than 'fruits' of development. The actual development level characterises the cognitive development retrospectively while the ZPD characterises it prospectively. (1978, p. 86)

In order to provide tailored learning opportunities for children, Vygotsky believed that it is necessary to establish two developmental levels (Meadows, 1993). The lower level provides a baseline measure of what a child can achieve independently on an ability test or task. The higher measure is the level the child can achieve with help and support. According to Vygotsky, the ZPD is:

> not a specific quality of the child, nor is it a specific quality of the educational setting or educators … It is … collaboratively produced in the interaction between the child and more knowledgeable others. The aim of this collaborative interaction is to lift the learner to become 'a head taller'. (1978, p. 102)

The child at the lower level of the ZPD is dependent on the teacher to guide and develop their learning. The adult is tasked with developing a self-regulated and increasingly competent learner. With this in mind, the adult's goal is to progressively reduce support as the child develops expertise. The child at the optimal level of the ZPD has achieved a degree of independence and ownership of their learning which renders further assistance unnecessary. At this point, new tasks and challenges can be identified to develop the child's learning further. Vygotsky believed that the ZPD offers a diagnostic tool to facilitate the development of a plan of learning to extend and support the learner. He acknowledged that individual children will require different levels of support and are capable of different levels of achievement. He asks the reader to imagine that:

> we have examined two children and we have determined that the mental age of both is seven years. This means that both children solve tasks accessible to seven-year-olds. However, when we attempt to push these children further in carrying out the tests, there turns out to be an essential difference between them. With the help of leading questions, examples and demonstrations one of them easily solves test items taken from two years above the child's level of development. The other solves problems that are only a half-year above his or her development. (Vygotsky 1956, pp. 446–7)

Figure 6.2 illustrates the child's potential for improvement with support. The child's potential is determined by a knowledgeable adult such as a parent, Early Years professional or teacher who will strive to plan, monitor and develop the child's ability. Whilst it is important to help the child improve upon their current ability level, it is equally important that goals within the ZPD are achievable and realistic rather than unachievable and aspirational. Beyond the ZPD remain all the problems and tasks that the child has yet to encounter and which exceed the child's current ability level, even with support.

Figure 6.2   A schematic view of the zone of proximal development

Exercise

Consider the reasons why some problems or tasks may be beyond the child's current ability level, even with support.

Although he did not address the issue of individual differences in detail, Vygotsky clearly acknowledged that children are individuals with different levels of potential. He pointed out that even when two children of the same age display a similar level of ability, their potential may be limited by personal or internal factors such as intelligence and motivation, or by external social and environmental factors. In essence, Vygotsky believed that a knowledgeable adult will tailor a programme to suit the child rather than expect every child to rise to meet unrealistic goals. In the figure below, you will note that child A and child B both started with the same level of ability and with support both made improvements. Whereas child A went on to make significant gains, child B made modest progress (see Figure 6.3).

In 1976, Wood et al. coined the term 'scaffolding' as a metaphor to explain the nature of the aid provided by an adult for a child who could not successfully complete a task alone. The concept arose from their observations of the strategies

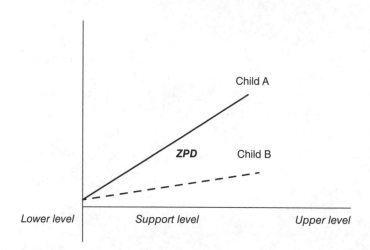

Figure 6.3   Individual levels of progress

mothers used to help their 3 to 4-year-old children complete a wooden block task. They noted that children were encouraged to complete as much of the task as possible alone before assistance was offered. Benson sums this view when he states that 'scaffolding is actually a bridge used to build upon what students already know to arrive at something they do not know; if scaffolding is properly administered, it will act as an enabler, not as a disabler' (1997, pp. 126–7).

Consider the examples below.

Examples

1. Tia (aged 3 years and 6 months) enjoys jigsaws. She has a large collection of 10- and 15-piece jigsaws at home and is frustrated with the 'baby' 5- and 10-piece jigsaws available in nursery. To extend Tia's learning, her teacher sources a number of 20- and 25-piece jigsaws including Tia's favourites: Hello Kitty, Elsa the Snow Queen from Disney's Frozen and Peppa Pig.

2. Alex (aged 4 years and 2 months) is making a spider for Halloween. He tries to cut out the spider's body but his first effort ends in disaster when the scissors slip and he cuts the body in half. His second and third efforts are no better and he is frustrated with the 'stupid scissors'. Maura, his key worker, shows him how to hold the scissors so they won't slip; she then demonstrates how to cut out the spider's body. Alex's fourth attempt is successful and with Maura's help he sticks on each of the eight fuzzy felt spider legs.

Support for Vygotsky's ZPD theory is provided in a number of studies, including Freund's seminal doll's house experiment. As part of her doctoral research, Freund (1990) explored mother–child interactions using two groups of children aged between 3 and 5 years. The task involved selecting and placing items of furniture in a doll's house. The first group of children completed a similar task with help from their mother (ZPD) before working on the experimental task alone. The second group had no previous guidance and worked alone on the task (Piaget's discovery learning). Freund found that children with prior experience and support from their mothers easily completed the task, whereas the second group were less proficient. She concluded that guided learning within the ZPD led to greater understanding/performance than working alone (discovery learning).

Effective scaffolding appears to have a number of general features which Applebee and Langer (1983) summarized as including:

1. **Intentionality**: The task has a clear overall purpose driving any separate activity that may contribute to the whole.
2. **Appropriateness**: Instructional tasks pose problems that can be solved with help but which students cannot successfully complete on their own.
3. **Structure**: Modelling and questioning activities are structured around a model of appropriate approaches to the task and lead to a natural sequence of thought and language.
4. **Collaboration**: The teacher's response to student work recasts and expands upon the students' efforts without rejecting what they have accomplished on their own. The teacher's primary role is collaborative rather than evaluative.
5. **Internalization**: External scaffolding for the activity is gradually withdrawn as the patterns are internalized by the students.

Vygotsky believed that children create their own ZPD during play. He believed that 'play creates a zone of proximal development for the child. In play a child always behaves beyond his average age, above his daily behaviour' (1987–98, p. 102 cited in Hogan and Tudge 1999). Although he cautioned against an over intellectualizing of children's play, he believed it was highly important in young children's development, particularly in the use of symbolic forms.

PEER COLLABORATION

The subject of peer collaboration was discussed at length in Chapter 5, where Piaget's views on peer collaboration are explored. For a full understanding of the advantages and disadvantages of peer collaboration, it is important that you refer back to that section. One of the main tenets of Piaget's theory was the belief that peer interaction was effective when one member of the dyad had achieved an understanding of conservation. Drawing on evidence from his own research, he concluded that non-conservers were more likely to attain conservation through their experience of working with a more expert peer than when working alone. Similarly, Vygotsky believed that collaboration was more effective when one member of the dyad had greater experience than the other. Whereas Piaget discussed peer interaction, Vygotsky focused on adult-led interactions, particularly between the teacher and the child.

Two key concepts underpin Vygotsky's theory. The first is the zone of proximal development previously discussed in this chapter. The second concerns the concept of intersubjectivity, which seeks to bring different perspectives together to form an agreed view. For example, Josh (aged 3 years and 3 months) is playing with his garage but the lift bringing the cars from the bottom to the top level isn't working. His dad has a look and asks him what the problem is; Josh explains that 'it's broken'. On examination, his dad finds a crayon lodged in the mechanism. Following his dad's instructions, Josh removes the crayon. Once free, the lift works again. Here, Josh and his father start from different perspectives but, working collaboratively, come to a mutual or intersubjective understanding.

According to Vygotsky,

> he continues to work in collaboration even though the teacher is not standing near him ... This help – this aspect of collaboration – is invisibly present. It is contained in what looks from the outside like the child's independent solution of the problems. (1987–98, p. 216)

A central theme of Piaget and Vygotsky's theory is the effectiveness of *asymmetric relationships*, which foster the transfer of knowledge from a more knowledgeable peer to a less experienced learner. Both theorists believed that a *symmetrical* relationship, which includes peers who bring the same knowledge to a problem, is no different from the child solving the problem alone. Similar to Piaget, Vygotsky was more concerned with the *process* than the *product* of higher-order thinking. For that reason, he tended to focus on the social interaction taking place during collaborative learning rather than on the benefit of the experience for the learner. Although much of the research on collaborative learning reports positive benefits (see Chapter 5 for a discussion), there are discrepancies about the conditions that mediate improvement. Support for the notion that mixed-ability groups are more collaborative and effective than similar-ability groups comes from a recent study by Kutnick and Blatchford (2014) into effective class groups. They concluded that cooperative groups, which involve children as co-learners, tend to be large, have teacher involvement, include boys and girls, comprise a broad mix of age ranges (see the section on Golden Key Schools in this chapter) and enjoy contextual support for collaboration. Conversely, less effective groups tend to be small; include children of similar ages, genders and abilities; and may be perceived by the wider group as exclusionary.

Another problem in collaborative relationships concerns the issue of ownership and the importance afforded each participant's perspective. For example, Jacob (aged 3 years and 5 months) is building a tower with bricks. He searches for smaller bricks to place at the top of his tower but each brick he selects is too large or too small and falls off. His brother Moses (aged 6 years and 7 months) decides to help. He points to the yellow angled bricks and asks Jacob to hand him one, then another and another. As Moses successfully places each brick in position, Jacob becomes increasingly agitated. Eventually he shouts at Moses to 'go away. They's mine bricks, not youse bricks'. In attempting to help Jacob, Moses took control of the problem, rendering Jacob's efforts redundant.

CRITICISMS OF VYGOTSKY

A number of criticisms have been levelled at the interpretation of Vygotsky's work. For example, it is argued that Vygotsky did not describe himself as a social constructivist; this label was attached by contemporary scholars during the translation of his work (Hua Liu and Matthews 2005). Translations of his work from Russian into English have led to an emphasis on some aspects of his work to the detriment of others and to superficial interpretations. By way of example, the ZPD thought to exemplify Vygotsky's theory appears less than nine times in all of the thousands of pages he wrote (Kamen and Murphy, 2012). It is also argued that, in keeping with his Marxist ideology, Vygotsky was concerned with society and people at the collective rather than the individual level (Resnick, 1996). Implicit in Vygotsky's theory is the rather optimistic notion that all social and cultural experiences will have a positive impact upon the developing child. Yet the cases of Victoria Climbé and Baby P remind us that some children live and die in appalling circumstances.

Vygotsky's emphasis on the importance of language in the development of learning has been roundly criticized by Fox (2001), who points out that if thought cannot exist without language, then a child is devoid of thought until they can speak. He continues by arguing that this theory 'ignores all the implicit knowledge we have of the world which we have never put into words' (pp. 29–30).

Moreover, Vygotsky's focus on spoken language ignored the role of social and experiential learning and the impact sign language has on a child's cognitive development. Acknowledging the role symbolic language plays in fostering children's cognitive development, the Reggio Emilia approach focuses on systematic symbolic interaction (Edwards et al., 2012). Using this approach, young children are encouraged to explore their environment and express themselves through multiple paths and all their 'languages', including the expressive, communicative, symbolic, cognitive, ethical, metaphorical, logical, imaginative and relational (Reggio Children, 2010).

Weblinks

An explanation of the Reggio Emilia philosophy is available at: www.aneverydaystory.com/beginners-guide-to-reggio-emilia/main-principles/ (accessed 11.4.15).

According to Daniels (2005), many of Vygotsky's theories are incomplete and lack sophistication. This may be attributed to his early death at the age of 38 and the fact that his understanding of psychology and psychological theories was derived from personal study, while his university training was in the arts and theatre.

VYGOTSKY IN ACTION: GOLDEN KEY SCHOOLS

Definition

Perestroika: a series of political and economic reforms in the former Soviet Union under the leadership of Mikhail Gorbachov, which encouraged trade between Russia and non-Marxist countries. Translates literally from Russian as 'restructuring'.

Led by Elena Kravtsova (Vygotsky's granddaughter), since 1989 and with *Perestroika*, over 30 Golden Key Schools have been established to develop Vygotsky's sociocultural theory of education. Kamen and Murphy (2012, p.4) detail how the Golden Key programme developed from a number of programmes and educational philosophies including: Swedish kindergartens, the English nurturing system, Steiner's anthroposophy, Waldorf's pedagogy and the seminal work of Vygotsky. Reflecting the core principles of sociocultural theory, Golden Key Schools are premised on the promotion of culture and history and cater for children between 3 and 10 years of age. Robbins (2010) and Kamen and Murphy (2012) describe the five principles in the programme as follows:

1. **Mixed age groups**: The school has mixed-age and single-age teaching to allow the older children to reflect their learning on to younger children, who benefit from learning from more advanced peers.
2. **Family principles**: Golden Key Schools are organized around family principles, including active parental involvement. Children are taught in 'families' of 15 to 25 children aged between 3 and 10 years of age rather than in age-specific classes. The children meet in their families every school day to discuss problems and to learn to solve problems. Since there are children of different ages in each family, the older children model behaviour and support the younger children.
3. **Meaningful events or happenings**: Lessons are centred on events that are highly meaningful to the child and touch their emotions. Subsequently, each lesson follows a plot directly related to the event.
4. **Interaction and interdependence**: The focus is on the interaction and interdependence of education and development. This ensures that lessons are age-appropriate and that learning takes place within the ZPD.
5. **Paired pedagogues**: Classes are taught by two teachers; one acts as an expert and the other as a novice, who asks questions to extend the children's knowledge and understanding.

Similarities can be drawn between the Vygotskian philosophy that frames Golden Key Schools and Reggio Emilia. Similar to Golden Key Schools, the teacher in the internationally renowned schools in Reggio Emilia, Italy, play a central role in helping children plan and execute their work. They guide discussions and activities and monitor outcomes. Reflecting the central tenet of Vygotsky's theory, teachers in Reggio schools scaffold learning and provide stimulating environments to promote discussions and challenge children's thinking (O'Brien 2002). Both approaches seek to develop children who are securely embedded within their social and cultural group.

Vygotsky's influence is not confined to Russia. He continues to have a presence in Early Years settings in many countries in the developed world. This is particularly evident in recent educational reforms in the UK – Desirable Outcomes for Children's Learning on Entering Compulsory Education. Department of Education and School Curriculum and Assessment Authority (SCAA, 1996); Early Learning Goals (QCA, 2000); National Strategies Early Years document (DfE, 2010) – predicated on the notion that instruction can and should precede learning. Similarly, his theory has had a significant impact on the development of a new school of thought, variously termed 'the new social studies of childhood,' 'the new sociology of childhood' and 'childhood studies', discussed in Chapter 9.

Summary

Like Piaget, Vygotsky believed that young children are curious and actively involved in their own learning and the discovery and development of new understandings/schema. Vygotsky's pedagogical theory is based on the Marxist view of relations between human consciousness and the material world. He believed that children develop in a social matrix formed by the interconnection of social relationships and interactions between themselves and other children. These experiences are internalized as thought. One of his most controversial claims concerns the notion that thought is internalized language. Interpreted literally, this theory implies that a child with a language delay or language difficulty is either only partially able to think or devoid of thought. Table 6.1 lists the strengths and weaknesses of Vygotsky's theory.

Whereas Piaget emphasized self-initiated discovery, Vygotsky focused on the role of the teacher. He did not believe that children were passive recipients of knowledge informed by knowledgeable teachers but viewed the teacher as a facilitator of learning. The social environment is given prominence in teaching, with effective teachers providing a stimulating and challenging learning environment. Reminiscent of Piaget's theory about assimilation and accommodation, Vygotsky believed that new knowledge builds on and extends previous knowledge. Through sensitive teaching and peer collaboration, a child can walk a 'head taller'. The zone of proximal development (ZPD) is perhaps the most widely referenced aspect of Vygotsky's work. Through observation or testing, an Early Years practitioner begins by determining the child's existing level of knowledge and, through skilful mentoring, extends the child's learning. He termed the difference between the child's existing knowledge base and higher-level thinking 'the ZPD'. The issue of understood learning was developed by a group of American researchers who sought to understand how learning and thinking can be scaffolded through the ZPD metaphor. Scaffolding is discussed in greater detail in Chapter 8. Similar to scaffolding, 'sustained shared thinking' (see Chapter 10) is another approach employed to enhance children's learning. Although the term is relatively new, the concept is well known to Early Years professionals and a statutory obligation of EYFS (2014). Although criticisms have been levelled against Vygotsky's work, they mostly concern the incomplete nature of his work. Nevertheless, for many, he remains 'the Mozart of Psychology'. Similarities in Vygotsky and Piaget's theoretical perspectives are listed in Table 6.2.

Table 6.1 Strengths and weaknesses of Vygotsky's theory

Strengths	Weaknesses
Adopts a child-centred approach. Children are viewed as active and powerful participants in the learning process.	
Emphasizes the role of culture and the environment in the child's learning.	
Offers a theory of cognitive development roughly associated with age. Vygotsky did not believe that development followed a fixed-stage,	Many early years theorists dispute suggestions of staged development, arguing it fails to take account of individual differences.

Strengths	Weaknesses
invariant approach. On the contrary, he believed that a difficult task may cause a child to revert to earlier forms of learning, such as counting on their fingers.	
Employs qualitative approaches, including observing and listening to children as they completed tasks.	1. He conducted very few studies to support his claims. 2. Evidence for his claims is supplied by his supporters, who interpreted his meaning.
Is based on a belief that learning can precede understanding. Children can be taught concepts that extend and develop their current learning.	
Focuses on process rather than product.	
Recognizes the central importance of play.	
Is based on a belief that language precedes thought.	This is a highly controversial claim. Children without speech or who have limited speech, according to this notion, would be incapable of thought.
Explains the internalization of language as thought.	
Identifies the importance of peer interaction and collaborative learning.	
Affords the teacher a central role in the child's learning. Teachers are considered facilitators who scaffold and develop learning.	
Identifies the importance of developing the child's potential.	The zone of proximal development is frequently misunderstood and given greater prominence by academics and students than afforded by Vygotsky.
	The theory has been translated and truncated to exclude Vygotsky's Marxist views. Translations have led to misinterpretations.

Table 6.2   Similarities in Vygotsky and Piaget's theoretical perspectives

Child-centred: Children are viewed as active and powerful participants in the learning process. **Cognitive conflict:** They both believed that cognitive development is initiated by cognitive conflict. Piaget termed the state of cognitive imbalance which drives learning 'disequilibration'. **Constructivism:** As constructivists, both believed that cognition is the result of mental construction. A constructivist teacher creates a context for learning in which students can become engaged in interesting activities that encourage and facilitate learning.	**Experiential learning:** They both believed that intelligence comes from actions. Experiential learning experiences might involve the child in baking cookies, growing watercress, playing games or creating art using junk. Through these activities, the child constructs knowledge. **Peer collaboration:** They both identified the importance of peer interaction and collaborative learning. They believed that effective peer collaboration was asymmetric, fostering the transfer of knowledge from a more knowledgeable peer to a less experienced learner.

(Continued)

Table 6.2   (Continued)

Process: They both focused on the process of learning rather than on the product. They were more concerned with how a child arrived at their solution to a problem than the answer.	**Social environment**: They both believed that interaction with the physical and social environment is critical for cognitive growth. Visits to the local fire station, park, theatre or seaside will extend the young child's social learning experiences.
Qualitative methods: Their qualitative approaches included observing children as they completed tasks and interviewing children.	

RECOMMENDED READING

Daniels, H. (Ed.) (2005). *An Introduction to Vygotsky*, 2nd edn. London: Taylor & Francis.

This is a must-read for students who hope to grapple with the complexity of Vygotsky's theory. It is a challenging read; nevertheless, it is accurate and thorough in its critique of Vygotsky's work.

Edwards, C., Gandini, L. and Forman, G. (Eds) (2012). *The Hundred Languages of Children: The Reggio Emilia Experience in Transformation*, 3rd edn. Santa Barbara, CA: ABC-CLIO (eBook available directly from www.abc-clio.com).

This book documents the development of the Reggio Emilia approach over a 50-year period, and the evolution of schools in Northern Italy predicated on the philosophical tenets of this approach. As you read, parallels can be drawn between Edwards et al.'s explanation of the practitioner's role in fostering children's thinking and Vygotsky's mediated learning theory.

Muthivi, A.E. (2010). Piaget, Vygotsky and the cultural development of the notions of possibility and necessity: an experimental study among rural South African learners. *South African Journal of Psychology, 40, 2*, 139–48. Available at: http://sap.sagepub.com/content/40/2/139.abstract (accessed 11.4.15).

This interesting article explores Piagetian and Vygotskian theories of learning in three groups of children in Grades 1, 3, 5 and 7. The notion, according to Piaget's theory, that poor academic achievement amongst black learners is due to cultural diversity is tested. Vygotskian explanations that place importance on sociocultural influences (such as teaching style significantly impacting a child's cognitive development) are also considered.

REFERENCES

Applebee, A.N. and Langer, J. (1983). Instructional scaffolding: Reading and writing as natural language activities. *Language Arts, 60 2*, 168–175.

Benson, B. (1997). Scaffolding (coming to terms). *English Journal, 86, 7*, 126–7.

Bruner, J.S. (1986). *Actual Minds, Possible Worlds*. Cambridge, MA: Harvard University Press.

Corsaro, W.A. (1992). Interpretative reproduction in children's peer cultures. *Social Psychology Quarterly, 55*, 160–77.

Daniels, H. (Ed.) (2005). *An Introduction to Vygotsky*, 2nd edn. London: Routledge Taylor & Francis.

DfE (2010). *The National Strategies Early Years Document*. Available at: www.education.gov.uk/schools/tools and initiatives/national strategies

Challenging practice to further improve learning, playing and interacting in the Early Years Foundation Stage London: Available at: http://webarchive.nationalarchives.gov.uk/201304011 51715/http://www.education.gov.uk/publications/eOrderingDownload/00113-2010BKT-EN.pdf

Dewey, J. (1959). *School and Society*. Chicago, IL: University of Chicago Press.

Edwards, C., Gandini, L. and Forman, G. (Eds) (2012). *The Hundred Languages of Children: The Reggio Emilia Experience in Transformation*, 3rd edn. Santa Barbara, CA: ABC-CLIO (eBook available directly from www.abc-clio.com).

EYFS Statutory framework for the early years foundation stage. (2014). Setting the standards for learning, development and care for children from birth to five Reference: DFE-00337-2014.

Fleer, M. (2014). 'Vygotsky's conception of play in context of slowmation'. Available at: www.youtube.com/watch?v=dY3EH7YQhww (accessed 11.4.15).

Flewitt, R. and Ang, L. (2015). Embracing diversity in the early years and primary classroom: a cross-cultural perspective. In D. Wyse, R. Davis, P. Jones and S. Rogers (Eds) *Exploring Education and Childhood*. London: Routledge.

Fox, R. (2001). Constructivism examined. *Oxford Review of Education, 27, 1*, 23–35.

Freund, L.S. (1990). Maternal regulation of children's problem-solving behavior and its impact on children's performance. *Child Development, 61, 1*, 113–26.

Hogan, D.M. and Tudge, J.R.H. (1999). Implications of Vygotsky's theory for peer learning. In A.M. O'Donnell and A. King (Eds) *Cognitive Perspectives on Peer Learning*. Mahwah, NJ: Lawrence Erlbaum. pp. 39–66.

Holzman, L. (2006). Lev Vygotsky and the New Performative Psychology: Implications for Business and Organizations. In D.M. Hosking and S. McNamee (Eds.) *The social construction of organization*. Oslo: Liber.

Hua Liu, C. and Matthews, R. (2005). Vygotsky's philosophy: constructivism and its criticisms examined. *International Educational Journal, 6, 3*, 386–99.

Kamen, M. and Murphy, C. (2012). Science education at the Golden Key Schools: learning science in Vygotskian-based elementary schools in Russia. In D.F. Berline and A.L. White (Eds) *International Consortium for Research in Science and Mathematics Education*. Columbus, OH: Ohio State University.

Kutnick, P. and Blatchford, P. (2014). Can the grouping of children in classrooms affect their learning: an introduction to social pedagogy, *Effective Group Work in Primary School Classrooms Professional Learning and Development in Schools and Higher Education, 8*, 1–21. New York: Springer.

Meadows, S. (1993). *The Child as Thinker: The Development and Acquisition of Cognition in Childhood*. London: Routledge.

Murphy, C. (2012). Vygotsky and primary science. In B.J. Fraser, K.G. Tobin and C.J. McRobbie, (Eds) *Second International Handbook of Science Education*, New York: Springer, pp. 177–187.

O'Brien, L.M. (2002). *A Response to Dewey and Vygotsky: Society, Experience, and Inquiry in Educational Practice*. Washington, DC: AERA.

Pagram, J. and McMahon, M. (1997). WeB-CD: an interactive learning experience for distance education students studying interactive multimedia. Poster presented at ICCE97 International Conference on Computers in Education, Kuching, Malaysia, 2–6 December.

Palinscar, A.S. (1998). Social constructivist perspectives on teaching and learning. *Annual Review of Psychology, 49, 1,* 345–75.

Pea, R.D. (1993). Practices of distributed intelligence and designs for education. In G. Salomon (Ed.) *Distributed Cognitions.* New York: Cambridge University Press. pp. 47–87.

Qualifications and Curriculum Authority (QCA). (2000). *Curriculum guidance for the foundation stage.* London: Author.

Reggio Children (2010). The Reggio Emilia approach. Available at: www.reggiochildren.it/identita/reggio-emilia-approach/?lang=en (accessed 12.4.15).

Resnick, L.B. (1996). Situated learning. In E. De Corte and F.E. Weinert (Eds) *International Encyclopedia of Developmental and Instructional Psychology.* Oxford: Elsevier. pp. 341–7.

Robbins, D. (2010). *Golden Key Schools.* Available at: http://faculty.ucmo.edu/drobbins/html/golden_key_schools.html (accessed 16.6.11).

Rose, S.A., Feldman, J.F. and Jankowski, J.J. (2003). The building blocks of cognition. *The Journal of Pediatrics, 143, 4,* 54–61.

School Curriculum Assessment Authority (SCAA). (1996). *Nursery education: Desirable outcomes for children's learning on entering compulsory education.* London: SCAA and Department for Education and Employment. ED 433 091.

Shepard, A. (2008). *The Princess Mouse: A Tale of Finland* (illust. L. Gore). London: Atheneum.

Schaffer, H.R. (2004). *Introducing Child Psychology.* Oxford: Blackwell.

Sutherland, P. (1992). *Cognitive Development Today: Piaget and his Critics.* London: Paul Chapman.

Toulmin, S. (1978). The Mozart of Psychology. *New York Review of Books, 28,* 51–7.

Tudge, J.R.H. (1992). Processes and consequences of peer collaboration. *Child Development, 63,* 1364–79.

Vygotsky, L.S. (1956). *Selected Psychological Investigations.* Moscow: Izdatel'stvoAcademii Pedagogicheskikh Nauk.

Vygotsky, L.S. (1962). *Thought and Language.* Cambridge, MA: MIT.

Vygotsky, L.S. (1971). *The Psychology of Art.* Cambridge, MA: MIT.

Vygotsky, L.S. (1978). *Mind in Society: The Development of Higher Psychological Processes.* Cambridge, MA: Harvard University Press.

Vygotsky, L.S. (1987–98). *The Collected Works of L.S. Vygotsky. Volume I: Problems of General Psychology. Volume II: The Fundamentals of Defectology. Volume III: Problems of the Theory and History of Psychology. Volume IV: The History of Development of Higher Mental Functions. Volume V: Child Psychology.* Edited in English translation by R.W. Rieber. New York: Plenum.

Wertsch, J.V. (Ed.) (1981). *The Concept of Activity in Soviet Psychology.* Armonk, NY: Sharpe.

Wood, E. (2011). Progression and challenge in play from 5–11. Inaugural lecture, Stranmillis University College, Belfast, 15 June.

Wood, D., Bruner, J.S. and Ross, G. (1976). The role of tutoring in problem solving. *Journal of Child Psychology and Psychiatry, 17, 2,* 81–100.

Want to learn more about this Chapter?
Visit the companion website at **https://study.sagepub.com/grayandmacblain2e** to gain open access to selected SAGE journal articles, author podcasts and weblinks to help further your study.

7   BANDURA, BRONFENBRENNER AND SOCIAL LEARNING

This chapter aims to:

- explore the work of Albert Bandura and how it contributes to our understanding of social learning
- examine the work of Urie Bronfenbrenner in relation to that of Bandura
- explore how Bandura and Bronfenbrenner's theoretical perspectives can help our understanding of children's learning and social development.

This chapter explores the work of two influential theorists who have attempted to explain the nature of social learning. In more recent years, the importance of social learning has come to be recognized as central to the progress made by all children (MacBlain, 2014), and perhaps most significantly by such groups of children as those whose childhood is characterized and defined by poverty and disadvantage and those with significant and complex special educational needs and/or disabilities (MacBlain et al., 2015). Whilst this has been brought about by an increase in research into how social factors impact upon learning, it has also been the result of monumental change across communities, cultures and society at large. The growth in digital technology, for example, has meant that for many children the social nature of their learning has become radically different. In addition, the increase in diversity within schools and communities has also meant that many children now have the opportunity to engage with and learn from children and adults of other cultures from an early stage. This chapter begins with the work of Albert Bandura, which though undertaken in previous decades remains highly relevant today. The more recent views of Urie Bronfenbrenner, who has offered us new ways of exploring how learning is impacted upon, is then also explored.

Bandura believed that social factors were central to the learning and development of the individual and, in the 1970s, he introduced his *social learning theory* (Bandura, 1977). In doing so, he moved significantly from some of his contemporaries who espoused a more purely behaviourist approach. For Bandura, learning did not always involve changes in behaviour and children could, for example, observe others without their observations necessarily leading to a change in their own behaviour. Unlike the early behaviourists, he suggested that motivation played a significant role in the link between children observing behaviours and subsequent changes in their own behaviour. Bandura saw motivation, therefore, as a key factor in the development and learning of young children.

Bronfenbrenner's theory differs from that of Bandura in a number of ways. In particular, he viewed factors in the child's wider social, political and economic environment as being of much greater importance than Bandura and other theorists working in the field of child development. Unlike Bandura, Bronfenbrenner's theory has at its core the view that a child's own biology is a key factor influencing their development. His theory, therefore, can be best understood as the interrelationship of children with the environments in which they live.

A question that continues to exercise many professionals is why so many children in modern societies succeed when so many others fail. Why, despite years of formal education, do significant numbers of children fail to develop their potential and live lives characterized by lack of social and emotional needs that are not met (MacBlain, 2014), low self-esteem (Kyung-Nyun, 2014) and disaffection often arising from social policy decisions (Bunje Bower, 2013) whilst others gain material success and status and develop confidence in their own abilities? What factors in their early years cause one child's life to differ so much from another's? The newspaper columnist James Chapman, writing in a British newspaper, the *Daily Mail*, recently commented:

> Some 46 per cent of children are born to unmarried mothers, according to research by the Centre for Social Justice. The think-tank said a child growing up in a one-parent family is 75 per cent more likely to fail at school, 70 per cent more likely to become a drug addict, 50 per cent more likely to have an alcohol problem and 35 per cent more likely to be unemployed as an adult. (2011, p. 6)

Such stark statistics need to be treated with considerable caution. Many children grow up in lone-parent families and are happy and successful. However, such newspaper articles do reflect a concern amongst some that many young children are failing to have access to important life chances that will enable them, as they grow older, to develop their potential (Buckingham, 2000; MacBlain et al., 2015).

A further and perhaps quite worrying assertion appeared more recently when their educational correspondent Laura Clark offered the following:

> Children as young as one are being labelled as having special educational needs by their nurseries … By the age of five, more than one in six children – 173,525 – has been diagnosed as having special needs … Most are diagnosed during their first year at school … Figures released yesterday by the Department for Education showed that 19.8 per cent of children across the school system – more than 1.6 million – have been given the label. (2012, n.p.)

Perhaps more worrying, however, is the following, again offered by Clark in the same newspaper:

> Ofsted revealed two years ago that schools may have wrongly labelled as many as 450,000 children as having special needs … the Government's former adviser on speech and language, warned that this was often 'used as an explanation for failure'. (2012, n.p.)

Some months earlier the journalist Peter Stanford, writing in another UK national paper, the *Daily Telegraph* had also commented:

> Many experts fear that funds earmarked to help children with learning difficulties are being redirected to cope with a new tide of social deprivation that is washing up in the classroom. Children from troubled homes, who turn up at schools with behavioural problems, are being routinely put on the SEN register alongside those with more specific learning difficulties, such as dyslexia and dyspraxia. (2012, n.p.)

It is concerning that the above comments appeared in national newspapers and they would appear to suggest significant problems in regard to understanding the nature of learning in many very young children. More especially, they suggest particular problems with the identification of learning needs in many young children and the importance of subsequent purposeful and effective interventions. For many young children experiencing failure in the early years, the social costs during their later years can at best be unfortunate and at worst life changing. The following two examples now present a number of issues common to many children and offer a focus for understanding the work of Bandura and Bronfenbrenner and how their work can support us in our own understanding of the complex nature of social learning.

> **Example**
>
> 1. Tracey, aged 6, is described by her teacher as 'a lively little girl who can try very hard'. She lives with her mother and two older step-brothers. Tracey's mother has just begun a relationship with a man she met recently. He is aggressive and verbally abusive and both she and her brother Matthew, aged 3, become frightened when he gets angry. Matthew attends playgroup and is beginning to imitate the aggressive behaviours of his mother's new partner. Tracey's mother is unemployed. Tracey's recent school report described her reading as very poor and noted that she could not say the alphabet in sequence. Tracey is also described by her teacher as 'not good at forming friendships' and as 'always seeking attention from the Learning Support Assistant'. When assessed by an educational psychologist following concerns about progress and occasional aggressive behaviour, she recorded low scores on vocabulary and verbal comprehension tests. Of note, however, were Tracey's abilities in areas of reasoning, which fell within the superior range, suggesting that she was very able but with specific learning difficulties compounded by delayed language development, impoverished vocabulary and poorly developed strategies for sustaining attention.
> 2. Ben, aged 6, is described by his teacher as 'articulate, socially skilled and exceptionally bright'. He lives at home with his parents, two older brothers and Gemma, his sister, who is aged 2. Both his parents have benefited from university education and hold professional positions where they earn well and have a wide circle of friends, all of whom work as highly paid professionals. Ben's parents are patient with him and take time to explain to him why they become upset when he behaves in ways that they disapprove of. Though only 6 years of age, Ben has already travelled widely and is used to being in the company of successful, motivated and articulate adults. Ben was able to read simple books at the end of his first year of schooling and his reading and spelling ages are currently well in advance of his chronological age – his reading age was recently measured as 8 years and 6 months, and his spelling age as 7 years and 6 months. His vocabulary is considered by his teacher to be 'very advanced'. Ben is sociable and has many friendship groups.

Clearly, the nature of Tracey and Ben's learning, and their social and emotional development, are complex and underpinning both cases are important external elements that contribute to, and impact upon, their learning and development. Our understanding of these important elements as with all children can be greatly enhanced by looking to and drawing upon the theoretical perspectives offered by Bandura and Bronfenbrenner. First, let us turn to the ideas offered to us by Bandura's social learning theory.

ALBERT BANDURA (b. 1925)

Albert Bandura was born in 1925 in Canada and is perhaps best known for his *social learning theory* and the Bobo doll experiment conducted in 1961. In this experiment, Bandura filmed a woman aggressively hitting a large toy doll known as a 'Bobo doll'. Bandura then showed this film to a group of young children who were given the opportunity to play in a separate room which contained a Bobo doll. These children then began to hit the doll as they had observed the woman doing. In this regard, they were imitating the aggressive behaviour of the woman. Of interest was the fact that the children were not being rewarded for hitting the doll. They were in fact engaging in behaviours they had observed but that had not been reinforced. Learning was, therefore, taking place, not as behaviourists of the time would have argued, as a result of reinforcement, but as a result of observation. Bandura believed that the stimulus–response explanation of learning proposed by the early behaviourists was overly simplistic and did not go far enough in explaining human behaviour and emotions. Take time to look at the video clip link below, in which Albert Bandura explains his thinking behind the Bobo doll experiment and offers some original 'clips' taken from the initial experiments.

Weblink

'Bandura's Bobo Doll Experiment', available at: www.youtube.com/watch?v=dmBqwWlJg8U (accessed 11.4.15).

Whilst Bandura acknowledged that classical and operant conditioning (see Chapter 4) could go some way in explaining social learning, he also argued that there were two other factors that were of great importance, namely *imitation* and *identification*. Bandura suggested that both of these factors provided for accelerated social learning in children. With the first of these, children imitate the behaviours of others whilst, with the second, new learning is assimilated into existing concepts that have already been internalized by the child. In this way, Bandura argued, whole patterns of behaving become internalized by children such that they then act upon new situations in the way they think that the adults from whom they have modelled their behaviour would behave. In the case of Tracey and Ben, they have internalized quite different patterns of behaviour that have been modelled by the adults in their families and by significant others they have come into contact with during those crucial pre-school years, and their first years of schooling.

Tracey's younger brother Matthew will also have learned from observing the behaviours that Tracey models, which may be characterized at times by anxiety and anger. On the other hand, Gemma, Ben's younger sister, will have observed Ben as being confident and enthusiastic and socially skilled. She will also have benefited from listening to Ben's more sophisticated use of language and from observing non-verbal communication such as his mannerisms and listening skills that he employs when he presents himself in social situations. In this way, her social learning is very different to that of Matthew.

Of course, it was recognized by Bandura that for positive and meaningful learning to take place, the behaviours of those adults being imitated by children need to be appropriate. Take the case of Tracey's younger brother, Matthew, who regularly witnesses his mother's partner being physically and verbally aggressive towards his mother. When Matthew observes arguments between his mother and her new partner, he often feels that he is to blame and that their arguments are due to his own behaviours. He may well even come to internalize a perception of himself as being a 'bad' child. This is unlikely to happen in the case of Gemma, Ben's younger sister, who will almost certainly come to internalize a view of herself as being capable and successful, and loved, as she observes the behaviours of others around her as being wholly appropriate, positive and purposeful. Unlike Matthew, Gemma is almost certain to receive regular positive feedback from her parents and older brothers, which will serve to reinforce those behaviours that her parents desire of her such as attentiveness, confidence and independence. In this way, these aspects of her personality and the manner in which she presents herself in social situations will have been imitated and identified with – in other words, they have become learned. Here, we can make reference to the approaches found in Steiner Waldorf settings. Miller and Pound have commented:

> Steiner practitioners observe that young children are nurtured by the security of rhythm and repetition – within which their inherent skills and abilities can flourish … Having well thought through and repeated routines builds habits that are useful (properly washed hands), respectful (creating a peaceful mood at the table) and comforting ('this is how we always do it here'). (2011, p. 92)

Whilst Tracey and Matthew, unlike Ben and Gemma, fail to have the security of rhythm and repetition in their home life, where most of their everyday experiences are characterized by chaos and inconsistency with, for example, irregular meals and bedtimes, they can, however, gain from feelings of security and nurturing in their primary school and playgroup, respectively.

According to Bandura's social learning theory, Matthew may come to imitate the aggressive behaviours of his mother's new partner and these may, in turn, be played out at his playgroup when he is with other children. It is possible that Matthew will identify with his mother's partner and may come to be viewed by others at his playgroup as an aggressive child, and he may start to live up to this perception by others. Bandura's social learning theory would suggest that Matthew is beginning to acquire a type of exterior, which has been learned through observing and imitating the behaviours of his mother's partner. Such was the case with the young children in the Bobo doll experiment referred to above, which Bandura used to emphasize how young children will observe and imitate the behaviours of others. It is an interesting, and worrying, aspect of human social and emotional development that individuals may, in stressful situations, 'identify with the aggressor' simply as a means of defending themselves.

Bandura suggested that children not only observe physical behaviours but that they also observe the verbal behaviours of others, which includes expectations that others make of them (Linden, 2005). He suggested that young children observe adults as they offer verbal narratives and descriptions of events and as they use language and gesture to communicate their ideas, thoughts, instructions, questions and so on. Given that Ben is frequently in the company of articulate and successful adults, it is certain that he will learn many positive aspects of behaving and interacting with others through observing their behaviours, as well as the responses they receive, which invariably will be characterized by the attentive and interested responses of others. It is worth noting that Bandura also proposed a type of symbolic modelling where children engage in imitation and identification of individuals who are not real but fictional, such as the type of characters found in fairy tales and children's stories. The ever-increasing number of visual stories and cartoons found in children's television, the cinema and computer games can be included within this type of symbolic modelling.

A further key element of Bandura's theory, which is directly relevant to practitioners working with young children, is that of *self-efficacy* (Bandura, 1997). Having a better knowledge and understanding of self-efficacy is very important for professionals working with young children in educational and care settings. Bandura saw self-efficacy as a child's belief in their abilities to do well and to succeed in certain situations, and as their capacity to exercise control over their own actions in order to gain success. He proposed that self-efficacy is directly related to how children think and act, as well as to their emotional state. In effect, Bandura has influenced the way in which we try to understand the goals that individuals – be they children, parents or professionals – aim to achieve. Children with poor self-efficacy, for example, have a tendency to avoid tasks that present them with a challenge, preferring instead to focus on the negative and frame their thinking within constructs whereby they come to convince themselves that they cannot achieve. Children with poor self-efficacy typically present themselves in social situations as having low self-confidence.

Directly linked to a child's capacity to gain success are the child's feelings about themselves and others, and the world around them. In recent years, there has been a resurgence of interest amongst psychologists and educators regarding self-efficacy, and particularly an increased recognition of how a child's self-efficacy influences and affects their learning and behaviour. Faced with having to organize their own time and with identifying learning goals and targets, children with poor self-efficacy will typically do less well than those with strong self-efficacy. They may, for example, demonstrate little interest in attempting tasks and seeing them through to completion, and may feel less committed to working with their peers. They may also demonstrate greater signs of anxiety than their peers when asked to engage in problem-based learning tasks. Colverd and Hodgkin have stressed how children in learning situations may:

> place limits on what they think is possible, believing a task is beyond their capability. Lack of self-belief affects their motivation and their commitment to learning. 'I can't do this, it's boring' signals 'I don't believe I can be successful with this and therefore I don't want to take the risk – it may or may not be boring'. (2011, p. 36)

Bandura believed that a key factor in developing a strong sense of self-efficacy was the development of 'mastery' through experiences, for example in observing others who are succeeding, having positive and affirming comments from others, and understanding one's own emotions and feelings. Self-efficacy as an integral part of a child's early learning experiences, therefore, has enormous implications for practitioners working with children in Early Years settings and primary schools.

Exercise

Take time to view the video link below, which offers useful insights into self-efficacy and how it affects individuals:

Weblink

'Self-Efficacy.mov', available at: www.youtube.com/watch?v=Jj4c4NEOSRE&list=PLjolwWg-dkTfXGgs-FtKaC7pxKlmS3ZQoH (accessed 11.4.15v).

After viewing the video clip:

1. Reflect upon occasions when you have observed children displaying 'good' self-efficacy.
2. Consider the nature of those learning experiences, including their play experiences that might have led to these children being able to display 'good' self-efficacy.
3. Consider how different types of play opportunities in the Early Years can affect children's self-efficacy as they grow older.

In order to understand social learning more fully as well as the impact upon children of their wider social environments, it is helpful to look more closely at learning within the wider social, political and economic contexts within which children grow up. Whilst Bandura's work tended to focus on the individual, other theorists have focused more upon more extraneous factors. One particular theoretical perspective that goes much further in exploring these wider contexts is that offered by Urie Bronfenbrenner. Bronfenbrenner's work offers a further dimension to that of Bandura's and provides the means for much greater critical reflection and understanding of how young children learn, and the cultural contexts and factors that influence the course of their development from early childhood through adolescence and into adulthood.

URIE BRONFENBRENNER (1917–2005)

Bronfenbrenner was born in Moscow, and when he was 6 years of age he moved with his family to the USA. Bronfenbrenner gained a scholarship to Cornell University in 1934 where he studied psychology. He subsequently served in the army from 1942 to 1946 in the latter years of the Second World War working as a psychologist. In 1979, Bronfenbrenner published a seminal text, *The Ecology of Human Development*, in which he set out his views on child development. Bronfenbrenner was co-founder of the Head Start programme and is perhaps best known for his *ecological systems model*, now redefined as the *bioecological model*.

Bronfenbrenner emphasized how children grow up in constantly changing and dynamic cultures in which they must interact with and relate to those around them in ever-shifting contexts (Bronfenbrenner, 1979; Bronfenbrenner and Ceci, 1994). As children grow and develop, the nature and quality of their interactions change and this process occurs within communities, cultures and wider societies, all of which have their own definable and recognizable characteristics (Johnston and Nahmad-Williams, 2009). Bronfenbrenner 'emphasizes the importance of studying "development-in-context", or the ecology of development' (Smith et al., 2003, 9). Take, for example, the cases of Tracey and Ben – consider that they are now older and in their first year of secondary school. Here it is important to emphasize how Early Years practitioners need to think ahead and see the children they work with not only as 'Early Years' children but as unique individuals who are in the beginning stages of the rest of their lives.

Example

Some years have passed and Tracey and Ben are now in their first year of secondary school where there are relatively high levels of disaffection amongst a small number of the older pupils, but high levels of achievement and aspiration amongst the majority of pupils who are aiming to move into the school's sixth form and then on to tertiary education. Tracey's mother has become more settled in her life and has gained employment. Her previous partner has left the family home and a new partner has moved in. Though he is not aggressive, he is unemployed and has been for over ten years. Ben's life has changed dramatically in that his mother has died. Money has become an issue and his father has had to take on extra part-time work in order to look after the family. Despite these challenges Ben continues to be highly motivated and focused and is developing some positive friendships with like-minded pupils in his year who are also focused and motivated. Following transfer to her secondary school, Tracey has become increasingly influenced by her new peer group, which consists mainly of children who have experienced problems in their primary schools relating to behaviour and lack of progress. She appears to be more drawn to the older pupils who are disaffected and during break times observes them closely.

Not only is the physical and geographical context of Tracey and Ben's new school very different to their primary school, the culture of their new school environment is also fundamentally distinctive with new rules to be learned, new expectations exercised by teachers, and more particularly, a whole new set of expectations from their peers. Differences in fashion are more pronounced in their new school and they have to start absorbing and understanding the hidden rules and behaviours of their peers and especially the older teenage boys and girls. In addition to these more immediate factors, society and its legal structure recognize that Tracey and Ben are now older and as such they will increasingly have expectations placed upon them to act and behave with much greater responsibility and accountability. The other children in the school, and particularly the older children, will act as role models for Tracey and Ben. It will be Tracey and Ben's early upbringing and the modelling of their own parents, and the relationships they had in their Early Years with significant others, that will now serve to give them stability and support them in resisting being drawn into potentially problematic social situations and maintaining a focus and good motivation in their new educational setting.

Whilst Bronfenbrenner placed significant emphasis upon the wider environment when attempting to explore child development, he also proposed that it is important to think of a number of layers that encompass children as they develop. These layers, both directly and indirectly, affect the biological maturation of every child. Bronfenbrenner's theory, therefore, requires that in order to fully explore child development, we need also to take into account the wider environmental influences upon the child. The layers that define Bronfenbrenner's theory are sometimes likened to Russian dolls, where smaller dolls are placed within much bigger ones (Linden, 2005). Bronfenbrenner gave a name to each of the layers that surrounded the child (see Figure 7.1). The closest and most immediate layer to the child is the *microsystem*.

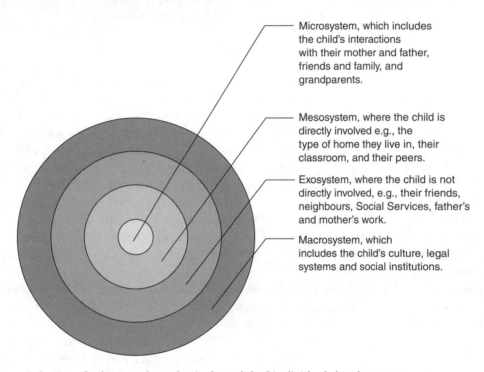

Microsystem, which includes the child's interactions with their mother and father, friends and family, and grandparents.

Mesosystem, where the child is directly involved e.g., the type of home they live in, their classroom, and their peers.

Exosystem, where the child is not directly involved, e.g., their friends, neighbours, Social Services, father's and mother's work.

Macrosystem, which includes the child's culture, legal systems and social institutions.

Figure 7.1   Bronfenbrenner's ecological model of individual development

Definitions

Microsystem: immediate environments (family, school, peer group, neighbourhood and childcare environments).

Mesosystem: a system comprising connections between immediate environments (i.e. a child's home and school).

Exosystem: external environmental settings which only indirectly affect development (such as a parent's workplace).

(continued)

(continued)

Macrosystem: the larger cultural context (Eastern vs Western culture, national economy, political culture, subculture).

Chronosystem: the patterning of environmental events and transitions over the course of life.

It is within the microsystem that the child has their most direct contact with, for example, their family, their nursery school or playgroup, their community and their neighbours. Bronfenbrenner proposed a two-way process within this layer that influenced the child, referring to these as 'bi-directional influences'. Whilst the child is influenced by the behaviours, actions and beliefs of their parents, the child in turn also influences the parents. Take the example of an infant in the cot who suddenly and for no apparent reason makes a joyful cooing noise. When the mother hears the noise, she comes running from the other room and lifts the child and gives lots of warm, nurturing hugs. In this situation, the child has initiated the interaction and the mother has responded. As such, the infant is in fact influencing the mother's behaviour. As Bronfenbrenner would suggest, the relation is bi-directional. Bronfenbrenner has suggested that these bi-directional influences are very strong.

The next layer outside of the microsystem is the *mesosystem*, which relates to the construction of connections between, for example, the child's mother and father and their first teacher, or between their local community and their school. Here, the child relates experiences gained in school to those gained in their family. The child is, therefore, drawing comparisons between their teachers and their parents, between their new school friends and friends in their neighbourhood, and between the wider family such as between brothers and sisters and cousins. If the child's family members are regular and frequent members of a sports club, for example, then there will be connections and comparisons made between those individuals within the club and their lifestyles and their own family context.

Outside of the mesosystem lies the *exosystem* – the child's wider social system. Here, for example, the work commitments of parents, or their levels of income, impact upon the child's microsystem. Within the exosystem the wider social experiences of children will also impact indirectly upon them. An example is the current economic climate in the UK where it is proposed that many public libraries will be closed and that the Forestry Commission will sell a percentage of its forested land to private developers, thus promoting fears amongst many that important resources and activities will become lost to many children, young people and their families. A further example can be seen in the UK when the previous coalition government in 2011 proposed significant changes to schooling through the introduction of 'free schools', much greater choice for parents, and a restructuring of the way in which teachers were to be trained. All of these external factors were to exert significant influence upon the lives of many children in the UK.

Outside of the exosystem lies the *macrosystem*, which comprises the child's culture, societal values, legal structures and so on. These all affect the inner layers. A child who grows up in a very traditional society or community that strongly advocates the importance of children being reared by both parents and rejects the idea of parental separation and divorce, may well receive less support of a practical nature than a child growing up in a community that is much more accepting of separation and divorce. Within the macrosystem, the ideological views that are historically dominant in the culture of an individual are viewed as being of great importance. Take, for example, children growing up in Northern Ireland where communities were, for many years, divided on the grounds of religion, or the southern states of the USA where generations experienced racial prejudice as part of their everyday lives, which in practice guided the thinking and education of whole communities of children and young people.

Bronfenbrenner identified a further layer, the *chronosystem*. The chronosystem is about time and how it interfaces with those environments in which the child grows up. As children age, they interact differently with their environments and can become more engaged in managing aspects of their environment and those changes that they must negotiate as they grow older. Here, transitions are very important, for example starting nursery school, playgroup or primary school for the first time or, in other cases, the transition from a two-parent family through the separation and divorce of parents over an extended period of time. As transitions and chronological events occur, the child is developing not just physically and cognitively but emotionally as well. It is worth considering how the chronosystem has exerted influence upon Tracey and Ben as they make the transition to secondary school.

Bronfenbrenner's theory can be criticized on the grounds that it does not pay adequate attention to the individual psychological needs of children, as is the case with the work of Bandura. Take, for example, the experiences of children who have lost parents through divorce or, more particularly, those who have lost a parent through death and find themselves entering a stage of grieving. Whilst Bandura would focus upon the individual child's self-efficacy and learning modelled through those around him/her, which would underpin their resilience and coping mechanisms, Bronfenbrenner might focus upon the argument that grief occurs in all cultures and in all societies and, therefore, existing social and economic systems are in place to support the child.

Exercise

Take time to view the following excellent YouTube video below, which offers further insight into Bronfenbrenner's model.

Weblink

'Ecological Systems Theory: Uri Bronfenbrenner', available at: www.youtube.com/watch?v=01BnvOrEDPM (accessed 11.4.15).

After viewing the clip, consider the following:

1. How might the working patterns of parents affect the learning of young children?
2. How can Bronfenbrenner's theory help us understand the nature of the learning experienced by young children growing up with different special educational needs and/or disabilities?

Summary

In attempting to further our understanding of social learning in young children, we can draw upon the work of a number of theorists such as Bandura and Bronfenbrenner. Their carefully considered and tested ideas and hypotheses offer effective frameworks to encapsulate and test our own ideas, thoughts and perceptions, from which we gain through our own personal experiences and learning. Bandura suggested that learning did not always involve change in behaviour and that children could observe others without their observations necessarily leading to changes in behaviour. He further suggested that motivation played a significant role in the link between observation and change in behaviour. Bandura saw motivation as a key factor in the development of children and young people and viewed self-efficacy as being central to educational development. Bronfenbrenner saw societies and communities across the globe as undergoing radical change. He argued that world economies have changed radically and we now have much greater emphasis upon the technological factors that drive our economies, but much of our working practice has not changed in tandem leading to enormous stress being experienced by many parents. Bronfenbrenner proposed that research into child development should take account of wider economic, social and political factors. Table 7.1 compares the similarities and differences between Bandura and Bronfenbrenner.

Table 7.1   Similarities and differences between Bandura and Bronfenbrenner

Similarities	Differences
Both Bandura and Bronfenbrenner acknowledge the part played by wider influences in society.	Bronfenbrenner placed much greater emphasis upon indirect influences such as the family environment and the community. He also viewed wider factors in society, such as the economic and political climate, as having a major influence upon children's learning and development.
Whilst not fully accepting the principles set out by more traditional behaviourists, they both emphasize the significance of social learning.	
They both viewed children's social interactions with others around them as being central to learning and development.	Bandura placed greater emphasis upon children's cognitive development, especially in terms of them acting upon information received from their environments. Unlike Bronfenbrenner, Bandura emphasized the importance of children imitating and identifying with others around them.
They both saw culture as playing a significant part in the education and schooling of children.	
Both theorists were also similar in that they did not view children's development in terms of stages.	Bandura placed greater emphasis upon self-efficacy than Bronfenbrenner.

RECOMMENDED READING

Bandura, A. (1997). *Self-efficacy: The Exercise of Control*. New York: Freeman.

This is a key text for any student or practitioner wishing to gain a much deeper understanding of self-efficacy and how it affects individual development.

Dowling, M. (2014). *Young Children's Personal, Social and Emotional Development*, 4th edn. London: Sage.

A useful resource for students and practitioners wishing to gain greater understanding of the social and emotional needs of children.

Miller, L. and Pound, L. (2011). *Theories and Approaches to Learning in the Early Years*. London: Sage.

An accessible and informative text, which will be of considerable help to students and practitioners wishing to develop their understanding of child development and the theoretical positions that underpin this most important stage in the lives of individuals.

REFERENCES

Bandura, A. (1977). *Social Learning Theory*. Englewood Cliffs, NJ: Prentice Hall.

Bandura, A. (1997). *Self-efficacy: The Exercise of Control*. New York: Freeman.

Bronfenbrenner, U. (1979). *The Ecology of Human Development*. Cambridge, MA: Harvard University Press.

Bronfenbrenner, U. and Ceci, S.J. (1994). Nature–nurture reconceptualized in the developmental perspective: a bioecological model, *Psychological Review, 101*, 568–86.

Buckingham, D. (2000). *After the Death of Childhood: Growing up in the Age of Electronic Media*. Cambridge: Polity Press.

Bunje Bower, C. (2013). Social policy and the achievement gap: what do we know? Where should we head? *Education and Urban Society*, 45, 1, 3–36.

Chapman, J. (2011). The collapse of family life: half of children see parents split by 16 as births outside marriage hit highest level for two centuries. *Daily Mail*, 18 April.

Clark, L. (2012). Nurseries label one-year-olds 'special needs', *Daily Mail*, 13 July.

Colverd, S. and Hodgkin, B. (2011). *Developing Emotional Intelligence in the Primary School*. London: Routledge.

Johnston, J. and Nahmad-Williams, L. (2009). *Early Childhood Studies*. London: Pearson Education.

Kyung-Nyun, K. (2014). Formation of educational expectations of lower socioeconomic status children, *Education and Urban Society*, 46, 3, 352–76.

Linden, J. (2005). *Understanding Child Development: Linking Theory to Practice*. London: Hodder Education.

MacBlain, S.F. (2014). *How Children Learn*. London: Sage.

MacBlain, S.F., Long, L. and Dunn, J. (2015). *Dyslexia, Literacy and Inclusion: Child-centred Perspectives*. London: Sage.

Miller, L. and Pound, L. (2011). *Theories and Approaches to Learning in the Early Years*. London: Sage.

Smith, K.S., Cowie, H. and Blades, M. (2003). *Understanding Children's Development*, 4th edn. Oxford: Blackwell.

Stanford, P. (2012). Can 20% of school children really have special needs? *Daily Telegraph*, 12 May.

Want to learn more about this Chapter?
Visit the companion website at **https://study.sagepub.com/grayandmacblain2e** to gain open access to selected SAGE journal articles, author podcasts and weblinks to help further your study.

8 BRUNER AND DISCOVERY LEARNING/CONSTRUCTIVISM

This chapter aims to:

- explore the contribution made to our understanding of education by Jerome Bruner
- explore the nature of the term 'learning' in relation to the work of Bruner
- examine how children represent the worlds they live in
- examine the relevance of Bruner's ideas for practitioners today.

JEROME BRUNER (b. 1915)

Jerome Bruner was born in 1915 in New York, USA and is considered by many to be one of the leading thinkers of our time. References to Bruner's work can be found in most academic texts that address learning and development. Regarded by most academics working in the fields of education and psychology as a key theorist, Bruner offered new ways of thinking about children's learning and how they are taught. For a time, Bruner worked with the US army during the Second World War and later worked as an academic at Harvard University.

It is important when examining different theoretical perspectives to understand and acknowledge the social and historical contexts within which they were created, the contemporary context within which they are being applied and, perhaps most importantly, their purpose. To fail to do so would be to miss a vital element in the temporal evolution of thought.

Like all theorists, Bruner did not write and function within a vacuum. Theorists are an integral part of what they write about and their theories are influenced and formed by how they see the world, and by their own unique personal journeys through life. For these reasons, it must be said at the outset that Bruner developed his ideas and theoretical views at a time when the world and, more particularly, the country of his birthplace, the USA, was undergoing enormous social, economic and political change. Racial tensions were evident across the Western world, with many children in schools in the USA being segregated because of colour and race. The USA was emerging from the aftermath of the Second World War and the Korean War and facing a drawn-out conflict in Vietnam. Materialism was on the rise and society was witnessing the emergence of the 'teenager'.

Social, economic and political change

Readers should at this point give some thought to the ongoing social, economic and political change that is happening around them both nationally and internationally and the impact this might have upon the nature of the learning experiences offered to young children both at home and in their formal learning situations. Readers might also reflect upon how more recent social, economic and political change across the globe has affected their own views in regard to the nature of learning and its relevance to young children growing up in the 21st century. MacBlain has, for example, commented thus:

> The effects of austerity in the UK can be seen in most places, with schools being no exception. Services that were once readily available have been increasingly cut, with more schools now having to 'buy in' services such as those offered previously by Local Authorities. School budgets are now under closer scrutiny than ever before, with many head teachers having to face the challenges that are being brought about by the wider economic and social factors that are contributing to increased poverty in some areas, most worryingly perhaps the growth in the drug culture that appears to permeate many areas of society and defines some more socially and economically deprived communities. In many respects the challenges facing teachers and schools, as well as parents, in the 21st century are considerable and require new ways of understanding childhood and the learning paths that are taken by many children. (2014, p. 206)

Bruner's purpose, it can be proposed, in developing his theoretical perspectives was, to some extent, about challenging the thinking of the time, which was in large part dominated by a legacy of behaviourism and psychodynamic perspectives originating in the works of Watson and Skinner, and Sigmund Freud and Carl Jung. Smidt has commented:

> What made Bruner unusual and special in terms of Western psychologists at the time was his recognition that meaning is not determined by the biological needs we inherit, nor is it determined by individual thought: rather, it comes about through an active search for meaning within the context of a culture. (2011, p. 10)

Bruner was also challenging many of the underlying ideas that policy and decision makers held in regard to the schooling and education of children at the time. Smidt has further commented: 'Bruner said that we should treat education for what it is, and for him what it was was political' (2011, p. 85). Readers may wish to reflect upon the more recent changes that have taken place with regard to schooling in the UK and especially England where the Coalition government, which came into power in 2010, introduced and developed the concept of *Free* schools and *Academies* and shifted the focus of training teachers significantly away from Higher Education Institutions such as universities and into schools (MacBlain, 2014). Each of these 'initiatives' have been informed if not driven by political ideals and, arguably, have had an enormous impact upon the nature of formal education and schooling and more importantly much of the learning experienced by children both in Early Years settings and schools.

The purpose to which Bruner applied himself was eloquently expressed some three decades ago by one of the author's professors:

> Bruner's thesis was that the study of children in problem-solving situations had concentrated too much upon the nature of the tasks and the stimuli presented to the child, and too little upon the dynamic qualities the child brought to the tasks in order to solve them. (Brown, 1977, p. 74)

To properly explore Bruner's thesis as well as the purpose of his work, we need to look more carefully at what we understand by the term 'learning'.

WHAT DO WE MEAN BY LEARNING?

Learning is a difficult word to define and yet it is used so frequently and by so many practitioners when they talk of their work with children both in and out of the classroom. Arguably, it is perhaps one of the most misunderstood words in popular usage within the field of education and is a term that is, all too frequently, surrounded by confusion. At the heart of this confusion lies a lack of specificity and clarity. What, for example, do we understand when a colleague tells us that a child has 'learned' their times tables or that a child has 'not learned' their spellings or is 'failing to learn' something. Should we not be more precise in our verbal exchanges with other colleagues and suggest, for example, that a child who is struggling in aspects of their learning might have underlying processing difficulties that are affecting their 'working memory' or the speed at which they process information or that they have come to acquire inappropriate, inefficient or unhelpful strategies for storing and then retrieving new information? To be able to share such insights does, however, require greater understanding of those cognitive processes that underpin learning. With the child who has 'failed to learn' their spellings, should practitioners, again, not be more precise when verbalizing to one another the child's difficulties and focus, for example, on the child's abilities and skills and their actual functioning in the area of 'phonological processing', which is where significant numbers of children with specific learning difficulties experience problems (MacBlain, 2014; MacBlain et al., 2015). To say that a child is failing to learn something is far too broad a statement and requires far more careful consideration and analysis on the part of practitioners and especially those working with young children when the foundations of learning are being laid down – yet it is a term that is so commonly heard. Such terms need to be more explicit and specific and to be much more informed by those using them not only in terms of what they are intending to convey but perhaps, more importantly, how others will understand and interpret them.

To properly understand 'learning' is to demonstrate knowledge and understanding of theoretical positions (as in the case of Bruner) that underpin the word's usage. This is not, however, as straightforward as it might seem, as different theorists have different ideas as to what learning actually is. Smith et al., for example, have defined learning as follows:

> Learning refers to the influence of specific environmental information on behaviour. Within a wide range of variation, the way an animal behaves depends on what it learns from the environment. Thus, individuals of a species may differ considerably in their learnt behaviour patterns. (2003, p. 34)

It is interesting to note that Smith et al. include the words 'environmental' and 'species'. More interestingly, they include the word 'behaviour' and the term 'behaviour patterns'. In addition, Smith et al. appear to place emphasis upon the notion of humans being a species, as in the case of animals. Such a view is very much in keeping with the behaviourist tradition and places particular emphasis upon changes in behaviour being central to the notion of learning. It is very different to how Bruner saw learning, as we shall see later.

The work of the early behaviourists, as discussed in Chapter 3, introduced us to a way of explaining learning in terms of stimuli and responses and the importance of identifying observable behaviours and subsequent reinforcement. In attempting to offer greater clarity to our understanding of the term 'learning', however, the psychologist David Fontana has made reference to 'descriptions' of learning in which he makes an important distinction between the behaviourist tradition (more directly, the notion of *operant conditioning*) and the cognitive tradition (more directly, the notion of *instrumental conceptualism*). Drawing directly on the work of Bruner, Fontana commented thus:

> This somewhat intimidating title (Instrumental Conceptualism) is used by Bruner to define one of the most coherent and consistent cognitive descriptions of learning and still one of

the most useful for teachers … Learning … is not something that happens to individuals, as in the operant conditioning model, but something which they themselves make happen by the manner in which they handle incoming information and put it to use. (1995, p. 145)

Having a clear understanding of what learning is, therefore, and those cognitive processes that underpin it is important for all practitioners working with children (Hayes, 2008). Equally important, however, is the need for practitioners to have a clear understanding of how behaviours are learned and subsequently reinforced.

Exercise

Weblink

Take time to view the YouTube video 'Jerome Bruner – How does teaching influence learning?' available at: www.youtube.com/watch?v=aljvAuXqhds (accessed 11.4.15), which offers an interview with Jerome Bruner only a week after his 99th birthday. Then, having watched the video, consider the following:

1. Reflect upon a specific instance or situation when you have observed teaching to directly influence the learning of a young child or children. Now, identify key factors that lead you to:

    i.   feel confident that the actual teaching has had a direct and positive influence upon the learning of the child or children.
    ii. feel confident that actual learning has taken place.
    iii. feel confident in understanding the type of approach taken by the teacher when working with the child or children.

2. Identify a number of different situations where you have observed children learning and consider how they were handling incoming information from other children and adults and putting it to use. First, however, consider what is meant by 'incoming information'.

HOW CHILDREN REPRESENT THEIR WORLD

Bruner did not view learning as something that happens to individuals but more as a process in which the individual is actively engaged. This idea is central to Bruner's theory of learning and differs markedly from that of the early behaviourists who saw learning more in terms of stimuli and responses. For those working with children, the key difference is that Bruner is chiefly concerned with what occurs within an individual's thinking between stimuli being emitted and the individual making a response. He is, in other words, concerned primarily with those cognitive processes that underpin and direct the actions of individuals.

Bruner was interested in the 'strategies' that children use when they are learning and, more specifically, when they are engaged in problem-solving tasks and experiences that underpin and lead to concept formation. Whilst the behaviourists were concerned essentially with how children's reactions to stimuli manifest themselves, Bruner was more concerned with how stimuli are represented through symbols and words and how these representations facilitate generalization and connection with other concepts. Representing stimuli in this way (i.e. through words and symbols) was, Bruner suggested, of a much higher order and he saw the inferences that children make through symbols and words as being key to their learning and cognitive development, and he referred to this as the *symbolic* mode. At the heart of Bruner's theory is the idea that individuals represent the world they live in, and their learning, through three 'modes'. He referred to these as the *enactive* mode, the *iconic* mode and the *symbolic* mode, which has just been referred to.

The *enactive* mode is concerned with actions, the *iconic* mode with images and pictures, and the *symbolic* mode, as we have just seen, which is far more complex, is concerned with words and symbols, and language. These modes do not follow on from one another as, for example, in the stages suggested by Piaget but, instead, are integrated with one another. In the enactive mode, for example, an infant's sight of an object is unavoidably linked with their physical movements and behaviours. Take, for example, an infant in a cot who is given a rattle. The infant will shake it and be alerted to the noise it makes. Each time the infant is given the rattle, he/she will shake it. In this way the actual movements being made become encoded within memory through the infant's reflex movements and through what some practitioners now refer to as *kinesthetic* or *muscle memory*, and are linked to the infant's sight of the rattle. The child's concept of the rattle, therefore, becomes internally represented as a combination of noise, image and physical movement. The enactive mode is, however, limited in that the infant cannot make links to other types of rattle. In this respect, the concept of 'rattle' for the infant remains located with the object upon which the infant is actually focusing. Such learning, it should be noted, is not restricted to infants, and the internal representations that we make as infants can remain with us throughout our lives.

With the iconic mode, a child can internally represent an object in the form of an image. Being able to do this allows the child to develop their cognition significantly. Having the ability to create and hold images means that the child can now apply their internal processing or thinking to objects that are not actually present in their environment. As with the enactive mode, however, the iconic mode has its limitations. Images formed by the child will be restricted to observable characteristics of an object, for example its colour, contours, textures and smell. Whilst the child may form internal images of their toys or their brothers and sisters, they will not be able to internally represent higher order concepts of, for example, kindness, joy, happiness and playfulness. They will need to internally represent these through language, which lies at the core of the symbolic mode. Brown explains the difference between icons, or images, that are central to the iconic mode and symbols, which are central to the symbolic mode, as follows:

> A photograph or a model of a cow would be an icon in that it would represent the animal in a very real and obvious way. The symbols C-O-W have no such characteristics. They only signify the existence of the animal by consensus of those who use the word. By eliminating the idiosyncrasies or special characteristics (for it will have to represent *a* cow) the symbol enables us to work with a general concept unrestrained by particulars. (1977, p. 75)

Exercise

Identify examples of the *symbolic*, *iconic* and *enactive* modes that you have observed in young children and consider:

1. How does play support the development of these three modes?
2. How might Early Years practitioners work with parents to support the development of these three modes in their children?

THE IMPORTANCE OF LANGUAGE

In drawing particular attention to Bruner's views of the function of language in young children, Smidt commented:

> Bruner reminds us that, 'Children learn to use language initially … to get what they want, to play games, to stay connected with those on whom they are dependent. In doing so, they find the constraints that prevail in the culture around them embodied in their parents' restrictions and conventions' (Bruner, 1983, p. 103). (2011, p. 66)

As language develops, children increasingly remove themselves from situations by way of their thinking. They can, for example, engage with others in talking about situations elsewhere, about experiences they have had in the past, and might have in the future, and so on. Very importantly, they can engage with others in problem solving and critical reflection, both of which are fundamental to higher-order thinking as proposed by Bruner. This developmental process is of enormous importance to Early Years practitioners and primary school teachers who create the linguistic environments for their children and who provide them with the opportunities to develop their language in tandem with their thinking. Take the case of Sally, who is in her third year at primary school.

Example

Sally is working in a group of five with her friends, Caroline, Michael, Julie and Mark. Her teacher has asked the class to work on a group task. Each group is given a single piece of A4 paper and a heavy textbook. The challenge for each group is to balance the book upon the paper. The children quickly become involved in the task and make random attempts at solving the problem. Though the teacher is interested in the strategies the children employ, she is more interested in the language they use. She listens to Sally's group as they work on the task:

Michael: 'This is mad, we can't do this.'

Mark: 'Yeah, no one can do this, it's stupid.'

Michael: 'Yeah, it's stupid.'

Sally: 'Wait, what if we change the shape of the paper?'

Julie: 'Yes, good idea. I know … what if we fold the paper like in a zigzag shape?'

Sally: 'Yeah, supposing we turn the paper on its side in a zigzag and then balance the book on top that will make the paper stronger.'

Caroline: 'That's right. That will do it.'

At this point, the group achieves success and by folding the paper in a concertina shape and standing it on its side, they can easily balance the book. This example illustrates very well the importance of the *Symbolic* mode and how it facilitates more sophisticated thinking. By beginning her sentence with 'Wait, what if …', Sally is engaging in hypothetical reasoning, which is higher order thinking than that of Michael and Mark who are simply reacting to the problem they have been presented with. Sally, on the other hand, is putting forward a hypothesis, which will be tested not only by her attempts at manipulating the materials before her but also by the responses and reactions of the others, such as, for example, Julie's response to Sally's suggestion to change the shape of the paper. Here, Julie is confirming Sally's original hypothesis. In this example, Sally and Julie have engaged in higher order thinking, which goes much further in facilitating effective problem solving. The type of verbal support given by Julie to Sally is also reinforcing Sally's sense of confidence in herself and her own abilities to take risks in front of others and try out new ideas.

At the very heart of this example is language, and it is through the carefully exercised use of language in such situations that a child's potential becomes increasingly realized. For this reason, the contexts and experiences that practitioners create for children to learn, the development of vocabulary and the techniques they employ when questioning and explaining are vitally important. It is essential, therefore, that practitioners working with young children take time to reflect upon their own use of language, in particular the types of questions they pose and the vocabulary and phrases they employ, as well as the situations they create in order to analyse their children's language and thinking processes. It is through the contributions made by such theorists as Bruner that we gain insights into the thinking and learning of young children and come to use theoretical frameworks within which we can explore our own practice and that of others.

It is worth emphasizing at this point, however, that there are many children who struggle with aspects of language and who can, for example, hold only a very small number of instructions and directions in working memory before losing the thread of what is being asked of them. For these children, many of whom will have learning difficulties of a specific nature arising from such conditions as dyslexia or dyspraxia, the Early Years practitioner will need to be especially vigilant. They will need to closely observe the actual responses of these children to their verbal instructions, questions and explanations, and most importantly the child's degree of understanding. Bruner saw the role of practitioners, therefore, as crucial to providing a system of support to facilitate and extend language development and he believed that language provided the central means by which children could develop their thinking and learning. Language, he argued, enabled children to internally represent their learning in sophisticated ways that facilitated abstract reasoning.

Directly related to the development of language is the emergence of literacy (Kaiser and Roberts, 2011; MacBlain, 2014; MacBlain et al., 2015). In order for young children to read and write, they need to be able to recognize written symbols and the sounds that are attributed to these symbols. Indeed, Bruner (1975) took great care to emphasize the importance of both reading and writing in the cognitive development of young children. He even went as far as suggesting that the cognitive structures of children who engage more in these two processes will typically be different to those of children who engage much more in less language-orientated processes such as drawing and making things using solid materials (Brown, 1977). Bruner also suggested that this latter type of child typically differed from those who tended to engage themselves largely in talking with others. The rationale for his views was that, whilst all young children engage in basic language interaction with others, this does not, as in the case of children who engage a lot in speaking and listening, have any very significant effect upon the development of the internal representations of their thoughts. However, when young children engage in creating written symbols, which represent their own as well as others' speech and language, then an important transformative process occurs.

By representing thinking in written form, either using words or mathematical symbols, the young child can then engage in higher order processing or thinking whereby they can, in turn, engage in analysis of the ideas they have produced and represented through symbols. Clearly, this suggests that making marks, as very young children readily and naturally do, is an important element in their development and one that must be encouraged by the adults responsible for them.

A further and important dimension of children's language and thinking that Bruner came to increasingly recognize was narrative. Smidt has drawn attention to Bruner's emphasis upon narrative as follows:

> For the past two decades Bruner has been systematically developing what some call a narrative view of culture and mind and has argued that reality is itself narratively constructed. (2011, p. 92)

The crucial role that narrative plays has been recognized for some time and is central to the thinking of many leading thinkers and theorists. It was, for example, recognized by Steiner (Chapter 2) over a century ago and continues to inform practice in Steiner Waldorf schools today. With regard to the importance of narrative, Smidt has further commented:

> The reason children become narrators is because they explore the expectations they have developed about how the world should be. They develop these expectations through their experiences and their interactions and the ways in which they look for patterns and regularities in the world. (2011, p. 99)

As we have seen, Bruner interpreted narrative in terms of 'reasoning', proposing that 'reality is narratively constructed' (Smidt, 2011, p. 13). This concept of narrative is immensely important for Early Years practitioners who are involved daily in the life events and unfolding stories of their children. Each day, Early Years practitioners and teachers are drawn into and involve themselves, wittingly or otherwise, in the narratives children create of their own lives. They do this at a number of levels, and in doing so they can exert enormous influence over their children. To many practitioners, this process is not, however, always readily apparent and, more typically, not fully understood.

Practitioners and their children share with one another, on a daily basis, verbal accounts of events experienced by themselves not only in relation to each other but also in relation to those significant others who are central to their lives. In doing so, the adults, it can be argued, play a central role through the medium of language in the construction of their children's knowledge, but perhaps more importantly they become involved in that subtle process whereby their children define and redefine the worlds within which they live. It is by understanding this process and fully acknowledging their part within it that practitioners can, with confidence, further define themselves as effective teachers and their children as effective learners.

Given that this process occurs as an integral functioning of day-to-day interactions, then it can be suggested that the process also offers excellent opportunities for practitioners to explore many hidden but important aspects of their children's social and emotional functioning, as well as their learning. More excitingly, narrative offers the practitioner a medium whereby insights and explanations of their children's life stories can be meaningfully related, understood and evaluated by themselves and others. By doing so, the practitioner can gain further insights into their own practice and their chosen pedagogies as well as their understanding of the nature of learning and problem solving.

Exercise

Weblink

Take time to view the YouTube video 'How children acquire and produce language (BBC, 2001)', available at: www.youtube.com/watch?v=2i1z37nYMrM (accessed 11.4.15), which offers most interesting insights into the importance of language acquisition in young children.

After having watched the video, consider:

1. How might Early Years practitioners work with parents to support them in developing their children's speech and language?
2. What particular steps might Early Years practitioners take to support children with delayed language in their own Early Years settings?

BRUNER AND EDUCATION

With regard to education, Bruner took great care to emphasize the importance of culture, which he argued shaped our thinking and the manner in which we construct our understanding of ourselves and the world in which we live. In this respect, his views relate closely to those of Bronfenbrenner discussed in the previous chapter. In fact, Bruner saw schools as being only part of this process by which culture inducts the child, and saw cultures as being:

made up of institutions (such as schools, hospitals, universities, libraries, banks, companies, shops, law courts, legal systems and more) where the roles that people can play are determined and where the respect accorded to these roles is worked out. (Smidt, 2011, p. 85)

Bruner suggested that we can only really make sense of what happens in schools when we view them within the wider context of the aims and intentions that societies have for their young, and he saw our conceptions of education as being a direct function of our conceptions of culture and its aims (Bruner, 1996). Take, for example, practitioners working in an inner-city area of extreme socio-economic disadvantage, who may well find that the popularly acknowledged aims of the surrounding culture are very different to those they might find, for example, when working in the pre-prep department of an expensive fee-paying public school.

Bruner viewed the manner in which children are supported with their learning in schools as being central to the development of their thinking and learning, and the development of their potential. Unlike Piaget, for example, who saw children moving through a number of stages during which their levels of cognitive development facilitated new learning, Bruner suggested that children could, in practice, be very involved in moving their own learning forward by undertaking more demanding and challenging tasks, provided they were properly supported.

Example

Angela has started her second year at primary school. Her teacher has decided to work on subtraction and has asked her class to complete a series of written numerical operations, which involve taking smaller single numbers from larger single numbers, such as 3 from 6. Angela completes these without any mistakes as she is using blocks to help her. Next day, the teacher asks Angela to complete numerical operations that require her to take smaller single numbers from larger double numbers such as 3 from 10 and 6 from 14. Angela becomes confused because the digits on the top row are smaller than the single digit on the lower row. The teacher comes to help Angela and introduces her to a method whereby she borrows and carries using the different columns. Angela performs this method alongside her teacher and when she has successfully completed two examples her teacher leaves her to help another child. The lesson finishes and the teacher does not introduce her class to further number work until a week later. By this stage, Angela has forgotten the method taught to her and when asked to complete some similar numerical operations, becomes confused.

Whilst Angela was able to carry out the method in the previous week, she has not conceptualized it. The problem is, in fact, too abstract for her and she has not been able to make the necessary steps to link it to existing internalized cognitive structures. The gap between these has been too great and she ought to have been directed to use much smaller graded steps, and have lots of reinforcement and over learning, which would have led to more effective learning and better retention, and subsequent recall. In effect, she needed more sustained support from her teacher over time with internalizing and accommodating her new learning as she progressed through a range of small steps.

It might be suggested that Bruner applied something of Vygotsky's thinking to educational settings. One example of this is Bruner's notion of 'scaffolding'. Whilst Vygotsky had offered insights into how adults supported children in their learning and, particularly, in their ability to reflect, he had not been specific as to how this might be managed by, for example, practitioners working with children. To this extent, his views remained very much of a theoretical nature. In practice, scaffolding is happening everywhere around us. We see parents structuring activities for their children, older siblings or friends structuring tasks for younger members of the family and attentive grandparents patiently taking their young grandchild through sequences of activities, which they have broken down into small steps and which they explain carefully along the way. It can typically be seen where older brothers or sisters are modelling and teaching their younger siblings to develop new skills and knowledge, such as knowing how to whistle, climb over rocks and so on.

Though scaffolding offers structure to learning, it does not imply a rigid structure. Take, for example, the very young child in a playgroup situation who plays or works alongside an adult. The adult models a particular activity and is observed by the young child who will then respond to the adult's spoken encouragement to try new strategies for solving a particular problem. In this case, the adult might also break down the child's learning into smaller, more manageable elements. In a sense, the adult is offering the child a scaffold, which will allow him to extend his knowledge and skills, and, perhaps more importantly, his understanding. As the adult breaks down the task and guides the child in attempting new ways of problem solving using different strategies, then the child will typically become more absorbed in the task; this sustains motivation, which in itself can then be even more motivating for the child.

Exercise

Weblink

Take time to view the two YouTube video links below, both of which offer excellent insights into, and examples of, scaffolding in different situations.

'Scaffolding Language Development', available at: www.youtube.com/watch?v=gLXxcsp CeK8 (accessed 11.4.15)

(Continued)

(Continued)

'Teaching Matters: Scaffolding', available at: www.youtube.com/watch?v=9gNjGD_W3dM (accessed 11.4.15).

Having viewed both video clips, reflect upon the similarities between the ideas expressed by Vygotsky and those of Bruner in regard to creating learning situations in which children develop their thinking through working alongside adults.

Closely linked to learning in more formal educational environments is the notion of motivation and the degree to which learners are interested in the tasks they are being asked to complete. Bruner viewed children's levels of interest in a subject as being one of the best stimuli to their learning. He saw the role of the teacher, therefore, as being very much about encouraging children to become actively, and purposefully, involved in what they do. By doing so, children become more intrinsically motivated. In other words, they become engaged because they want to be and because they experience inner feelings of satisfaction. This process is vitally important for children's future learning in the Early Years because it lays down foundations for the way in which children will approach learning tasks in more formal settings when they attend primary and then post-primary school. This process is also closely linked to the development of self-efficacy discussed previously in relation to Bandura, and the role of the teacher as 'mediator' proposed by Feuerstein and discussed later in Chapter 9. Unlike Piaget, Bruner saw the social and cultural aspects of schools and Early Years settings within which children develop and learn as being of much greater significance.

A further significant feature of Bruner's work is the importance he placed upon learning through discovery and by engaging in problem solving. Here, the child uses their previous knowledge and life experiences to build new knowledge and skills and further develop their thinking. Discovery learning is viewed by those who strongly advocate it as being a means for strengthening the internalization of meaning and the conceptualization of new facts into existing knowledge. Smidt commented:

> For Bruner, meaning has always been at the heart of any investigation into mind and cognition. When we talk of meaning we are talking about making sense of something, of understanding or comprehending it. (2011, p. 10)

On first consideration, some might consider the notion of learning through discovery as being a wholly good and beneficial thing. However, there are those who would suggest that there are a number of drawbacks. For example, children may, during their episodes of discovery learning, acquire misconceptions and these may go unnoticed by the adults managing their learning. In addition, discovery learning may suit some learning styles much more than others and there may be children who prefer to work in more didactic ways. Furthermore, there may be some parents and schools who view discovery learning as under-used time, preferring instead that their children engage with more formal situations where information is directly taught and their children are expected to complete identifiable tasks and make identifiable progress in comparison to their peers.

CONNECTING WITH BRUNER IN THE 21ST CENTURY

What then can Bruner offer to practitioners in the 21st century, and how can practitioners assimilate his ideas into their own understanding of what they do? Perhaps more importantly, how does having knowledge of Bruner's ideas impact upon practice? To explore these questions, we need to see the work of Bruner, as in the case of all of the theorists and philosophers we have encountered, within the context of the 21st century and our own immediate cultures, communities and internalized world views of the realities that surround us. Smidt commented:

> Bruner said that the world (and everything in it) is not just as you see it but it is as you see it in context and in relation to your thoughts. So things may look different depending on how you feel, who you are with, what you have just been doing, what you are thinking about and so on … There is a link between perception, mind and learning. (2011, p. 9)

What, then, are our perceptions of childhood and how realistic are these? It is now generally accepted that parents in modern industrialized societies typically spend less time with their children than did their own parents and grandparents, as was the case when Bruner was originally constructing his views on learning and development. This is, in part, due to the changes in working patterns over the last decades. James commented:

> Since 1998 the number of people in Britain working more than sixty hours a week has more than doubled (from 10 to 26 per cent), and full-time Brits work an average of forty-four hours, the most in the European Union. (2007, p. 273)

Many parents now feel that because they are spending less time with their children, they should place much greater emphasis upon what they actually do with them (Buckingham, 2000). This perceived need has been driven, in part, it is argued, by an exaggerated sense of needing to 'up the quality' of the time they spend with their children. Indeed, Buckingham has also pointed towards the notion of this time with children as a commodity in which some parents feel that they need to be viewed by others around them as being heavily involved with their children. More recently, in the UK, the concept of the 'Yummy Mummy' has emerged and now offers a popularized term to represent a type of parenting characterized, some would say, by competitive parenting. Added to this is the number of children growing up in reconstituted families, which can bring its own challenges. Only a decade ago, 10 per cent of families in the UK with dependent children were stepfamilies (Johnston and Nahmad-Williams, 2009, p. 218). Such changes in the dynamics of family relationships and parenting are relatively new to us and, though similarities with previous decades can be observed, it is, nonetheless, important to recognize that the nature of these changes is now characteristically different. As such, we must take these into account when drawing upon Bruner's ideas to help us interpret and understand our own observations, perceptions and evaluations of how children are thinking and learning.

Play as a feature of young children's activities has also altered dramatically in the last decades. It is generally recognized that young children now play less outside of their homes so that their parents can keep a close eye on them. Many children spend more time nowadays watching television or engaging with electronic games, computers and the Internet. According to Zwozdiak-Myers:

> there seems little doubt that the default for contemporary children's play is interior whereas for previous generations, particularly in the second half of the twentieth century, it was exterior. (2007, p. 6)

Given the emphasis that is now placed upon materialism and the use of technological playthings, and the need for parents to feel that they must spend more time with their children, it can be suggested that many parents have become prisoners of their children's demands. Bruner also emphasized the importance of children learning through the process of enquiry and encouraged practitioners to accept and feel comfortable with intuitive thinking as being an important element in learning. Such views, however, stand in stark contrast to actual practice in some areas of the education system. The popular author Oliver James, for example, has drawn attention to the pressure that many children are placed under by their parents and by the competitive nature of certain elements of our society:

> A London private nursery school was recently exposed in a newspaper as doing tests on two-year-olds to see whether they would be suitable for entry at three. The test was to leave the toddler alone in a room with five others; the ones that failed were deemed to be those who went after their mother when she left the room. (2007, p. 280)

> **Definition**
>
> **Metacognition:** a learner's knowledge about their own mental abilities such as memory and attention. For example, knowing you have a bad memory, you may write notes to yourself.

Directly related to this is the view (Fisher and Rush, 2008) that too many teachers of young children continue to overly concern themselves with the delivery of content and do not engage enough with those reflective processes, and metacognitive structures, which are at the heart of learning. In addition, it can be suggested that too many teachers and Early Years practitioners fail to give priority to these processes and structures of which they themselves are a dialectical part (Fisher et al., 2010). This being the case, many young children may well continue failing to have their individual learning needs met, and fail to reach their true potential (Long et al., 2007). Fisher et al. have, for example, commented as follows:

> Students preparing to enter the teaching profession should have as a major priority the need to devote real time to embracing theoretical views on learning ... To do so would potentially free them from vague and distorted notions of what learning actually is and lead to much greater understanding of the nature and function of knowledge, the purpose of learning, and the manner in which individuals at different stages of their development process information and construct meaning of the world around them, and act rationally to improve their lives through effective learning. (2010, p. 94)

Despite policy and decision makers continuing to debate theories of teaching and learning and how effective different pedagogies are, the central debate in the UK remains dominated by simplistic and polarized views of teaching and learning as being either traditional and teacher-led or modern and child-centred (Geens et al., 2009). It can be asked then, to what extent do the ideas of such theorists as Bruner really influence policy and decision making?

> **Exercise**
>
> Consider in which ways Early Years practitioners might need to develop their practice to meet the changing and diverse needs of young children in the 21st century.

Summary

It is important to fully recognize that theorists do not construct their ideas, propositions and theories in isolation to the worlds they inhabit. It is equally important to understand that practitioners need to view theoretical perspectives within their own immediate situations and the cultures and societies in which they practise. Bruner, as we have seen, grew up in a rapidly changing society in the USA and, unlike Vygotsky, for example, had access to what some might argue was a freer and more open society. Whilst Bruner formulated his thinking within a society characterized by a growing sense of materialism, Vygotsky's thinking emerged within a society built largely upon a Marxist philosophy. Despite living in vastly different cultures, it is fair to say that Vygotsky had a huge influence upon Bruner's thinking and the way in which he shaped his theory. Perhaps one of the greatest differences between these two key figures, though, was Bruner's absolute belief in the importance of culture as being central to the learning of children. Like Vygotsky, Bruner has offered practitioners a great deal in terms of understanding those cognitive processes that underpin learning in young children. The subtle, but significant, differences between their theoretical perspectives again highlights the view that the term 'learning' requires careful consideration and reflection when used to describe and explain children's behaviours to others.

 ## RECOMMENDED READING

Bruner, J.S. (1960). *The Process of Education*. Cambridge, MA: Harvard University Press.

Bruner, J.S. (1983). *Child's Talk: Learning to Use Language*. New York: Norton.

Both of these texts offer in-depth accounts of Bruner's theoretical perspectives. Whilst the former focuses upon the wider education process as envisaged by Bruner, the latter concentrates more upon the importance of language in relation to thinking and culture.

MacBlain, S.F., Long, L. and Dunn, J. (2015). *Dyslexia, Literacy and Inclusion: Child-centred Perspectives*. London: Sage.

This text offers excellent insights into the holistic needs of children struggling to access literacy.

REFERENCES

Brown, G. (1977). *Child Development*. Shepton Mallet: Open Books.

Bruner, J.S. (1975). Language as an instrument in thought. In A. Davies (Ed.) *Problems of Language and Learning*. London: Heinemann.

Bruner, J.S. (1996). *The Culture of Education*. Cambridge, MA: Harvard University Press.

Buckingham, D. (2000). *After the Death of Childhood: Growing Up in the Age of Electronic Media.* Cambridge: Polity Press.

Fisher, A. and Rush, L. (2008). Conceptions of learning and pedagogy: developing trainee teachers' epistemological understandings. *The Curriculum Journal, 19, 3,* 227–38.

Fisher, A., Russell, K., MacBlain, S.F., Purdy, N., Curry, A. and MacBlain, A. (2010). Re-examining the culture of learning in ITE: engaging with the new demands of the 21st century. *Critical and Reflective Practice in Education, 2,* 92–102.

Fontana, D. (1995). *Psychology for Teachers.* Basingstoke: Palgrave McMillan.

Geens, W., James, S. and MacBlain, S.F. (2009). Journeyman to master: the changing shape of a PGCE primary course. *The International Journal of Learning, 16, 8,* 629–40.

Hayes, D. (2008). *Foundations of Primary Teaching.* London: Routledge.

James, O. (2007). *Affluenza.* London: Vermilion.

Johnston, J. and Nahmad-Williams, L. (2009). *Early Childhood Studies.* London: Pearson Education.

Kaiser, M.Y. and Roberts, M.Y. (2011). Advances in Early Communication and Language Intervention. *Journal of Early Intervention, 33, 4,* 298–309.

Long, L., MacBlain, S.F. and MacBlain, M.S. (2007). Supporting the pupil with dyslexia at secondary level: mechanistic or emotional models of literacy. *Journal of Adolescent and Adult Literacy, 51, 2,* 124–34.

MacBlain, S.F. (2014). *How Children Learn.* London: Sage.

MacBlain, S.F., Long, L. and Dunn, J. (2015). *Dyslexia, Literacy and Inclusion: Child-centred Perspectives.* London: Sage.

Smidt, S. (2011). *Introducing Bruner: A Guide for Practitioners and Students in Early Years Education.* London: Routledge.

Smith, K.S., Cowie, H. and Blades, M. (2003). *Understanding Children's Development,* 4th edn. Oxford: Blackwell.

Zwozdiak-Myers, P. (ed.) (2007). *Childhood and Youth Studies.* Exeter: Learning Matters.

Want to learn more about this Chapter?
Visit the companion website at **https://study.sagepub.com/grayandmacblain2e** to gain open access to selected SAGE journal articles, author podcasts and weblinks to help further your study.

9 NEW PERSPECTIVES: CHILDHOOD STUDIES

> **This chapter aims to:**
> - outline the development of the social studies of childhood
> - explore how this approach facilitates our understanding of the child
> - discuss the ethical implications of research involving young children
> - highlight the strengths and weaknesses of this approach.

Thus far, we have examined the philosophies and theories that shape our understanding of children's learning. A thorough perusal of the theoretical perspectives posited by Pavlov, Watson, Thorndike, Skinner, Piaget, Vygotsky, Bandura, Bronfenbrenner and Bruner reveals that no single theorist offers a complete explanation of children's learning. Each perspective has strengths and weaknesses, and in attempting to understand aspects of children's learning, scholars typically draw on several learning theories. In recent years, discontent with the methods employed by developmental psychologists and the lack of attention afforded children and childhood by sociologists provided the impetus for the emergence of a new disciplinary approach, variously termed 'the new social studies of childhood', 'the new sociology of childhood' and 'childhood studies'. These terms reflect the contradictory views of scholars currently working within this disciplinary approach. For Muñoz (2006), the new sociology of childhood is a sub-discipline of sociology, whereas for James (2007) the new social studies of childhood is a multidisciplinary approach that embraces contributions from a range of disciplines including psychology, geography, history, anthropology and sociology. Concurring with James, Tisdall (2012) succinctly captures these sentiments in the title 'childhood studies.' Removal of the word 'new' is deliberate and attributable to the fact that this counter-paradigm emerged more than 20 years ago in the 1980s (Gray, 2014; Tisdall, 2012). Acknowledging our preference for a title that reflects the 'multidisciplinary nature of this evolving field', in our first edition of this book (Gray and MacBlain, 2012) we used the term 'the new social studies of childhood'. Given the sustainability of this dynamic discipline and its impact on theory and practice, throughout this chapter we employ the more appropriate title 'childhood studies'.

In placing the child at the heart of the discussion, we quite deliberately marginalize interdisciplinary debates which, in positioning one discipline against another, cloud the central issue: young children's lives. The chapter begins with a brief overview of the history of childhood and the influences that have shaped and challenged societal notions of childhood. It continues by examining the methodological tools devised by scholars working within the childhood studies and introduces the newly developed ethical code for researchers working with vulnerable groups. The final section explores the fit and tensions between the childhood studies and conventional theories of child development. Table 9.1 at the end of this chapter provides a useful, though not definitive, summary of the strengths and weaknesses of the childhood studies.

The study of children and childhood has a short history. In their seminal publications, both Ariès (1986 [1962]) and Zelizer (1994 [1985]) describe childhood as a modern concept. They point out that prior to the 17th century, childhood was not perceived as a distinct category of life. On the contrary, children tended to be perceived as undeveloped adults or adults-in-waiting. By the time of the industrial revolution, a number of laws had been enacted to ensure the protection and later the education of children. In *Pricing the Priceless Child: The Changing Social Value of Children*, Zelizer notes that between the 19th and 20th centuries, a transition occurred from perceptions of the child as being economically 'useful' to economically 'useless' but emotionally 'priceless' (Zelizer, 1994 [1985]). He suggests that the real 'value' of children lies in their ability to give meaning and fulfillment to their parents' lives. Whilst definitions of children are frequently based on biological distinctions, McDowall Clark disputes any suggestion of a 'universally agreed definition of childhood' (2010, p. 8), pointing out that practices with regard to children vary from country to country and culture to culture. This is a view shared by Prout, who observes how:

> the diversity of forms that childhood can take is expanding, or at least becoming more visible. As a consequence there is a need to revise the assumption that childhood is a unitary phenomenon. (2005, p. 3)

Social inequity appears in many guises, not least in international employment patterns. Global estimates on child labour indicate that 168 million children aged between 5 and 17 were involved in various forms of labour in 2012; figures exclude legally employed children (Diallo et al., 2013). Whilst this represents a sharp decline from 215 million in 2008, there are 85.4 million children employed in hazardous occupations that may have adverse effects upon 'the child's safety, health and moral development' (2013: 11).

Western notions of work as a step to independence are challenged by a report on the state of the world's street children by Thomas de Benitez (2011). She describes how street children in Brazil frequently juggle three jobs to survive. Although these children show considerable resilience in finding seasonal work, work at cultural festivals and tourist centres, Thomas de Benitez cautions against romanticizing this as autonomy or agency. Despite their struggle for survival, street children are subject to social stigma and the perception that they are 'outcasts, beggars and petty criminals that society needs to clean up' (UNICEF, 2010: 34). 'Clean up' would appear to be a euphemism used to mask the fact that street children are preyed upon by death squads paid to clean up the streets (Zimmerman, 2008).

Although there has been a significant decrease in child labour, particularly in children aged between 5 and 11 years old, many children in developing countries find their childhood and education curtailed at an early age by social, cultural and economic conditions. Yet the dominant construction of childhood in the developed world is of childhood as a time of innocence, play, education and economic dependence (Woodhead, 2005). Summing up his views on the diversity of children's experiences, Woodhead notes that:

> [w]hile universal accounts of normal development offer a powerful basis for realising rights in early childhood, they also have limitations. Firstly, they tend to overlook the diversities in children's experiences, including differences in the ways children learn, play and communicate ... Secondly, any particular account of young children's development is always partial, and can never encompass the varieties of childhood. Thirdly, specific cultural patterns of early development and care risk being normalised and universalised. (2005, p. 88)

Recognizing that childhood is not a natural or universal feature has important implications for Early Years practitioners. Woodhead (2005) points out that early childhood settings are culturally constructed; they are dynamic and evolving social contexts, with no two operating in exactly the same way. Children attending Early Years settings have rich and diverse life experiences, which are constructed and mediated by their peers and the adults in their setting – who in turn are products of their own cultural history and circumstances, which adds structure to their lives and meaning and direction to their experiences.

Exercise

Weblink

'"UK nursery kids are 'chaotic' and must learn respect" says MP Elizabeth Truss'. Available at: www.youtube.com/watch?v=1xjS865Avmw (accessed 11.4.15).

Watch this video contrasting the early learning experiences of young children in France and the UK. What are the cultural beliefs that inform early provision in both countries? Can you identify any common factors in the services in each country? What key questions would you ask the MP Liz Truss?

To highlight global disparities in children's lives, the United Nations declared 1979 the Year of the Child. By 1989, the United Nations had published the *Convention on the Rights of the Child* (UNCRC, 1989). By 2009, this rights-based treaty had been ratified by 195 member states; Somalia ratified the treaty in February 2015. In accepting the Convention, member states agreed to adopt the 54 articles and two optional protocols, which afford children and young people substantive human rights, including the right to protection from violence; to leisure, play and culture; to education; and to freedom of expression on all matters that affect them. For example, Article 13 of the Convention asserts the child's right to freedom of expression: this right shall include freedom to seek, receive and impart information and ideas of all kinds, regardless of frontiers, either orally, in writing or in print, in the form of art, or through any other media of the child's choice. Despite the almost universal ratification of the UNCRC, children's rights are not universal. Burr (2004) argues that the UNCRC reflects Western values and a particular model of childhood that holds no value in non-Western countries. This is particularly evident in cultures that place an emphasis on the collective rather than individual rights of its citizens.

Although early childhood was not specifically mentioned in the original UNCRC document, this was later remedied and a set of recommendations was subsequently included in General Comment No. 7 in 2005 (published in 2006). This asserted that in their Early Years children have the same rights as others to express their views freely and to have those views given due weight in accordance with their age and maturity (Lundy, 2007). Section 3 of the document highlights concerns that children are not being given adequate attention by states in terms of their laws, policies and practices. The UK government further endorsed these rights in the Children Act (2004), Every Child Matters (2003) and the Children Bill (2004).

The growing attention afforded children and childhood led a number of sociologists to question the almost total absence and marginalization of children from sociological literature (Muñoz, 2006; Ryan, 2008). Nikitina-den-Besten (2009) attributes the failure of sociologists to examine the lives of children to the macro-level approach typically adopted by research focused on global systems, politics, economics and family life. Others argue that it is their lack of economic power that has silenced and marginalized children, and women before them, from sociological study (McDowall Clark, 2010; Smith, 2011). As the focus on children in research gathers pace, questions are raised concerning children's role as active participants in the construction of society.

Definitions

Methods: the tools, materials or artefacts used to gather data.

Methodology: a system of principles or methods of procedure in any discipline, such as education, research, diagnosis or treatment. They may include ethnography, experimental approaches, action research or case studies.

Ethnography: a generic term for a set of research tools that places emphasis on uncovering participants' understanding of their social and symbolic world.

THE EVOLUTION OF CHILDHOOD STUDIES

As previously discussed, childhood is not a unitary concept. As sociologists began to question the lack of visibility of children in their research, they also queried the transmission and construction of knowledge. Christensen and Prout (2005) articulate the swift progression of thinking from children being viewed as a natural or biological phenomenon to being understood as products of 'history, society and culture'. Children were now seen as active participants in the interpretation and construction of their own cultural knowledge. As the focus shifted to examine children's lives, it became clear that it was more complex and intricate than had been assumed by some sociologists. By way of explanation, Giesecke (1985 cited in Christensen and Prout 2005, p. 49) pointed out that children, like adults, live in a society of competing, complementary and divergent values and perspectives gleaned from the media, the consumer society and adult and peer relationships.

According to Muñoz (2006, p. 10), childhood studies has three key aims:

1. It seeks to contribute to the social sciences in general by incorporating the voice of one of the most frequently forgotten groups in society: the child.
2. It aims to contribute to the multidisciplinary approach needed to address a complex phenomenon such as childhood by providing a sociological explanation.
3. It makes children visible as active members of society, according to the principles of the UNCRC; it recognizes children as individuals with rights.

Thus far, sociologists informed by this rights-based approach have focused on socialization processes or on the analysis of institutions responsible for this socialization: the family and schools. In adopting this perspective, sociologists focus on the processes that shape childhood rather than on childhood *per se*. The most influential approaches, to date, include:

- **The sociology of childhood**: Theorists working within this theoretical framework believe that the child should be the unit of investigation. Children are perceived as social actors and therefore researchers should focus on the relationships between a child's social world and the world of other children and adults.
- **The deconstructionist sociology of childhood**: This approach explores societal beliefs about children and childhood. To understand the construct of childhood, these theorists attempt to understand how society transmits its notions to the child.
- **The structural sociology of childhood**: This perspective considers childhood to be a distinct period in life. Researchers link significant aspects of the child's life (such as poverty) with macro-level contexts and attempt to explain them in terms of their significance to macro-level mechanisms (Muñoz, 2006).

Corsaro (2014) suggested another approach, termed *interpretive reproduction*. Advocates of this approach view the child as actively interpreting their cultural practices. Corsaro believed that children interact with a number of childhood cultures, which are interconnected like a spider's web. He was one of the first sociologists to take early childhood as the starting point for his thesis on culture.

The methods employed by theorists working within these three theoretical paradigms also differ. Whereas structuralists employ quantitative data gleaned from secondary sources, others employ qualitative ethnographic or individual and group interviews. Advocates of childhood studies as a distinct discipline eschew quantitative research approaches, typically preferring to involve children in the interview process or to observe them in their natural environment. Framing interview questions to avoid ambiguity or misinterpretation presents its own problems. Research suggests that, in the main, children do their best to please adults and will even answer questions that make no sense at all (Greene and Hill, 2005; McLeod, 2008). Hughes and Grieve (1980) asked children nonsense questions such as 'Is red heavier than yellow?' and 'One day two flies were crawling up a wall. Which fly got to the top first?' Even though they made no sense, the majority of children attempted to answer these questions. Waterman et al. (2001) found that children are 76 per cent more likely to answer nonsense questions than adults (20 per cent). Children may often attempt to answer such questions due to the phrasing of the question or to the fact that children are used to answering adults, who may not always make sense to them.

Recently, the first author conducted a series of focus groups with young children aged between 4 and 6 years of age (Gray, 2012). In preparation for these interview discussions, two groups of children agreed to act in the role of children's advisers to the project. The first task was to consider the form that questions should take for our young interviewees. We asked whether we should use puppets, paintings, photographs or other methods to gain a real understanding of the children's experiences of the after-school club they were attending. Whilst older children (aged between 9 and 10 years) suggested role play, drawings, stickers and camcorders, younger children (aged between 7 and 8 years) suggested that we simply 'ask them. Just ask the questions and they'll tell you the answers'. One interpretation of this practical response is that adults and older children tend to over-complicate the interview process and to underestimate children's ability to understand properly phrased questions. As McLeod points out, 'the adult who wants to listen needs to learn to keep their mouth shut and their eyes and ears open' (2008, p. 106). Consider McLeod's point in terms of the following example drawn from the experiences of one Early Years practitioner in New Zealand:

> I turned ready to free Lys from her clothing but was met by a serious attempt to remove her sweatshirt herself. Without any thought I began to aid Lys by shifting the bottom edge for her. Lys stopped; looked straight at me, making sure I was going to listen and stated boldly, 'No Lys'. Of course, I stopped immediately and was truly embarrassed by having doubted Lys's abilities. 'Sorry Lys', I apologised … She was working steadily on freeing her left arm. Her elbows had become entangled in the folds of the material, her face serious as she persisted in her struggles. My hands trembled … itching to help, but Lys had warned me, she could do it. I watched in awe as her gutsy persistence paid off. (Hatherly and Sands, 2002, 12)

The practitioner in this example assumed that Lys required help to remove her sweatshirt. Taking her cue from Lys, she stepped back and even though she was 'itching' to intervene gave Lys ownership of the task. This example neatly demonstrates the reciprocal nature of learning from child to adult and adult to child.

Greene and Hill (2005) also point to the shortcomings of observations of children that impose adult interpretations on children's behaviour. They argue that adults can never adopt a 'fly on the wall' approach or neutralize themselves. Their very presence may be sufficient to disrupt the specific behaviour they wish to observe. Rather than impose an adult agenda, it is possible, as the children in the example above suggested, to simply ask children to explain their behaviour.

In a recent study undertaken in a socially deprived area, we asked children to draw a picture of their favourite places to play. Older children (aged between 7 and 8 years) drew pictures of the local park, their after-school club, their street or local playing fields. Younger children (aged between 4 and 6 years) drew their house, their garden, their mum and their siblings. When asked why they had chosen to draw their house, one child explained:

> 'See that's where I play. I can't go the park if my big sister doesn't go too. You have to cross the busy road and I'm not allowed to cross the road by myself. I'm not allowed, so I play at home with my mummy and my little sister. Sometimes my friends come in and I play with them or I play in the garden on the swing or in the street with my friends.'

As adults, we might have concluded that the younger children hadn't understood the task. By asking the children to explain their pictures, we determined that they had understood and that their play area was limited to their home, garden or the street outside their house.

Mindful of previous methodological shortcomings, Christensen and Prout (2005) believe theorists working within the childhood studies paradigm have made some progress in this area by moving the perspective away from child–adult relationships to explore children's interrelations and interactions with each other. They claim that contemporary approaches see socialization as a collective rather than an individual process. This is a notion contradicted by Frønes (1993), who argued that there is no single childhood but multiple childhoods formed by the personal experience and interpretation of culture and society. You will note similarities between Frønes's claim and the views penned by Vygotsky, Bronfenbrenner and Bruner, who agreed that children are not passive recipients of culture but active participants in practices involving them with others.

For Bronfenbrenner, context includes any group whose members share the same 'values and beliefs, resources, hazards, lifestyles, opportunity structures, life course options and patterns of social interchange' (1993, p. 25). In the main, sociologists are more interested in the macrosystem of Bronfenbrenner's ecological model. Discussed in Chapter 7, this includes the child's culture, legal systems and social institutions. In contrast, psychologists are more interested in the microsystem; this includes the child's interactions with their mother, father, friends, family and grandparents. As in sociology, in recent years a number of psychologists have critiqued the methods and tools used to study children's behaviour (see Burman, 2008; Christensen and James, 2000; Christensen and Prout, 2005). To bridge these differing perspectives, researchers working within childhood studies devised new methodologies and tools of enquiry.

METHODS AND METHODOLOGIES

Although he was discussing psychological theory, Vygotsky (1987–98) argued that new theories require new methodological approaches. Conversely, Christensen and James (2000) believe that research into children's lives does not require a specific set of tools. This latter view is contrary to the theoretical stance adopted by the majority of sociologists and psychologists who have grown increasingly disenchanted with the methods employed by traditional developmental psychologists. Opponents point out that laboratory and experimental methods objectify children. Additionally, they argue, these methods ignore the influence of culture and context on the child's behaviour and on their interactions with others. It is a quarter of a century since Hill (1997) drew parallels between psychological descriptions of infancy and factory workers. She asserted that the experimental approach favoured by psychologists tends to focus on the acquisition of skills in children which later develop into more complex skills rather than on the processes involved. She drew parallels between this approach and an assembly line, arguing that both focus on production and target setting. Similarly, Burman (2008, p. 22) criticizes psychologists who describe infancy in terms of 'the normal child, the ideal type' (2008, p. 22). She asserts that the information which informs these trends is from comparative scores of an age-graded population. Scores are summed and averaged to represent normal patterns of development. Consequently, the picture of normal development presented is little more than 'an abstraction, a fiction or myth'. Here you will note similarities between the views expressed by Hill, Burman and Piaget. Employed to test children's understanding of test items, Piaget became interested in how they came to their conclusions (process) rather than in their answers (product). He was the first to eschew experimental approaches in favour of observations of and interviews with children.

In the past, many of the research methods used by developmental psychologists were not child-centred and were heavily criticized on the grounds that scientific methods borrowed from the natural sciences were employed to study young children who were merely considered 'objects' rather than 'participants' in the research process (Burman, 2008). Similarly, it was argued that research was conducted 'on' rather than 'with' children. Within a social constructivist approach, however, the methods employed tend to be naturalistic, and methodological tools are employed for research conducted in real-world situations rather than in laboratory settings.

Over time, the distinction between 'method' and 'methodology' has become increasingly blurred. Since they represent two distinct aspects of research, at this juncture it seems appropriate to clarify them. A methodology may be considered a system of principles or methods of procedure in any discipline, such as childhood studies, education, psychology or sociology. It can include ethnographic or experimental approaches, action research or case studies. It is the methodological stance adopted by the researcher that influences their choice of method. Ethnographers, for example, employ a range of naturalistic tools including observations and interviews, whereas experimental researchers select materials that offer solid, quantitative data such as achievement test scores, computer test scores and so on.

Researchers operating within childhood studies typically adopt the rights-based approach advocated by the UNCRC, which introduces the challenge of finding an effective approach to elicit the child's voice. More recently, reflecting the multidisciplinary nature of childhood studies, a range of naturalistic and innovative tools have been used to engage children in the research process. Working with 3- and 4-year-old children in five European countries, Pascal and Bertram (2009) used multi-voice, intercultural, critical incidents, cultural circles (akin to circle time), storytelling, wishing tree, listening posts, guided tours and focused observations – amongst other tools – to elicit the voices of children. Bitou and Waller (2011) worked with a group of 12 younger children, aged between 2 and 3 years, in Early Years settings in Greece and England over a three-year period. Their methods involved participant observation, video and photographic evidence, walking tours and participatory games. To involve the children, the researchers frequently acted as novices who required the help and support of the children. Working with children with special needs and, in a few cases, limited speech, Gray and Winter (2011b) used thumbs-up and -down stickers, smiley faces and drawings to encourage children between 3 and 5 years of age to express their views.

Each of the studies mentioned above employed a multi-method, triangulated approach to increase the rigour and fidelity of the research (Gray and Winter 2011a). Many of these techniques are far from new and were originally introduced into research involving children by Piaget (1954). As well as the observations and interviews mentioned previously, he kept detailed diaries from his observations of his own children and devised tasks to test their understanding (see Chapter 4 for a discussion of Piaget's theory). As Moss et al. point out, 'listening to young children requires of adults some revaluing and relearning of the hundred languages of childhood' (2005, p. 5). This notion receives support from other proponents of multiple, mixed-method approaches to participatory research with children (Bussell, 2008; Crotty, 1998; Punch 2002). Multiple, mixed-method approaches are argued to have a number of advantages over single-method approaches (Clark et al., 2003). For example, the shortcomings of a single method approach are easily overcome when the same issue is explored using a range of methods. It is also believed that they produce more robust results, offer adults and children choice, and provide a framework for listening which can be focused on children's lived experiences embedded in real-world settings (Bussell, 2008; Clark et al., 2003).

CRITICISMS OF CHILDHOOD STUDIES

Childhood studies provided a welcome counter-paradigm to traditional approaches involving children. Studies framed within childhood studies provide insight into, amongst many other areas, children's perceptions of their Early Years setting (Einarsdóttir, 2005a, 2005b; Gray and Winter, 2011b), children's experiences of indoor and outdoor play spaces (Waller, 2006), children's rights to participate in the research process (Lundy, 2007; Te One, 2011) and the tools and methods used to release the voice of the child (Clark, 2005, 2011; Degotardi, 2009; Dunphy and Farrell, 2011; Holloway and Jefferson, 2000). It affords children rights previously denied them in research. No longer are they viewed as objects of study; instead they are increasingly involved as participants in the process.

McLeod (2008, p. 45) notes how the drive to include children in research led the UK government to introduce a torrent of initiatives which elevated listening to the voice of the child to a 'new orthodoxy'. Developing this point, Spyrou (2011) argues that the preoccupation with children's voices has led researchers to ignore the processes which produce children's voices in research, the power imbalances that shape them and the ideological contexts that inform their production and reception – or, in other words, issues of representation.

James acknowledges that the approach 'has been replicated in any number of studies about any number of topics by any number of social scientists' (2010, p. 264). Whilst not contesting the value of this work, he claims the paradigm has reached a crossroads, where searching questions must be asked to develop the field. According to James (2010), a key obstacle to progression concerns the lack of agreement on what constitutes childhood. Far from a unitary concept, childhood, according to James, involves a range of maturational stages denoted in terms such as 'newborn', 'toddler', 'pre-schooler', 'preteen', 'teenager' and 'young adult', amongst others. Since context, time and place influence the childhood experience, a body of research explores the plurality of childhood. Aldridge (2012), for example, explored the childhood experiences of children caring for a parent with mental problems, whilst Thomas de Benitez (2011) used a range of ethnographic methods to capture the voice of street children living in Brazil and Russia.

James (2010) and Qvortrup (2008) critique the plurality approach on the basis that it tends to obscure issues of relevance to children globally. It also tends to privilege some forms of childhood over others. James notes the abundance of research into kindergarten policies in Scandinavia, changing children's culture in Germany, and the reconstruction of childhood in the UK (2010, p. 2). By contrast, Thomas de Benitez (2011) points to the dearth of evidence on the plight of street children forced, through no fault of their own, to survive by whatever means available. Similarly, there remains a paucity of research on the child's right to religious freedom enshrined in Article 14 of the UNCRC. Langlaude (2012) argues that in emphasizing the child's right to autonomy, the committee positions the child as an adult. It also ignores the complexity of religiosity which is informed by the family, the religious community, the state and, ultimately, the child. The lack of voice afforded young children with disabilities was highlighted by Gray (2015). She contends that the provocation is for researchers working within childhood studies to debate, challenge and redefine claims regarding agency, participatory research and giving voice to the child. Whilst James (2010) argues the need to articulate the focus of childhood studies, Gray acknowledges that troubling the accepted discourse may prove uncomfortable for many within the discipline. Ultimately, she claims, it will strengthen and inform the emergence of a strong theoretical base to frame the participatory research discourse.

Another criticism levelled against this evolving paradigm comes in Gray and MacBlain (2012). At that point, we identified the lack of a discipline specific code of ethics as a weakness of the approach. Until quite recently, there was no framework which focused explicitly on the ethical challenges of conducting research with very young children and their families, and in a wider context than purely educational settings. We are delighted to report that between 2012 and 2014 a working group was formed under the leadership of Professor Chris Pascal, with the first author and EECERA (European Early Childhood Education Research Association) trustees. In an editorial alerting readers of the *International Journal of Early Years Education* to this development, Gray opines that:

> this development marks a seismic shift in thinking for practitioners operating within the new social studies of childhood. It marks the evolution of a discipline, which is no longer 'new' and which is emerging with its own identity, practices and procedures. (2014)

Whilst undoubtedly subject to ongoing revision, the first draft of this code is available for Early Years professionals and researchers working in the field of childhood studies at www.eecera.org/documents/pdf/organisation/EECERA-Ethical-Code.pdf (accessed 11.4.15).

In terms of the focus of this text, in a thorough review of the literature we noted that researchers operating within the context of childhood studies do not address the development of learning or the hidden mental processes which support and extend the child's learning. We contend that practitioners working with children require some knowledge of the processes involved in children's learning so that they can support, develop and scaffold the child's development. We did, however, note that a number of scholars working within the broader context of Early Years have written about the development of young children's thinking and learning, including Robson (2012), Fleer (2013), Dowling (2013), Fabian and Mould (2009) and Nutbrown (2006). In a text entitled *Extending Thought in Young Children: A Parent–Teacher Partnership*, Athey (2003) examines the quality of educational interaction between teacher and child, parent and child and parent and professional. Throughout the book, she reports evidence from research conducted at the Froebel Institute in London. Acknowledging the work of Piaget, Athey explores the development of schematic thought and how action turns into thought. Her work is heavily referenced by Nutbrown, who also explores schema formation. Nutbrown notes that:

> one of the clearest ways to understand progression in children's learning is to look at individual children over a period of time, observing their schematic interests, seeing how these relate to the development of their behaviour, their speech and their thinking. (2006, p.37)

Definition

Microgenetic approach: examines change as it occurs, thus attempting to identify and explain its underlying mechanisms. For example, observing a child solve similar problems over a period of time will enable a professional to identify the child's progress or repeated mistakes.

In this statement, Nutbrown concurs with Vygotsky's proposition that adults play an important role in progressing children's thoughts and appears to share his commitment to the *microgenetic approach*. This approach involves repeated observations of the same child over time. It enables a researcher to monitor small changes in children's ability on tasks over a prolonged period. Although time-consuming, it provides a rich insight into the child's development. By way of example, Pine et al. (2007) conducted a microgenetic study into the relationship between children's speech and gestures. Through close observation of 21 children, they surmised that children's gestures are rarely produced without speech and that there appears to be no correlation between the type of gesture made and the spoken word.

Exercise

Undertake a microgenetic study of a child in your setting for short periods of time over a week. Note the types of gestures the child makes and then observe the relationship between the child's gesture and speech. Are your findings similar or different to those reported by Pine et al. (2007)?

Exercise

In Chapter 1, you were asked to consider which theorist best explains how children's learning develops. Has your opinion changed?

 Summary

Few would dispute that children are active participants in the learning process. From the first moment of birth, they interact with, influence and shape their environment and the people who share that environment. In 1989, the UNCRC provided the tools for governments and policy makers worldwide to acknowledge the rights of the child to express their views on matters that affect their lives. This fuelled a new approach to research, involving children as active rather than passive participants. Collectively, they provided the impetus for the evolution of a new movement, which began in Europe and culminated in the development of a new theoretical framework termed 'childhood studies'. Although it has had a profound effect upon the way children are viewed in the research process, this approach continues to evolve and develop. More recently, a new set of ethical guidelines for researchers working within this newly evolving paradigm was produced. This marked a seismic shift in the development of a discrete discipline focused on early childhood. The strength of this approach lies in the multidisciplinary nature of this newly evolving field. In order to develop and grow, the strengths that each discipline brings to our understanding of children should be valued to ensure that we gain a rounded rather than narrow picture of child development. In essence, we believe that the strength of disciplines such as sociology and anthropology (which explore the child's interactions with society and the collective) can be complemented by psychology (which takes the individual child as the focus of study). Table 9.1 lists both the strengths and weaknesses of childhood studies.

Table 9.1   Strengths and weaknesses of childhood studies

Strengths	Similar to	Weaknesses
Adopts a child-centred approach; children are viewed as active and powerful participants in the learning process	Vygotsky, Bronfenbrenner, Bruner	
Emphasizes the role of culture and the environment in the child's learning	Vygotsky, Bronfenbrenner	
		Fails to explore covert processes such as learning, memory and attention
Employs qualitative approaches, including observations and listening to children as they complete tasks	Piaget, Vygotsky, Bronfenbrenner, Bruner	
Focuses on process rather than product	Piaget, Vygotsky, Bronfenbrenner, Bruner	
Recognizes the central importance of play	Piaget, Vygotsky, Bronfenbrenner, Bruner	
Identifies the importance of peer interaction and collaborative learning	Piaget, Vygotsky, Bronfenbrenner, Bruner	
Identifies the importance of developing the child's potential	Piaget, Vygotsky, Bronfenbrenner, Bruner	
		Considers the child at the collective rather than individual level
		Lacks ethical guidelines for practitioners
		Fails to regulate practitioners working within this new paradigm
As a newly evolving discipline, it can draw on the best practice within a range of existing disciplines		

Throughout this text, we have attempted to highlight the strengths and weaknesses of a number of key learning theories. We do not attempt to argue the superiority of any single approach but believe that each offers valuable insights into some aspect of children's learning. At this point, you may have a clear preference for a theory of learning or may feel conflicted and, like Nutbrown and Athey, prefer to draw on the strengths of several theories. In the final analysis, you may be forgiven for believing that further research is warranted if we hope to understand what goes on between the young child's ears.

RECOMMENDED READING

Clark, C. (2011). Multimodal map making with young children: exploring ethnographic and participatory methods. *Qualitative Research, 11, 3*, 311–30. Available at: http://qrj.sagepub.com/content/11/3/311.full.pdf+html (accessed 11.4.15).

This paper reports findings from a longtitudinal study that applied the principles of the ethnographic and participatory approaches. Researching the 'insider' perspective involved tuning into different modes of communication to create opportunities for this knowledge to be communicated by young children and adults in the design and review of learning environments. This article first explores map making, one of the methods used in the Mosaic approach as a site of multi-modal communication. Second, it investigates how the maps, as informant-led representations can promote cultural brokerage.

EECERA (2014). Ethical guidelines for early childhood researchers. Available at: www.eecera.org/documents/pdf/organisation/EECERA-Ethical-Code.pdf (accessed 11.4.15).

The ethical guidelines for those working with young children are essential reading for practitioners and researchers across disciplines. It is written in an accessible way but highlights key points of interest to those working with young or vulnerable groups. This is a first draft and comments are welcome. If you note missing information or areas for expansion please contact the first author.

Dowling, M. (2013). *Children's thinking*. London: Sage.

This is an excellent text. Employing a very accessible writing style, Dowling considers all aspects of the thinking journey from birth through to 7 years of age. Relationships with primary and secondary adults are explored in terms of how they contribute to the child's early learning experience.

James, A.L. (2010). Competition or integration? The next step in childhood studies? *Childhood, 17, 4*, 485–99. Available at: http://www.kingscollege.net/pomfret/3311/pdf/readingjames.pdf (accessed 11.4.15).

In an article that remains relevant today, James observes how childhood studies is approaching a crossroads, reaching a point in its history and development when searching questions must be asked about how the field is now perceived and whether there is any longer a shared understanding of what was once a unified project. As he explores competing constructions of childhood, James highlights the influence of the postmodernist tradition on the interpretation of childhood as complex and multifaceted. This article raises important questions about how childhood is understood and interpreted in the 21st century.

REFERENCES

Aldridge, J. (2012). Children of parents with mental health problems: research, policy and practice issues (notes for International Working Group on Parental Mental Health and Child Welfare). Available for download (accessed 4.5.15).

Ariès, P. (1986 [1962]). *Centuries of Childhood: A Social History of Family Life*. London: Penguin.

Athey, C. (2003). *Extending Thought in Young Children: A Parent–Teacher Partnership*. London: Paul Chapman.

Bitou, A. and Waller, T. (2011). Researching the rights of children under three years old to participate in the curriculum in Early Years education and care. In D. Harcourt, B. Perry and T. Waller (Eds) *Researching Young Children's Perspective: Debating the Ethics and Dilemmas of Educational Research with Children*. London: Routledge. pp. 52–67.

Bronfenbrenner, U. (1993). The ecology of cognitive development: research models and fugitive findings. In R. Wonziak and K. Fischer (Eds) *Development in Context: Acting and Thinking in Specific Environments*. Hillsdale, NJ: Erlbaum. pp. 3–44.

Burman, E. (2008). *Deconstructing Developmental Psychology*, 2nd edn. London: Taylor & Francis.

Burr, R. (2004). Children's rights: international policy and lived practice. In M.J. Kehily (Ed.) *An Introduction to Childhood Studies*. Maidenhead: Open University Press. pp. 145–59.

Bussell, S. (2008). Research with children: thinking about method and methodology. In *Involving Children and Young People in Research*. Compendium of papers and reflections from a Think Tank co-hosted by the Australian Research Alliance for Children and Youth and the New South Wales Commission for Children and Young People, 11 November.

Christensen, P. and James, A. (2000). *Research with Children: Perspectives and Practices*. London: Falmer.

Christensen, P. and Prout, A. (2005). Anthropological and sociological perspectives on the study of children. In S. Greene and D. Hogan (Eds) *Researching Children's Experience: Approaches and Methods*. London: Sage. pp. 42–60.

Clark, A. (2005). Listening to and involving young children: a review of research and practice. *Early Child Development and Care, 175, 6, 489–506*.

Clark, C. (2011). Multimodal map making with young children: exploring ethnographic and participatory methods. *Qualitative Research, 11, 3, 311–30*. Available at: http://qrj.sagepub.com/content/11/3/311.full.pdf+html (accessed 11.4.15).

Clark, A., McQuail, S. and Moss, P. (2003). *Exploring the Field of Listening to and Consulting with Young Children*. Research Report 445. London: Department for Education and Skills.

Corsaro, W. (2014). *The Sociology of Childhood*, 4th edn. Thousand Oaks, CA: Sage.

Crotty, M. (1998). *The Foundations of Social Research: Meaning and Perspective in the Research Process*. Crows Nest, NSW: Allen & Unwin.

Degotardi, S. (2009). Relationship theory in the nursery: attachment and beyond. *Contemporary Issues in Early Childhood, 10, 2, 144–55*.

Diallo, Y., Etienne, A. and Mehran, F. (2013). *Global Child Labour Trends 2008 to 2012*. International Programme on the Elimination of Child Labour (IPEC). Geneva: International Labour Office. Available at: www.ilo.org/ipec (accessed 11.4.15).

Dowling, M. (2013). *Children's thinking*. London: Sage.

Dunphy, L. and Farrell, T. (2011). Eliciting young children's perspectives on indoor play provision in their classroom: reflections and challenges. In D. Harcourt, B. Perry and T. Waller (Eds) *Researching Young Children's Perspectives: Debating the Ethics and Dilemmas of Educational Researchwith Children*. London: Routledge. pp. 128–42.

Einarsdóttir, J. (2005a). Playschool in pictures: children's photographs as a research method. *Early Child Development and Care, 175, 6, 523–41.*

Einarsdóttir, J. (2005b). We can decide what to play! Children's perceptions of quality in an Icelandic playschool. *Early Education and Development, 16, 4, 469–88.*

Fabian, H. and Mould, C. (2009). *Development and Learning for Very Young Children*. London: Sage.

Fleer, M. (2013). *Early Learning and Development: Cultural-Historical Concepts in Play*. New York: Cambridge University Press.

Frønes, I. (1993). Changing childhoods. *Childhood, 1, 1–2.*

Gray, C. (2012). *School readiness: the voices of the child*. Conference Presentation, European Early Childhood Education Research Association: 22nd Conference, Oporto, Portugal, 29 August–1 September.

Gray, C. (2014). Evolution, revolution and development: changing perspectives on early childhood studies – theory, research and policy. *International Journal of Early Years Education, 22, 4, 343–5.*

Gray, C. (2015). Participatory research with vulnerable and marginalised groups. In M. Fleer and B. van Oers (Eds) *International Handbook of Early Childhood Education and Development*, Volume 1: Methodologies. New York: Springer.

Gray, C. and MacBlain, S. (2012). *Learning theories in childhood*. London, Sage.

Gray, C. and Winter, E. (2011a). The ethics of participatory research involving young children with special needs. In D. Harcourt, B. Perry, and T. Waller (Eds) *Researching Young Children's Perspectives: Debating the Ethics and Dilemmas of Educational Research with Children*. London: Routledge. pp. 26–37.

Gray, C. and Winter, E. (2011b). Ethics and participatory research with young children with and without a disability. *European Journal of Early Years Research, 20, 3, 309–320.*

Greene, S. and Hill, M. (2005). Researching children's experience: methods and methodological issues. In S. Greene and D. Hogan (Eds) *Researching Children's Experiences: Approaches and Methods*. London: Sage. pp. 1–21.

Hatherly, A. and Sands, L. (2002). So what is different about learning stories? The first years. Nga Tut Tuatahi. *New Zealand Journal of Infant and Toddler Education, 4, 1, 8–12.*

Hill, M. (1997). Participatory research with children. *Child and Family Social Work, 2, 71–183.*

Holloway, W. and Jefferson, T. (2000). *Doing Qualitative Research Differently: Free Association, Narrative and the Interview Method*. London: Sage.

Hughes, M. and Grieve, R. (1980). On asking children bizarre questions. *First Language, 1, 149–60.*

James, A. (2007). Giving voice to children's voices: practices and problems, pitfalls and potentials. *American Anthropologist, 109, 2, 261–72.*

James, A.L. (2010). Competition or integration? The next step in childhood studies? *Childhood, 17,* 4, 485–99. Available at: http://chd.sagepub.com/content/17/4/485.full.pdf+html (accessed 11.4.15).

Langlaude, S. (2012). Children and religion under Article 14 UNCRC: a critical analysis. *International Journal of Children's Rights, 16,* 4, 475–504.

Lundy, L. (2007). Voice is not enough: conceptualising Article 12 of the United Nations Convention on the Rights of the Child. *British Education Research Journal, 32,* 6, 927–42.

McDowall Clark, R. (2010). *Childhood in Society.* Exeter: Learning Matters.

McLeod, A. (2008). *Listening to Children: A Practitioner's Guide.* London: Jessica Kingsley.

Moss, P., Clark, A. and Kjørholt, A. (2005). Introduction. In A. Clark, A. Kjørholt and P. Moss (Eds) *Beyond Listening: Children's Perspectives on Early Childhood Services.* Bristol: Policy. pp. 1–17.

Muñoz, L.G. (2006). The new sociology of childhood: contributions from a different approach. *Politica y Sociedad, 43,* 1, 9–26. (Translation from the original Spanish available at www.enmcr.net)

Nikitina-den-Besten, O.N. (2009). What's new in the new social studies of childhood? *NHTEP, 5,* 2009. Available at: www.isras.ru/files/File/Inter/05/Nikitina-den-Besten_Eng.pdf (accessed 11.4.15)

Nutbrown, C. (2006). *Threads of Thinking: Young Children Learning and the Role of Early Education.* London: Sage.

Pascal, C. and Bertram, T. (2009). Listening to young citizens: the struggle to make real a participatory paradigm in research with young children. *European Early Childhood Education Research Journal, 1,* 2, 249–62. Available at: www.informaworld.com/smpp/title~content=t776628938 (accessed 10.1.14).

Piaget, J. (1954). *The Construction of Morality in the Child.* New York: Basic Books.

Pine, K.J., Lufkin, N. Kirk, E. and Messer, D. (2007). A microgenetic analysis of the relationship between speech and gesture in children: evidence for semantic and temporal asynchrony. *Language and Cognitive Processes, 22,* 2, 234–46.

Prout, A. (2005). *The Future of Childhood: Towards the Interdisciplinary Study of Children.* London: Falmer.

Punch, S. (2002). Research with children: the same or different from research with adults? *Childhood, 9,* 2, 321–41.

Qvortrup, J. (2008). Childhood in the Welfare State. In A. James and A.L. James (Eds) *European Childhoods: Cultures, Politics and Childhood in Europe.* Basingstoke: Palgrave Macmillan.

Robson, S. (2012). *Developing Thinking and Understanding in Young Children,* 2nd edn. London: Routledge.

Ryan, P.J. (2008). How new is the new social study of childhood? The myth of a paradigm shift. *Journal of Interdisciplinary History, 38,* 4, 533–76.

Smith, A. (2011). Respecting children's rights and agency: theoretical insights into ethical research procedures. In D. Harcourt, B. Perry and T. Waller (Eds) *Researching Young Children's Perspective: Debating the Ethics and Dilemmas of Educational Research with Children.* London: Routledge. pp. 11–25.

Spyrou, S. (2011). The limits of children's voices: from authenticity to critical, reflexive representation. *Childhood, 18,* 2, 151–65.

Te One, S. (2011). Supporting children's participation rights: curriculum and research approaches. In D. Harcourt, B. Perry and T. Waller (Eds) *Researching Young Children's Perspective: Debating the Ethics and Dilemmas of Educational Research with Children.* London: Routledge. pp. 85–99.

Thomas de Benitez, S. (2011). *State of the World's Street Children Report: Research*. Street Children Series 2. London: Consortium for Street Children. Available at: www.google.co.uk/url?url=http://www.aviva.com/media/upload/State_of_the_Worlds_Street_Children_Research_final_PDF_online.pdf&rct=j&frm=1&q=&esrc=s&sa=U&ei=4NgxVJinIorPaPi7grAL&ved=0CBQQFjAA&usg=AFQjCNGmPScAi5btfrv-hT4qLkbKzIAz9w (accessed 6.10.14).

Tisdall, E. (2012). The challenge and challenging of childhood studies? Learning from disability studies and research with disabled children. *Children & Society, 26, 3,* 181–191.

UNICEF CEE/CIS (2010). *Blame and Banishment: The Underground HIV Epidemic Affecting Children in Eastern Europe and Central Asia*. Geneva: UNICEF CEE/CIS.

United Nations Convention on the Rights of the Child (UNCRC) (1989). *Convention on the Rights of the Child*. New York: UNICEF.

Waller, T. (2006). Don't come too close to my octopus tree: recording and evaluating young children's perspectives on outdoor learning. *Children, Youth and Environments, 16, 2,* 75–104.

Waterman, A., Blades, M. and Spencer, C. (2001). Is a jumper angrier than a tree? *The Psychologist, 14,* 474–7.

Woodhead, M. (2005). Children and development. In J. Oates, C. Wood and A. Grayson (Eds) *Psychological Development and Early Childhood*. Oxford: Open University Press. pp. 9–46.

Zelizer, V. (1994 [1985]). *Pricing the Priceless Child: The Changing Social Value of Children*. Princeton, NJ: Princeton University Press.

Zimmerman, A. (2008). Welcome to Brazil, a paradise of impunity for all kinds of criminals. Paper presented at the Criminal Law Workshop held by the John Fleming Centre for Advancement of Legal Research at the Australian National University College of Law, 7–9 February. Available at: www.brazzil.com/info/188–february-2008/10042.html (accessed 21/7/13).

Want to learn more about this Chapter?
Visit the companion website at **https://study.sagepub.com/grayandmacblain2e** to gain open access to selected SAGE journal articles, author podcasts and weblinks to help further your study.

10 THEORY IN PRACTICE: LEARNING AND THE REFLECTIVE PRACTITIONER

This chapter aims to:

- examine the importance of reflective practice in the work of Early Years professionals
- explore the social and economic context within which young learners develop
- look at key factors that are important in creating effective learning environments for young children
- bring together the concepts of learning and reflection as used in professional practice taking account of the importance of emotional intelligence and sustained shared thinking
- explore the relationship between theory and practice.

A little over a decade ago the following comments were offered in relation to the importance of meeting the individual learning needs of young children:

> '... systematically helping children to learn so that they are helped to make connections in their learning and are actively led forward, as well as helped to reflect on what they have learnt ... Practitioners teach children in many ways. The different ways to teach may be selected at the planning stage or may be a perceptive response to what children do and say ... The strategies used in learning and teaching should vary and should be adapted to suit the needs of the child.'
>
> **The Quality and Curriculumn Authority, 2000, p. 20**

Underpinning the effective and purposeful teaching and learning of young children is the engagement by Early Years practitioners in critical reflection, and directly related to this is the importance of active and meaningful participation of children in what they do, as indicated by QCA in their above statement. With younger children, the activities they engage in, and the type and quality of their play, are crucial. Equally important, however, is the nature of the environments that are created for them and the extent to which they are encouraged to involve themselves in problem-based exploratory learning, both on an individual basis and, perhaps more importantly, with their peers and with the adults around them. This second point takes on much greater credence for it is now the case in the UK and especially in England that the delivery of the Early Years curriculum is becoming much more formalized with a growing emphasis upon children's academic achievement and a much tighter monitoring of practice by Ofsted. For many practitioners working in Early Years settings this represents a significant challenge and along with this challenge comes the belief, held by many practitioners, that there is an increasing erosion of autonomy on the part of the practitioner and a lessening of creativity (MacBlain et al., 2015).

Whilst the concept of 'learning' was explored earlier, it is now also worth considering at this point what is meant by engaging in critical reflection, and why this might be so important for Early Years practitioners and teachers of young children. Daudelin, cited in Zwozdiak-Myers (2007, pp. 160–1), has commented that:

> [r]eflection is the process of stepping back from an experience to ponder, carefully and persistently, its meaning to the self through the development of inferences. (1996, p. 39)

This definition is very useful as it points towards a number of concepts that can serve as signposts for understanding key elements that underpin sound professional practice with young children, namely: 'stepping back', 'carefully and persistently', 'meaning' and 'inferences'. These concepts are especially useful as they can provide an entry point through which Early Years practitioners can explore and evaluate their own professional practice. They also offer a means by which practitioners can engage in effective and purposeful evaluation of the learning they observe taking place around them, the opportunities they provide for their children and the environments they create.

What becomes quickly apparent when listening to effective Early Years practitioners and primary teachers is the nature of the conversations they have when talking about the children they work with. They are clear about the purpose of the environments they create and they know exactly what they are trying to achieve when they set tasks for their children. Conversations are typically characterized by meaningful and objective discussions and there is far less evidence of descriptive talk and narrated accounts when talking about learning, and about the individual needs of the children. The nature and purpose of these 'professional' conversations are extremely important and reflect a deep and systematic understanding of children's emotional, social and developmental needs as well as how they learn and in what contexts learning can be optimized. Effective practitioners take time to step back and carefully observe the behaviours of their children and take time to reflect upon their own behaviours and the purposes of their actions. They take great care when making inferences based on observations and they continually look for new meanings in what they do.

BECOMING A REFLECTIVE PRACTITIONER

It is always a point of debate as to whether we are born reflective or whether we acquire those dispositions that make us reflective. A useful entry point to this debate can be found in the work of Reuven Feuerstein (Feuerstein et al., 1979, 1980), who drew heavily upon the original ideas of Vygotsky. Before looking in detail at the work of Feuerstein, however, it is worth highlighting two crucial elements that underpin critical thinking and effective practice with young children, namely the nature and quality of practitioners' observations, and the importance of purposeful listening. One further element in critical thinking and effective practice proposed some decades ago by Schön (1987) is the need for practitioners working with young children to also have a deep knowledge and understanding of themselves.

The importance of undertaking purposeful and meaningful observation and listening is recognized throughout the literature. Dowling (2005, p. 30), for example, has commented that '[t]he task of really getting inside children's minds and under-standing them can only properly be achieved through observing their actions and conversing with them', whilst Penny Lancaster has suggested that:

> [l]istening to young children fits a rights-based approach in relating to children. It ... advocates a move away from viewing young children as passive recipients of adults' decisions, where choices and decisions need to be made on their behalf. (2006, p. 69)

Lancaster further suggests that in order to respect the child's voice, practitioners need to have 'understood how they [the children] have made sense of their experiences' (2006, p. 72). This point is extremely important and emphasizes the need for Early Years practitioners to take time to 'really hear' what children are saying and to give their children 'space' in which they can process information at an appropriate level and within their own time. To fail to do so may well result in children learning to become passive agents in the adult–child relationships that exist around them. In extreme cases, such as with children who are experiencing significant social and emotional trauma in their lives, they may even fail to have their situations recognized and responded to. In the very sad and extremely severe case of the child Victoria Climbié, who was physically abused and then died, Penny Lancaster noted:

> Victoria Climbié needed someone to listen to her life experiences, her concerns, her feelings and her perspective of her situation, but no one did. Her rights were overlooked and the care she received was steered by adult demand. (2006, p. 65)

Equally important to listening to young children is the need for reflective practitioners to develop their observation skills and to take time to understand

and consider carefully what they are observing. Careful, considered and purposeful observation will inform and underpin effective planning, assessment and intervention, and will also facilitate the identification of appropriate learning objectives for the future. Cathy Nutbrown, in respect of the importance of observation, argues:

> Observation and assessment are the essential tools of watching and learning with which practitioners can both establish the progress that has already taken place and explore the future. (2006, p. 99)

In reporting on observation in the classroom as undertaken by Montessori teachers, Feez noted:

> When learning to observe, trainee Montessori teachers sit where they will not disturb, distract or interact with the children in any way. They record everything, including small details others might not recognize as being important. In particular, they record:
>
> - everything that interests each child, no matter how apparently insignificant
>
> - how long a child sustains interest in each activity they choose, whether for seconds, minutes or hours
>
> - how a child moves, especially movement of the hand
>
> - how many times a child repeats the same activity
>
> - how a child interacts with others. (2010, p. 24)

This approach to the observation of young children can be used by practitioners as a model for their own practice.

Weblink

For an excellent example of observation taking place in an Early Years setting, see '210 Observation EYFS'. Available at: www.youtube.com/watch?v=jNMsEEWxr_I (accessed 11.4.15).

Having recognized the importance of purposeful and meaningful observation and listening in the practice of Early Years practitioners, it is now worth turning to the work of Reuven Feuerstein, who in recent decades has come to exercise significant influence upon many practitioners and academics working with and researching the learning of young children. Feuerstein's background was in clinical psychology and he studied at the University of Geneva under Jean Piaget and Barbel Inhelder. Following the Second World War, Feuerstein worked with child survivors of the

Holocaust and went on to hold the position of Director of the Centre for Development of Human Potential in Jerusalem. Feuerstein has proposed that theories are based on those belief systems and values held by individuals within societies and that these belief systems are essential in the determining of action, which can be construed as effective. In this respect, it is worth Early Years practitioners taking time to reflect upon their own belief systems regarding childhood and how, for example, they might assess the intellectual functioning of young children and especially those children who present with difficulties in the areas of language and behaviour.

Feuerstein suggests that belief systems need to view human potential as having almost no limits whilst recognizing that artificial barriers remain in place which can work to prevent change in children realizing their potential. He further suggests that all children, no matter what their age and no matter what their degree of difficulty, can become effective learners. By adopting such belief systems, we can argue that Early Years practitioners and teachers become 'freed' from constrained thinking that limits their vision of what is possible for all young children. In doing so, they can be even more engaged in critical analysis of their own practice and the learning of their children. When this process is embarked upon, a number of consequences can occur, most notably recognition of the concept of what Feuerstein calls 'structural cognitive modifiability'. This refers to the belief that the brain's cognitive structure can be altered by an enabling process which permits the learner to 'learn how to learn'. Learning, essentially, becomes cumulative and affects performance throughout an individual's entire life (Burden, 1987).

Such an approach, Feuerstein argued, is directed at changing the structural nature of cognitive development. Feuerstein views 'structural change' in terms of an individual's manner of 'acting upon' sources of information and then responding to these. The central factor involved in learning how to learn is the idea of *mediated learning* experience, and it is this that underpins Feuerstein's *social interactionist theory* of learning:

> the way in which stimuli emitted by the environment are transferred by a 'mediating' agent, usually a parent, sibling or other caregiver. This mediated agent, guided by his intentions, culture, and emotional investment, selects and organises the world of stimuli for the child ... Through this process of mediation, the cognitive structure of the child is affected. (Feuerstein et al., 1980, p. 16)

The crucial factors in mediating learning are: that the mediator must be aware of, make known and ensure the learner has comprehended what is intended (intentionality and reciprocity); that the mediator must explain why she is going to work at a task (investment of meaning); and that the act must be shown to have value over and above the here-and-now (transcendence) (Burden, 1987). It is important, therefore, for Early Years practitioners to reflect upon their own philosophies of teaching and learning and how they, themselves, mediate the learning experience of their children. How, for example, do Early Years practitioners, as mediating agents, select and organize the world of the child, and how do they help the child to learn how to learn?

Weblink

For an excellent insight into how Feuersteins's ideas can be used in practice, view the excellent YouTube video link, 'Down Syndrome Film "Looking Up On Down" (Glow Films/Feuerstein Institute film by David Goodwin)'. Available at: www.youtube.com/watch?v=IqSQI6VJgLk (accessed 11.4.15).

Exercise

Consider the difference between a child's 'ability' and their 'potential'. How might Early Years practitioners use the learning environment to develop each of these?

DEVELOPING YOUNG LEARNERS

Crucial to the practice of any Early Years practitioner is an informed understanding of development in the first years. Gaining an informed understanding of a child's development requires knowledge and critical understanding of the narratives that parents offer in regard to their children. Most parents are only too willing to talk at length and in detail about the events in their children's lives, and in doing so they provide useful and relevant information about the early milestones in their children's development and even about possible causes for concern. Reflective practitioners can take opportunities when listening to parents to engage in careful and meaningful discussion, which will lead to better understanding not only of the child but also the home environment and the child's wider family and community (Johnson, 2010). In doing so, however, it is important for practitioners to critically reflect upon the inferences they find themselves making as a result of their discussions and observations. It is important to 'step back' and understand what parents are truly saying about their children. This has become increasingly important in the last decades as we witness huge changes in society.

The world into which children are now born is, perhaps more than ever, one of immense complexity, a complexity that we can all too often fail to properly absorb and comprehend (MacBlain and Purdy, 2011). How we understand and define childhood and, more importantly, the inferences we make about this time in the lives of individuals, are fundamental to sound professional practice. Miller and Pound, in making reference to the work of Kellet (2010), have emphasized that:

> childhood is a construction that arises from historical, cultural and economic conditions (Kellet, 2010) and ... educators can hold multiple views or constructions of children ... It is reflection which helps us to understand and reconcile what are sometimes apparently irreconcilable views. (2011, p. 5)

Do we, for example, view childhood as a time of joy and excitement, fun and security, or do we, in the light of our own experience and that of others' reported in the media, view it through less rose-tinted glasses and adopt what some might argue is a more realistic but cynical view?

As we set about reflecting upon how we might develop young learners, we also need to understand how children are influenced not just by their personal experiences, but also by the social, historical, economic and cultural contexts that surround them, which is at the core of Bronfenbrenner's theory discussed in Chapter 7. Across the globe, societies, communities and, perhaps more importantly, families, are changing at a rate unprecedented in history. It has been estimated, for example, that in the year 2001 in Britain there were some 3.1 million children living in lone-parent households (MacBlain and MacBlain, 2004). In the spring of 2002, it was further estimated (National Statistics, 2003) that one-fifth of dependent children in Great Britain lived in lone-parent families, almost twice the proportion as in 1981. In the subsequent 10 years from 1981, the number of families headed by a single parent rose by over 70 per cent, with lone-parent families making up 19 per cent of all families in the UK (Brown, 1999, p. 66). This percentage is now much greater (MacBlain and MacBlain, 2004; MacBlain and Purdy, 2011). The rate of divorce has also been increasing at what many consider to be an alarming rate. Just over a decade ago, Rowntree predicted that 'If recent trends continue, more than a third of new marriages will end within twenty years and four out of ten will ultimately end in divorce' (1998, cited in Brown, 1999, p. 66). Ten years before Rowntree's predictions, Wells (1988) estimated that in England and Wales alone, some 40–50 children each day lost a parent following bereavement. More recently, Holland (2001) has suggested that approximately 3 per cent of the school population will have experienced the death of a parent during their school years. Added to these two groups has been the increasing number of children in lone-parent households where parents have chosen to live separately and remain unmarried.

In effect, the structure of families is changing, with many sociologists and educationalists now preferring to use the term 'households' instead of families. This has enormous implications for the early social experiences of children as well as their learning and emotional development. At the beginning of the 21st century, Buckingham (2000) alerted us to the fact that in Britain today there has emerged an 'underclass' where many children are failing to be properly represented. Buckingham has further alerted us to the fact that in the 13 years between 1979 and 1992, the number of dependent children growing up in households where income was not even half of the average income in Britain rose from one in every ten to one in every three. He also cites the incidence of children in Britain growing up in dwellings that are unfit for human habitation as being around the one million mark. This figure is now higher.

In reflecting upon the development of young learners, it is also important to acknowledge the influence of technology. Most young children, even some as young as 5 or 6 years of age, now have access to mobile telephones, computers, social media and 24-hour television. One regularly hears of the concerns expressed publicly by organizations such as parent groups and teaching unions about the diet of violence and sexualized activity available to young children through different media platforms. In addition, there are significant numbers of children now entering Early Years settings and schools who have poorly developed listening skills and delayed language development, and who display a lack of maturity and preparedness for more formal learning environments (Palmer, 2006). The result of delays in language and immaturity also means, for many children, that they typically begin school at a disadvantage and can, in all too many instances, struggle with the acquisition of literacy and with forming purposeful friendships. In 2006, in a letter to the British newspaper, the *Daily Telegraph*, 110 teachers, psychologists and 'other experts' called upon the government 'to prevent the death of childhood'. The letter contained the following:

> Since children's brains are still developing, they cannot adjust – as full-grown adults can – to the effects of ever more rapid technological and cultural change. They still need what developing human beings have always needed, including real food (as opposed to processed 'junk'), real play (as opposed to sedentary, screen-based entertainment), first-hand experience of the world they live in and regular interaction with the real-life significant adults in their lives. (Fenton, 2006, p. 1)

On the other hand, there are also significant numbers of children entering Early Years settings who have experienced high levels of input from their parents in terms of access to positive role modelling, educational experiences and sophisticated social situations, which aids them in developing their self-confidence and self-efficacy. Akin to this is the notion that young children have become a lucrative market. The young child in the 21st century typically now has much greater spending power than ever before. Only a decade ago, Buckingham (2000) estimated the size of the UK market for children's spending in the area of consumer goods to be in the region of £10 billion pounds. This is now significantly greater. Many parents and professionals now point to a run-away sense of materialism in the youth of today.

Exercise

Examine your own perceptions of childhood and consider how childhood might have changed over the last 50 years. To what extent do we see childhood as an idyllic time, and should we be more realistic about our perceptions and examine more closely the life experiences of those children who are growing up in families where there is little emotional support?

CREATING A LEARNING ENVIRONMENT

The culture of Early Years and primary school settings has undergone massive change in the past three decades. There has, for example, been an increasing diversity of pupil needs as evidenced by the growing number of children now included in mainstream settings who have a wide and diverse range of special educational needs and/or disabilities. In 2008, for example, it was estimated that in England alone there were approximately one and a half million pupils with special educational needs in schools, representing approximately one-fifth of the school population. In addition, over 50 per cent of the 223,600 children (just under 3 per cent of the school population) with statements of special educational needs had been included within mainstream schools (DCSF, 2008). Moreover, in regard to linguistic diversity there are currently around 900,000 children in schools in England learning English as an additional language, suggesting that there are some 200 languages being spoken (MacBlain and Purdy, 2011).

Given the changing nature of the range of needs presented by young children in mainstream settings, it is extremely important for Early Years practitioners to reflect upon the learning environments, and particularly 'enabling environments', that can be created for all children and the degree of effectiveness or otherwise of these. In doing so, they can be guided by the work of theorists and philosophers against whose work they can compare their own thoughts, belief systems and practice. It would be useful at this point to look back at some of the key figures introduced in Chapters 2 and 3 and reflect upon how their ideas and philosophies of learning and development were so closely interwoven with the environments they felt were necessary for children to learn effectively. It is also worth reflecting upon how society has changed since they introduced their ideas and how society now influences our thinking about learning. Palmer has offered a sobering note in regard to young children entering schools in the UK and, perhaps, a challenge to Early Years practitioners about how they assist in the preparation of very young children for their future schooling:

> Everywhere I went it was the same story: four- and five-year-olds were coming to school with poorer language skills than ever before; they weren't arriving with the repertoire of nursery rhymes and songs little ones always used to know, and children of all ages found it increasingly difficult to sit down and listen to their teacher or to express complex ideas in speech or writing ... I also discovered that this issue was bothering teachers across the developed world. (2006, p. 105)

As emphasized in Chapter 3, current practice in the field of education and learning has changed markedly within the last decade and will continue to change markedly over the next decades. Take the views of Dewey, who advocated that school should be an 'extension of the home', or Steiner, who saw the function of education as that of responding to the changing physical, cognitive and emotional needs of children. Set against significant changes in modern societies, with an increased emphasis upon technology and materialism, we can once again see the importance and wisdom of Steiner's ideas.

Equally, the pioneering work of the McMillan sisters, with their emphasis upon play outdoors and healthy living, can be viewed against recent legislation and practice in the UK regarding the importance of appropriate nurturing and care for children before they reach statutory school age. However, it should be noted that even in the latter part of the 20th century much had not improved for young children in the UK. In addressing the situation for pre-school children in the UK during this time, Mayall felt able to comment that:

> [i]n the 1970s and 1980s, when other European countries were providing universalist high quality state-run nurseries, British pre-school children were (and still are) the victims of a ramshackle patchwork of poor services. Indeed ... they could not be called services, but rather an ad hoc system which operated certainly not in the interests of children, nor even of the people who ran them. (2002, p. 13)

> **Example**
>
> Arthur is 6 years of age and has just started his second year at the local primary school. He is struggling to acquire basic literacy skills in reading and writing, and appears to have particular difficulty with rhyming words and with words that contain several syllables. In addition, Arthur has marked difficulties with organization and with concentration and attention. He has been described by his previous two teachers as 'a real fidget' and as having 'very poor, almost no concentration span'. They have both emphasized to his new teacher that they constantly have to repeat instructions to him and that he is 'just too easily distracted by those around him'. His parents, on the other hand, emphasize how he can remain absorbed in construction activities 'for ages' and proudly tell their friends that he is 'brilliant at working things out in his head'. There are signs that Arthur is beginning to dislike going to school.

Arthur is typical of a number of young children in their early stages of formal education who are perceived as having difficulties when in fact they have failed to acquire suitable and efficient strategies for managing particular elements of their learning. Following assessment by an educational psychologist, Arthur was found to be predominantly a visual learner but with very poor short-term memory, which led to difficulties in following instructions given by his teachers when these were spoken quickly and in succession. At the time of assessment, he was also found to be intellectually very able with scores on a range of sub-tests falling in the superior range of functioning. Sadly, these key elements of Arthur's functioning were not identified with the result that poor short-term memory and underlying processing difficulties, which affected the speed at which he worked, were interpreted as poor concentration and organization, and as a general lack of motivation and interest. By the time Arthur started his second year in primary school, he had already acquired and internalized a range of inefficient and ineffective strategies for accessing literacy and numeracy.

A major barrier to Arthur's progress is the perception that others have of him and the way in which his learning environment has been created, organized and maintained. Arthur has difficulty with the wide range of activities that are presented to him throughout the week and avoids planning ahead because this causes him anxiety and makes him confront his difficulties in this area. In addition, he is now perceived as not being very able and as a bit of a 'plodder'. Because he is forgetful and has difficulty attending to activities for long periods of time, he distracts others around him. This pattern of distracting has been learned and is being reinforced on a daily basis by the other children around him who observe him distracting others and laugh at him. The laughter is very rewarding for Arthur because it makes him the centre of attention and he enjoys the celebrity status that it offers.

The emotionally intelligent learner

It is been recognized for quite some time (Bandura, 1977; Goleman, 1996; Miller and Pound, 2011; Palmer, 2006) that the manner in which children develop their understanding of emotions, and then manage these, significantly impacts upon their learning. Indeed, it is now generally recognized (Brouzos et al., 2014; Colverd and Hodgkin, 2011; James, 2012) that our emotions influence and even frame the way in which we see the world around us as well as those who inhabit our worlds. This point is well made by Smidt, who refers to the work of Bruner (see Chapter 8) as follows:

> Bruner said that the world (and everything in it) is not just as you see it but it is as you see it in context and in relation to your thoughts. So things may look different depending on how you feel, who you are with, what you have just been doing, what you are thinking about and so on … There is a link between perception, mind and learning. (2011, pp. 8–9)

Exercise

Weblink

Take time to view the excellent and highly informative YouTube video link 'Emotional Intelligence, Creativity and the Arts', available at: www.youtube.com/watch?v=U9VgzE-Ras9s (accessed 11.4.15), This features a conversation between Peter Salovey, President-elect, Yale University (one of the key figures in the emerging field of emotional intelligence), Marc Brackett, Director of the Yale Centre for Emotional Intelligence, and Ínigo Sáenz de Miera Cárdenas, Director, Fundación Botín.

This is an excellent introduction to emotional intelligence, what it is, how it affects thinking and learning in individuals, and most particularly, its relevance to creativity (see 'Play, creativity and thought' in Chapter 5) As well as being able to listen to the conversation between these leading academics, the video offers the opportunity for readers to view and listen to questions being directed at these prominent figures by a number of journalists. This discussion, which focuses upon creativity, is of particular relevance to practitioners working with young children today as recent directives emerging from the coalition government have emphasized a return to more formal education and learning; many practitioners currently argue that there has been a growing reduction in the opportunities for creativity in the class room.

Arguably, the need for young children to become engaged in recognizing and understanding their emotions, and then managing these, has become even more important in recent decades. In part, this has been brought about by the monumental growth in technology, the increasingly materialistic nature of society and the ease with which even very children can communicate with one another. In a relatively recent report, *An Intelligent Look at Emotional Intelligence*, commissioned by the Association of Teachers and Lecturers, Professor Guy Claxton commented as follows:

> In school, young people's emotions are much more present in classrooms – and playgrounds – than they used to be. For example:
>
> - With what sociologists call the 'decline of deference' (and what teachers simply label as 'bad behaviour'), pupils and students bring more of their complicated emotional selves into the classroom with them.
>
> - Living with the consequences of 'inclusion', teachers are sometimes faced with challenging behaviour and displays of strong emotion that they struggle to know how to deal with. (ATL, 2005, p. 6)

These views expressed by Claxton have even greater resonance when we consider the following, recently offered by Cowie:

> The Innocenti Report published by UNICEF (2010) provided evidence that, in comparison with other countries in the developed world, children in the UK scored very poorly in terms of emotional health and well-being. The UNICEF study found that UK children rated their own health as being low, and they also described themselves as the least content in the developed world and as more likely to feel lonely and excluded ... An international study of child well-being in the developed countries (UNICEF, 2007) reported that the UK ranked in the bottom third ... Today's young people seem to face severe stresses that were unknown a generation ago. (2012, pp. 1–2)

In attempting to offer insights into the reasons why so many children in developed countries experience difficulties with their emotional well-being, James has offered the following most attractive, though 'common-sense' notion of 'love bombing', a term that is in itself self-explanatory:

> When it comes to dealing with disobedient or shy or clingy or aggressive or impatient children, love and control, it seems, really are the answer. What is more, because so many parents are, or have had periods of, living very busy or miserable or complicated lives, most of us need to reconnect with our children from time to time. Love Bombing does the job. (2012, p. 2)

Compare James' proposition of 'love bombing' with that offered by Curran:

> IT IS EXTRAORDINARY TO ME that in the last 15 years of brain research, all those billions of dollars spent in laboratories has shown to me one single important message. It can best be set out as follows:

- If a child is in an environment where they are *understood* as an individual human being then,

- Their *self-esteem* will be improved, and

- If their self-esteem is good they will gain *self-confidence*, and

- If they are in an environment where their self-esteem is good and they have self-confidence, they will feel *engaged* with that environment.

And what does all that add up to? Well, love as it happens. (2012, p. 5)

Developing his ideas further, Claxton, cited above, went on to emphasize how the emotional intelligence of children differs from more traditional and popularized explanations and representations of intelligence, which has too frequently been the means by which adults make judgements about children's abilities, and more worryingly, their potential. He proposed two quite fundamental ways in which this is the case. First, he advocated how emotional intelligence:

> values different ways of being bright. It asserts that understanding someone else's point of view, or knowing how to deal with stress, are forms of intelligence, just as useful – indeed, quite possibly more so – than being able to solve logical brainteasers fast under pressure. (ATL, 2005, p. 9)

Second, Claxton advocated how emotional intelligence is not like the popularly held perception of intelligence being fixed in some way, as in the case of the intelligence quotient (IQ), but instead:

> focuses on the extent to which emotional competence can be developed. Whereas a child of 'low (intellectual) ability' tends to be seen as a prisoner of their genes, Emotional Intelligence is of interest to so many teachers because they believe they can do something to help. (ATL, 2005, p. 9),

This second point is crucial and goes a long way in explaining why this fairly novel concept of emotional intelligence – or as it is sometimes referred to, 'emotional literacy' – has grown in popularity with teachers and Early Years practitioners. Through promoting emotional intelligence and steering away from more traditional notions of intelligence as something that is fixed and that children are born with, teachers and Early Years practitioners have been able to recognize and celebrate the fact that what they do with children and the manner in which they do it impacts significantly upon their pupils' learning.

As was emphasized in the previous section, the creation of effective and purposeful learning environments is crucial not only to surface learning but also to the holistic development of the 'whole child', and thereby, their emotional well-being and well-becoming (MacBlain et al., 2015). Such a view, however, emphasizes the challenges and responsibilities placed upon teachers and Early Years practitioners in regard to creating learning environments where children are supported in realizing their potential, as opposed to acquiring abilities that simply allow them to get by in their lives. Such a view also draws us to think about the ideas expressed by philosophers and theorists over the generations, many of whom placed enormous value upon the emotional and holistic development of children and the manner in which their teachers created stimulating, effective and purposeful environments. Here, Montessori and Steiner (Chapter 3) immediately jump to mind and offer a stark contrast to the ideas of the behaviourists (Chapter 4), which came to dominate much of the learning of countless number of children throughout the 1940s, 1950s, 1960s and 1970s, and even the 1980s. Some would now argue that the behaviourist approach to learning is making a comeback through recent changes in thinking brought about by the previous Secretary of State for Education, Michael Gove.

Exercise

Weblink

Observe the two YouTube video links 'Montessori Vs Conventional School', available at www.youtube.com/watch?v=3NGRpzQ9vCE (accessed 15.4.15) and 'Montessori Vs Conventional Pre-school', available at www.youtube.com/watch?v=QtDfZMNrmhk (accessed 15.4.15), which offer some interesting views and observations regarding Montesssori methods and environments and how these meet the needs of young children.

Then consider how the principles that underpin teaching and learning in Early Years settings and primary schools relate to your understanding of emotional intelligence and how young children cope with their emotions as they progress through secondary school. Consider also the view that Montessori schools are more effective in developing emotional intelligence than mainstream state schools.

Sustained shared thinking

As I write this section I am reflecting upon my observations of my one-year-old grandson Thomas, who up until a few minutes ago was playing with his mum. Both were absorbed in solving the type of routine problem that young mums and their children meet on a daily basis. We had been renting a cottage for the week in the Lake District and Thomas had been brought over by his mum to visit myself and his grandmother. Being in a new and somewhat strange environment, he rather reluctantly began to look around and soon began to explore – he has only just begun to take his first steps. When Thomas spots my guitar in the corner of the room he makes straight for it and starts to hit the strings with his hand. As he does so his mum moves over beside him and starts to talk with him about the guitar – she shows him how to gently pluck the strings, which he imitates and she voices a number of words, which Thomas again imitates as best he can. They play with the guitar, and as Thomas plucks the strings his mum sings along with the noise he is making and, once again, he tries to imitate her singing. They play like this for what seems to be a long time and it is a joy to observe. Through her activity with Thomas she is maintaining his interest and developing his learning and thinking in all manner of ways. She is, in effect, increasing his learning by sustaining the activity through her own interactions with him. Such patterns of behaviour can be observed between parents and their children every day. By sustaining the activity and by introducing to Thomas new words, noises, rhythms, ways of understanding the new object and responding to it in different ways that she has modelled and so on, Thomas' mother is extending his thinking. They are both, in effect, sharing in the learning and thinking that is happening. Recently, our understanding of such vital everyday activities between adults and children has been formalized into what is now regarded as an important element in the education of young children, namely *sustained shared thinking*.

Sustained shared thinking has been defined as:

> [a]n episode in which two or more individuals 'work together' in an intellectual way to solve a problem, clarify a concept, evaluate activities, extend a narrative etc. Both parties must contribute to the thinking and it must develop and extend the understanding. (Siraj-Blatchford et al., 2002, p. 8)

In the above example Thomas's experience with his mother can be understood in terms of his learning about the guitar as 'new' thinking, which is being amplified through his interactions with his mother and with the new object or concept. Compare Thomas' experience with that of another child, where the mother shouts at the child to 'leave the guitar alone and come away from it – you're not to touch that, leave it alone or you'll get a smack'. It is important to point out that 'sustained' learning experience is now recognized as having a significant impact upon future learning as well as social and emotional development. In both cases the children are having very different experiences that will last and affect their future development in very different ways.

Examples of sustained shared thinking can be located within the area of 'pretend play' where one or more children or adult-child dyads engage in imaginary play activities that seek to develop the manner in which children represent the world around them and are assisted in doing so by the others with whom they are inter-acting and who can move their thinking forward. Morrissey (2014) has offered some interesting research findings in regard to how very early pretend play in preschool children links to the measurement of intellectual functioning in the pri-mary years. Here research, which is part of a wider study, offers some interesting observations and findings, which readers may wish to pursue with regard to the role of 'pretend play' and emotional intelligence as opposed to IQ, which is the measure employed by Morrissey (for a detailed discussion of IQ see, MacBlain, 2014, Chs 6 and 7).

Weblink

The YouTube video 'Franchesca – Sustained Shared Thinking', available at www.youtube.com/watch?v=SmZsDfVTa8I (accessed 11.4.15), offers an excellent example of sustained shared thinking in practice.

PUTTING THEORY INTO PRACTICE

As adults and practitioners, we typically explain social situations, the behaviours of children and their parents, and cycles of behaviour through our own internalized world views. We form opinions and we make judgements, which arise from our own experiences. All too often, however, these inferred judgements are more a reflection of our own emotional responses to others' behaviours, as opposed to careful and objective interpretations of what is, in actuality, happening. This of course has implications for the way in which we manage behaviours as well as social situations.

> **Example**
>
> Joe (aged 3 years and 6 months) is the youngest of three. He is attending a local pre-school. Joe's nursery school teacher has been concerned about Joe's behaviour and has referred him to the educational psychologist for assessment. When she met with the educational psy-chologist, she described Joe's behaviour as 'often unacceptable, he can be a real nuisance at times both to me and the other children. He is easily distracted and upsets the others, and on occasions his behaviour can be dangerous. Joe has almost no concentration and cannot stick at something for more than two minutes.'

What is interesting about the comments made by Joe's teacher is that they tell us little of any use about Joe. Instead, they are more a reflection of the teacher's emotional responses to Joe's behaviours. In this situation, the educational psychologist will be left with very little understanding of Joe's actual behaviours, what triggers them and how his behaviour patterns are reinforced. The educational psychologist will have to probe the teacher much further and take time to observe Joe in the classroom situation as well as outside of the classroom during unstructured time to gain objective information.

Drawing on theory to critically reflect upon one's own work with children is a vital element in ensuring best practice. It is theory and research that guides us with our understanding and knowledge and allows us to challenge not only our own ideas but those of others, in informed and meaningful ways. To illustrate this point, it will be useful to focus upon some specific aspects of one notable thinker who has influenced thinking and practice in the development of young learners. The work of Montessori lends itself to such a proposition. This is not to exclude others who have also exercised considerable influence, as in the case of Froebel who has been referred to, for example, by Miller and Pound as follows:

> Froebelians continue to influence official documents in a behind-the-scenes way … from the Hadow report (1933) onwards, through to Plowden (Central Advisory Council for Education, 1967); *Starting with Quality* (DES, 1990); *Curriculum Guidance for the Foundation Stage* (DfEE, 2000); *Birth to Three Matters* (DfES, 2002); *The Early Years Foundation Stage* (DCSF, 2008). (2011, p. 64)

Miller and Pound have drawn further attention to the more recent emergence of Froebelian training, which they contextualize as:

> Given the central control of teacher training, and the move towards this for other practitioners in the early childhood field, the Froebel Certificates have recently been re-established at Roehampton University and are developing in Edinburgh … the next generation of Froebelians is emerging, trained, in the practical apprenticeship way, in reflective practice through in-service training. (2011, p. 64)

Montessori put forward the notion of different 'Planes' or stages through which young children progress. It was during the first Plane (0–6 years) that Montessori saw children as developing their abilities in such important areas as short-term memory, spoken or expressive language, and receptive language or the ability to receive instructions, questions and directions, and respond to these with understanding. Montessori believed that it was during this first Plane that adults working with young children typically see the greatest steps in learning taking place. Here, we can take this notion of 'seeing' steps in learning and link it directly to the earlier definition provided by Daudelin (1996) at the beginning of this chapter. Let us now look more closely at this stage and link Montessori's theoretical view to the realities found in actual practice. By doing so, it is possible to explore our own thinking and practice in direct relation to one approach that is considered by many to be successful.

Within the first Plane, Montessori identified 11 'sensitive' periods during this stage, which practitioners can use as a framework for engaging in critical reflection of young children. Actively engaging with parents about their child's behaviours during this period can offer Early Years practitioners invaluable insights regarding early cognitive development, motor coordination and social skills as well as other important factors such as the quality of early attachment (Herbert, 2005; Pearce, 2009). During this period, from birth to around 12 months, children are developing their ability to crawl and walk. They are also exploring their environment through touching, grasping and holding objects, and moving. Others have recognized the importance of these physical and sensory activities for some time and have built these activities into their work with children. Goddard Blythe, cited in Miller and Pound (2011, p. 90), have, for example, commented that:

> [t]he Steiner Waldorf curriculum focuses on the ability of young children to learn through imitation and through activity. Movement facilitates integration of sensory experience ... Actions carried out in space help us literally to 'make sense' of what we see. Sight combined with balance, movement, hearing, touch and proprioception ... help to integrate sensory experience and can only take place as a result of action and practice. (2008, p. 140),

It is during this first stage or Plane that young children between the ages of 1 and 4 can also be observed to fixate upon particular objects and detail. This is an important element in their development because they are acquiring attention and concentration as well as developing their visual skills and internally representing visual features such as contours and shapes within the brain. In addition, and of equal importance, is the fact that by fixating on objects young children are also engaging in a process of verbal mediation whereby they attach verbal utterances and labels to these objects. The effective practitioner will observe young children fixating upon objects and will focus and reflect upon the language the child uses and such other factors as the child's determination and concentration and their growing familiarity with particular objects and how they act upon these. During this period, the young child also progresses from making random sounds to babble, then words and phrases, followed by sentences, indicating an understanding of their own thoughts and ideas, and those of others.

Montessori also believed that in young children between the ages of 2 and 4, there can be observed a need for consistency and a desire for sameness. The emphasis for professionals working with young children at this sensitive period would appear very obvious in that they would need to pay very careful attention to the environments they create during this period. Some children can become distressed when their environments are radically changed. During this period, young children appear to respond well to routines. Again, the professional practitioner might reflect upon the importance of regular and established routines both at home and in the classroom and how young children, particularly those from homes where there is much chaos and disorganization, must adapt.

Montessori thought that between the ages of 2 and 6 children appear to demonstrate a natural interest in elements of music, such as beat, rhythm and singing. 'Grace and courtesy' and 'refinement of the senses', which might appear to us to be outdated concepts, can also, Montessori suggested, be observed during this stage. Here, the young child aged between 2 and 6 imitates those positive and considered behaviour patterns of others, which facilitates the internalization of these behaviour types into their own schema, and at around 3 to 4 years of age become absorbed by sensory stimuli such as touch and taste. Other factors that Montessori identified during this stage were:

- an apparent fascination with writing where the young child at around 3 to 4 years of age can be observed trying to copy letters and words or numbers and symbols
- an interest in reading where the young child between 3 and 5 years of age can be observed to display interest in the sounds of letters and words
- an interest in spatial relationships between 4 and 6 years of age where the young child internally represents relationships between objects and their immediate environments.
- a development of basic concepts in mathematical thinking using concrete materials between 4 and 6 years of age.

It is then during the second Plane that the curriculum begins to reflect the type of curriculum more commonly found in the majority of state primary schools and it is during this stage that the child's learning and thinking become more abstract in nature. In a sense, therefore, the child is at a stage where they are going beyond simply reacting to sensory stimuli within their immediate environments. These ideas have close similarities to those of Bruner's symbolic mode referred to in Chapter 8. More formalized learning becomes apparent at this stage.

Independence, and the ability to look after oneself, are also key features of this philosophy. In Montessori nurseries, for example, children are encouraged to engage with such tasks as putting on their clothes and tidying up, which assist in their own development and contribute to their immediate communities. Montessori teachers also stress the importance of children developing at their own pace, and they encourage children to internalize at a very young age the notion that learning is something to be embraced and enjoyed. What then are the implications for young children who experience difficulties in these areas because of poor coordination or because they have never been taught by their parents or caregivers to engage in these activities at home?

Repetition of tasks is another important feature of the Montessori method as this works to underpin the foundations of future abstract reasoning. There is an important distinction to be made here, however, in that new skills are not taught through an uninteresting repetition of activities but through the creative over-learning of exercises that facilitate and prepare the child to internalize new concepts and new understanding. When new concepts are introduced to the child, a three-step process is used, namely introducing the new idea, comprehending it in concrete terms and finally comprehending it in abstract terms. Teaching and learning are very individualized for each child and the Montessori method places great emphasis upon observation skills that are developed through the five senses.

It is interesting at this point to reflect upon how Montessori's ideas 'fit' with the current requirements of the Early Years Foundation Stage (EYFS) and the educational philosophies supported and espoused by the current government in the UK. Though similar, there are significant differences, perhaps most notably, for example, in the way children's progress is assessed and recorded. In addressing this particular point, Miller and Pound have drawn attention to the fact that advocates of the Montessori principles have worked closely with the Office for Standards in Education (Ofsted) in the UK and with local authorities to encourage the use of approaches based upon these principles and, in turn, it has been recognized that these principles lead to sound and effective practice:

> In 2008, 88% of Montessori nurseries were considered by Ofsted to be 'outstanding' or 'good'. Concerns remain that local authorities have the power to oversee EYFS provision and to monitor its quality when assessing nurseries' eligibility for state funding for 3- and 4-year- olds' places. Interpretations of the EYFS can vary from one local authority to another and ... can easily ignore the particular nature of Montessori education. (2011, p. 31)

However, Miller and Pound have also called for caution:

> External pressures from government guidance or a management hierarchy can lead practitioners to focus on curriculum 'delivery' or 'coverage' as the main focus of their practice. Such a view would have been anathema to the foundational theorists ... but in England it has become a feature of the Early Years Foundation Stage (EYFS) (DfES, 2008) and the National Curriculum in primary schools, causing uncertainty for many practitioners. (2011, p. 165)

It is also worth noting that those who have trained to work as Montessori teachers are not eligible to work as teachers in state schools in the UK.

Since Miller and Pound wrote the above there have been monumental changes in the education system, most particularly England, brought about by the Coalition government. A cautionary, and perhaps rather worrying, note was sounded in the year following the election of the Coalition government by Cox, who commented in regard to how 'new initiatives' have come to impact upon teachers, and thereby, the learning of children:

> There is no shortage of initiatives in the world of education. These are often sold to teachers in the way that any other goods are marketed – through a catchphrase or acronym. Whether it is 'excellence and enjoyment' …'thinking skills' … AfL (Assessment for Learning) or APP (Assessing Pupil Performance) … these initiatives are being interpreted within a context that is largely dominated by performance. The practices and values of policy makers, who have embraced an intensely competitive market-driven system over the last 20 years, are shaping teachers' actions in the classroom. (2011, p. 184).

Since Cox wrote the above, much of teacher training has been moved out of Higher Education Institutions (HEIs) such as universities and into schools with the growth of the *School Direct* training programme where prospective teachers are taken on by schools and are now being trained largely within the school and with some input from higher education institutions. This has major implications for the manner in which teachers are now being trained and for how they will be trained in the future. In addition to the training of teachers being changed, the current government also introduced the concept of *Free Schools* and accelerated the growth in *Academies*, all of this at the cost to Local Authority control over education, which has been considerably reduced.

Exercise

How does a knowledge and understanding of different theoretical perspectives support practitioners in developing effective practice with young children?

Why might it be important for Early Years practitioners to adopt belief systems that emphasize potential as opposed to ability?

Why is it important for young children to learn how to learn, and what role can Early Years practitioners play in facilitating this?

 ## Summary

This chapter has brought together the concepts of learning and reflection that underpin good practice in Early Years and primary school settings and examined the nature of *emotional intelligence* and the importance of *sustained shared thinking* and its impact upon young children. Key factors in developing young learners and the importance of creating purposeful and meaningful environments were explored in relation to a number of theorists and key figures who have influenced our thinking and who have provided us with the necessary foundations and landscape to further explore our practice both now and in the future.

As we move into the second decade of the 21st century, it is worth considering how differing theoretical perspectives and our interpretation of these might influence professional practice in the future. To do so would be to engage at an even deeper level of critical reflection. Our societies and communities, and the way in which we choose to educate our children, will change dramatically over our own lifetimes as has been the case in recent generations. Changes in technology, political policy and, perhaps most importantly as Bruner might suggest, culture will have an enormous impact upon the learning and development of our children and young people in the forthcoming decades.

 ## RECOMMENDED READING

Alexander, R. (Ed.) (2010). *Children, their World, their Education: Final Report and Recommendations of the Cambridge Primary Review*. Abingdon: Routledge.

An up-to-date review of the current situation regarding primary education gained from extensive consultation.

EYFS Statutory framework for the early years foundation stage. (2014). Setting the standards for learning, development and care for children from birth to five Reference: DFE-00337-2014.

A necessary piece of reading for all practitioners working with children in the Early Years.

Montessori Schools Association/DCSF (2008). *Guide to the Early Years Foundation Stage in Montessori Settings*. London: Montessori St Nicholas/DCSF.

A very useful reference for practitioners wishing to gain a much greater understanding of the work undertaken by Montessori practitioners, and the principles that underpin such work.

REFERENCES

Association of Teachers and Lecturers (ATL) (2005). *An Intelligent Look at Emotional Intelligence*. London: Association of Teachers and Lecturers.

Bandura, A. (1977). *Self-efficacy: The Exercise of Control*. New York: Freeman.

Brouzos, A., Misailidi, P. and Hadjimattheou, A. (2014). Associations between emotional intelligence, socio-emotional adjustment, and academic achievement in childhood: the influence of age. *Canadian Journal of School Psychology, 29, 2,* 83–99.

Brown, E. (1999). *Loss, Change and Grief*. London: David Fulton.

Buckingham, D. (2000). *After the Death of Childhood: Growing up in the Age of Electronic Media*. Cambridge: Polity Press.

Burden, R.L. (1987). Feuerstein's instrumental enrichment programme: important issues in research and evaluation. *European Journal of Psychology of Education, 2, 1,* 3–16.

Central Advisory Council for Education (England) (1967). *Children and their Primary Schools (The Plowden Report).* London: HMSO.

Colverd, S. and Hodgkin, B. (2011). *Developing Emotional Intelligence in the Primary School.* London: Routledge.

Cowie, H. (2012). *From Birth to Sixteen: Children's Health, Social, Emotional and Linguistic Development.* London: Routledge.

Cox, S. (2011) *New Perspectives in Primary Education: Meaning and Purpose in Learning and Teaching.* Maidenhead: Open University Press.

Curran, A. (2012). Autism and the brain's working: how far have we got? *Debate, 144,* 5–6.

Daudelin, M. (1996). Learning from experience through reflection. *Dynamics, 24, 3,* 36–48.

Department for Children, Schools and Families (DCSF) (2008). *Special Educational Needs in England.* London: DCSF.

Department for Children, Schools and Families (DCSF) (2008). *The Early Years Foundation Stage.* London: DCSF.

Department for Education and Employment (DfEE) (2000). *Curriculum Guidance for the Foundation Stage.* London: DfEE.

Department for Education and Skills (DfES) (2002). *Birth to Three Matters: A Framework to Support Children in their Earliest Years.* London: DfES.

Department of Education and Science (DES) (1990). *Starting with Quality: The Report of the Committee of Inquiry into the Quality of the Educational Experience Offered to 3- and 4- year olds.* London: HMSO.

Dowling, M. (2005). *Young Children's Personal, Social and Emotional Development,* 2nd edn. London: Sage.

EYFS Statutory framework for the early years foundation stage. (2014). Setting the standards for learning, development and care for children from birth to five Reference: DFE-00337-2014.

Feez, S. (2010). *Montessori and Early Childhood.* London: Sage.

Fenton, B. (2006). Junk culture 'is poisoning our children'. *Daily Telegraph,* 12 September.

Feuerstein, R., Rand, Y. and Hoffman, M.B. (1979). *The Dynamic Assessment of Retarded Performers: The Learning Assessment Potential Device, Theory, Instruments and Techniques.* Baltimore, MD: University Park Press.

Feuerstein, R.R., Rand, Y., Hoffman, M. & Miller, R. (1980). *Instrumental Enrichment: Intervention Programme for Cognitive Modifiability.* Baltimore, MD: University Park Press.

Goddard Blythe, S. (2008). *What Babies and Children Really Need.* Stroud: Hawthorn Press.

Goleman, D. (1996). *Emotional Intelligence: Why It Can Matter More Than IQ.* London: Bloomsbury.

Hadow, W. (Chair) (1933). *The Report of the Consultative Committee: Infant and Nursery Schools.* London: HMSO.

Herbert, M. (2005). *Developmental Problems of Childhood and Adolescence.* London: BPS/Blackwell.

Holland, J. (2001). *Understanding Children's Experiences of Parental Bereavement.* London: Jessica Kingsley.

James, O. (2012). *Love Bombing.* London: Karnac.

Johnson, J. (2010). *Positive and Trusting Relationships with Children in Early Years Settings.* Exeter: Learning Matters.

Kellet, M. (2010). *Rethinking Children and Research: Attitudes in Contemporary Society.* London: Continuum.

Lancaster, Y.P. (2006). Listening to young children: respecting the voice of the child. In G. Pugh and B. Duffy (Eds) (2013) *Contemporary Issues in the Early Years: Working Collaboratively for Children*. London: Sage.

MacBlain, S.F. and MacBlain, M.S. (2004). Addressing the needs of lone-parent pupils, *Academic Exchange Quarterly, 8*, 2, 221–5.

MacBlain, S.F. and Purdy, N. (2011). Confidence or confusion: how prepared are today's NQTs to meet the additional needs of children in schools? *Journal of Teacher Development, 15, 3*.

MacBlain, S.F., Long, L. and Dunn, J. (2015). *Dyslexia, Literacy and Inclusion: Child-centred Perspectives*. London: Sage.

Mayall, B. (2002). *Towards a Sociology for Childhood: Thinking from Children's Lives*. Maidenhead: Open University Press.

Miller, L. and Pound, L. (2011). *Theories and Approaches to Learning in the Early Years*. London: Sage.

Morrissey, A. (2014). Scaffolding, analysis and materials: contributing factors in an unexpected finding of advanced infant/toddler pretend play? *Journal of Early Childhood Research, 12, 2,* 195–213.

National Statistics (2003). *Social Trends*. London: The Stationery Office.

Nutbrown, C. (2006). Watching and listening: the tools of assessment. In G. Pugh and B. Duffy (Eds) (2013) *Contemporary Issues in the Early Years: Working Collaboratively for Children*. London: Sage.

Palmer, S. (2006). *Toxic Childhood*. London: Orion.

Pearce, C. (2009). *A Short Introduction to Attachment and Attachment Disorder*. London: Jessica Kingsley.

QCA (2000). *Curriculum Guidance for the Foundation Stage*. London: QCA.

Rowntree, J. (1998). *Foundations – Divorce and Separation: The Outcomes for Children*. York: Joseph Rowntree Foundation.

Schön, D.A. (1987). *Educating the Reflective Practitioner*. San Francisco, CA: Jossey-Bass.

Siraj-Blatchford, I., Sylva, K., Muttock, S., Gilden, R. and Bell, D. (2002). *Researching Effective Pedagogy in the Early Years (REPEY) DfES Research Report 365*. London: HMSO.

Smidt, S. (2011). *Introducing Bruner: A Guide for Practitioners and Students in Early Years Education*. London: Routledge.

United Nations Children's Fund (UNICEF) (2007). *Child Poverty in Perspective: An Overview of Child Well-being in Rich Countries*. Florence: UNICEF Innocenti Research Centre.

United Nations Children's Fund (UNICEF) (2010). *The Children Left Behind: A League Table of Inequality in Child Well-being in the World's Richest Countries*. Innocenti Report Card 9. Florence: UNICEF Innocenti Research Centre.

Wells, R. (1988). *Helping Children Cope with Grief*. London: Sheldon.

Zwozdiak-Myers, P. (ed.) (2007). *Childhood and Youth Studies*. Exeter: Learning Matters.

Want to learn more about this Chapter?

Visit the companion website at **https://study.sagepub.com/grayandmacblain2e** to gain open access to selected SAGE journal articles, author podcasts and weblinks to help further your study.

11 THE CHANGING NATURE OF LEARNING

This chapter aims to:

- explore aspects of the changing nature of childhood in the 21st century
- examine the changing nature of the contexts within which learning in the Early Years and during the primary phase takes place
- examine how play and children's interests are evolving and impacting upon learning.

Children do things differently now. Indeed, many features of the learning one observes in young children today would be unrecognizable to those teachers and Early Years practitioners working with children even a decade ago and yet the key principles of learning remain much the same. This is why we look to theory, underpinned by philosophy to assist us in shaping our interpretations and understanding of learning and to offer us choice in the decisions we make, about how children are educated (Newby, 2010, p. 71). In seeking to understand the place of theory in education and its relevance for teachers wishing to gain a deeper understand of children's learning Jarvis offered the following only a decade ago:

> Education differs from comparable professions, such as medicine and psychology, in that although there is a thriving field of professional research, it takes place largely in isolation from professional practice. It is a rare doctor that does not peruse the medical research literature at least occasionally, and it would be unusual for a psychologist not to at least dip into current psychological literature – this is a requirement if they have chartered status … but teachers largely ignore education research. (2005, p. 204)

Since Jarvis offered the above comment there have, however, been significant strides in the field of educational research, which have resulted in a much more informed body of practitioners who actively pursue and benefit directly from such research-based initiatives as the *Early Years Foundation Stage* (EYFS) curriculum in England, *evidence-based* teaching, assessment and interventions for children with special educational needs evidenced by important and radical new legislation and the new *Special Educational Needs and Disability Code of Practice: 0 to 25* (DfE/DfH, 2014).

There can be few who would not argue that Western industrialized societies in which children's learning now takes place are vastly different from those of previous generations, and even decades. Perhaps the greatest changes in learning have been brought about by the monumental growth in digital technology, which has not only come to transform much teaching and learning but, arguably, has also come to define the way in which information is communicated. More specifically, the growth in digital technology has influenced our thinking in regard to what it means to be literate in the 21st century (Flewitt et al., 2014; MacBlain et al., 2015).

CHILDHOOD IN THE 21ST CENTURY

Children now have access to opportunities, experiences and information that previously would have been considered unimaginable. Indeed, the world has become a very small place and is shrinking by the day. Diversity is increasing and can be found almost everywhere. It is not unusual now for teachers and Early Years practitioners to find themselves working with children from a range of other countries who bring with them their own native language and customs, cultural differences and family traditions, and importantly, the expectations of their parents for how learning will benefit their children in the future. Alongside these expectations can be found, in most cases, high aspirations for their children. The experiences and early learning patterns of many children newly arrived in schools from other cultures can, therefore, be substantial. Equally, it is not unusual for teachers and Early Years practitioners to find themselves working with children who are widely travelled and who have experienced different cultures, foods and customs whilst holidaying abroad with their parents.

For many children living in the 21st century, however, the realities of modern living can at best be difficult and at worst deeply problematical. Reflecting wider modernized society, the nature of childhood for many children is becoming increasingly complex and with this complexity comes, for some, significant challenges. In making particular reference to the UK, Cowie commented:

> Today's young people seem to face severe stresses that were unknown a generation ago. Suicidal thoughts are common among young people, as are feelings of hopelessness and futility … There are disturbing statistics on the number of children and young people who run away from home or care … These amount to around 100,000 episodes each year in the UK, with around a quarter running away before the age of 13, and one in ten running away before the age of ten. (2012, p. 2)

Cowie goes on to report how, in 2012, the National Society for the Prevention of Cruelty to Children (NSPCC) was dealing with 30,000 cases, equalling some 0.25 per cent of the population. These statistics are worrying and represent a challenge for those who view childhood purely as a time of fun and joy characterized by security and stability and a lack of responsibility; they do, in fact, offer an emerging reality that for many young children remains very much outside of such popularized notions of childhood, all too often characterized by different elements of the media (MacBlain, 2014).

Reflection point

Examine the following paragraph taken from MacBlain (2014, p. 231) and then consider how practitioners in Early Years settings and primary schools can work in partnership with parents and external agencies such as social services and health professionals to ensure the safeguarding of all those children with whom they work.

A recent report, *What About the Children?*, produced by Ofsted and the Care Quality Commission (CQC) (Ofsted, 2013) took evidence from nine local authorities and partner agencies, as well as canvassing the views of parents, carers, children, and practitioners and managers. The report indicated that one in six of the adult population, some nine million individuals, experience mental health problems and that estimates suggest that 30 per cent of those adults have dependent children (between 0 and 18 years of age). The report also indicates that evidence drawn from a number of small studies of individuals with health difficulties suggests that a significant number, 'at least 25% and probably substantially more, especially among young women' of adults in acute psychiatric hospital settings might be parents (Ofsted, 2013, p. 9). The report makes reference to recent findings published by the National Society for the Prevention of Cruelty to Children (NSPCC) (Cuthbert et al., 2011) in which it was estimated that 144,000 babies under the age of one year live with a parent 'who has a common mental health problem'. The report went on to make reference to the National Treatment Agency for Substance Abuse (2011), which collects data on those individuals using drug and alcohol services. This report estimated that around 200,000 adults are currently in receipt of some form of treatment for substance misuse problems and that around 30 per cent of these are parents with children living with them. The recent review undertaken by the NSPCC (Cuthbert et al., 2011) estimated that during the previous year some 19,500 infants under the age of one year were living in a home with a parent who was a user of Class A drugs and that some 93,500 infants under the age of *one year lived in a home with a parent who was a problem drinker.*

A further and very noticeable change across most Western industrialized societies, and especially the UK, that has arguably affected the experience of childhood for many children has been the increase in hours worked by their parents. Less than a decade ago James, for example, commented that:

> [s]ince 1998 the number of people in Britain working more than sixty hours a week has more than doubled (from 10 to 26 percent), and full-time Brits work an average of forty-four hours, the most in the European Union. (2007, p. 273),

Such working patterns continue to define the lives of many families and may frequently be driven by a need to earn more money in order to meet the rising cost of living and in a significant number of cases the requirement to manage the very high cost of mortgages, which was less the case in previous decades. The cost of housing in parts of the UK, for example, for many young parents who are first-time buyers is at best highly expensive and at worst prohibitive, especially in London and the south of England. This often means that both parents have to work. More recently, the Office for National Statistics offered the following:

> Over the past 40 years there has been a rise in the percentage of women aged 16 to 64 in employment and a fall in the percentage of men. In April to June 2013 around 67% of women aged 16 to 64 were in work, an increase from 53% in 1971. For men the percentage fell to 76% in 2013 from 92% in 1971. In April to June 2013, looking at the not seasonally adjusted series, around 13.4 million women aged 16 to 64 were in work (42% part-time) and 15.3 million men (12% part-time). For those who worked full-time there were differences in the average hours worked per week. For example, full-time men worked on average 44 hours per week whilst full-time women worked 40 hours per week. While there have been increases in the number of women in work, the percentage of them doing a part-time role has fluctuated between 42–45% over the past 30 years. (2013, p.1)

CHANGING LANDSCAPES IN THE EARLY YEARS

The UK, and most particularly England, is not short on initiatives. Three major initiatives that have had a considerable impact upon the learning of young children, and continue to do so, are: *High Scope*, which originated in Michigan, USA in the 1960s; *Sure Start*, which originated in England in 1998; the *Statutory Framework for the Early Years Foundation Stage in England*, which became mandatory in September 2012 and more recently the EYFS Statutory framework for the early years foundation stage (2014).

Here, one is reminded of the ideas of the early philosophers, thinkers and theorists who saw learning and, most particularly, change in education as a means of improving society. At the heart of the philosophy underpinning *High Scope* has been the belief that learning should be an active process as opposed to a passive one, which is central to the ideas expressed by Vygotsky (see Chapter 5), and more recently by Bruner (see Chapter 7). Miller and Pound drew attention to the benefits gained by children within the High Scope approach and importantly the active involvement of those working with the children:

> HighScope practitioners are as active and involved as children in the Early Years setting … The HighScope approach promotes independence, curiosity, decision-making, co-operation, persistence, creativity and problem solving in young children. (2011, p. 103)

Exercise

Consider how the principles underpinning the High Scope approach could be compromised in Early Years settings through an increasing emphasis from government for more formal teaching in the area of literacy.

Weblink

An excellent resource for readers wishing to gain a much deeper understanding of the High Scope curriculum in Early Years settings can be accessed through this video link:

'Getting to Know High Scope's Preschool Curriculum', available at: www.youtube.com/watch?v=U7YaobYTPgk (accessed 11.4.15).

A further initiative introduced in the UK just over a decade ago in 1998 is *Sure Start*, with much of its origins in the *Head Start* programme in the USA of which Bronfenbrenner (see Chapter 6) was a key figure. Whilst originally aimed at children and families in England, other regions of the UK have embraced it and even adapted the approach to meet their own particular needs. Sure Start was originally developed with the purpose of giving those children who were in particular need of a better start in life, the best possible beginning they could have. Improvements in child care support for families including aspects relating to health and emotional well-being were seen as being central to the effectiveness of this approach. Considerable attention was also given to the development of communities. The funding originally provided for this initiative was significant, being around £540 million between the years 1999 and 2002. It was estimated at the time that around 150,000 young children who were living in significant deprivation could benefit. Whilst the government of the day initially agreed to provide funding for Sure Start over a 10-year period this did not happen, and the then Chancellor of the Exchequer reported in 2003 that the government would be relocating Sure Start to local government by 2005 with the intention of establishing Sure Start centres in all communities.

Weblinks

Two excellent resources for readers wishing to gain a much deeper understanding of the original principles behind setting up Sure Start centres and the hopes and aspirations behind these are:

'DfE Children's Plan Two Years On: Early Years – Sure Start Children's Centres', available at: www.youtube.com/watch?v=dzGEZ8D1HN0 (accessed 11.4.15).

'Sure Start Children's Centres', available at: www.youtube.com/watch?v=Zi_JHgZ8jQs (accessed 11.4.15).

In recent years a further major initiative was introduced in England, though not the rest of the UK: *The Statutory Framework for the Early Years Foundation Stage*. This became mandatory in September 2012 for all Early Years providers working in England in maintained and non-maintained schools, independent schools, and all providers on the Early Years Register, though it was recognized that there could be some exemptions to this last group. Though welcomed by many, this initiative divided practitioners, policy and decision-makers and academics, due mainly to the perceived over-emphasis upon more formalized and direct teaching/learning approaches. It has now been superseded by the EYFS Statutory framework for the early years foundation stage (2014) *Setting the standards for learning, development and care for children from birth to five Reference*: Department for Education (2014). (Statutory Framework for the Early Years Foundation Stage. London: DfE. Available at: www.gov.uk/government/uploads/system/uploads/attachment_data/file/335504/EYFS_framework_from_1_September_2014).

The introduction of the new Framework built upon previous good practice and had at the centre of its rationale the universal belief that every child deserves the best possible start in life as well as the necessary support to enable them to fulfil their potential. The Framework embraces the view that children today are not only developing more quickly than ever before but that life experiences following birth and during those years prior to beginning formal education at age 5 are crucial to their futures. Such a view is of course not new and can also be located within the works of the early thinkers (see Chapter 1). What appears to be new is the increased emphasis being placed by government on ensuring that all Early Years providers offer provision that is effective and purposeful and central to the social, emotional and educational development of children in their care. Positive and effective parenting is also viewed as being key to the development of children during the Early Years, as is the importance of children having access to learning that is of a high quality.

It is of particular note that Ofsted will have regard to the EYFS in that they will inspect the implementation, and application, of the new Framework and then report on the quality and standards of provision being offered. Following their inspections Ofsted will then publish their findings and may in some instances issue a 'notice to improve' or a 'welfare requirements notice'. Any provider then found not complying to a 'welfare requirements notice' will be committing an offence. The Framework proposes four over-arching principles, which are considered to be central to practice in Early Years settings:

- every child is a unique child, who is constantly learning and can be resilient, capable, confident and self-assured
- children learn to be strong and independent through positive relationships
- children learn and develop well in enabling environments, in which their experiences respond to their individual needs and there is a strong partnership between practitioners and parents and/or carers
- children develop and learn in different ways and at different rates. (DfE, 2011, p. 3).

Exercise

Identify some of the practical considerations that face Early Years practitioners working with children from severely disadvantaged or dysfunctional homes. What steps might practitioners take to develop closer partnerships with the parents of these children?

The *Statutory Framework for the Early Years Foundation Stage* also proposed seven areas central to the learning and development of young children and how these should inform and shape best practice in Early Years settings. They are: communication and language; physical development; personal, social and emotional development; literacy; mathematics; understanding the world; and expressive arts and design.

The first three of these are considered as 'Prime' areas, which are particularly crucial, with the next four considered as 'Specific' areas, which providers should use in supporting children with developing the first three. The Framework stresses the need for providers to pay particular attention to the individual needs of children in addition to their actual stage of development. This is important and readers may wish to consider the range of needs experienced by those children who, for example, grow up in homes where their parents may be abusive and neglectful or those children who from their early stages of development take on the role of 'carer'. Information gained from consideration of these areas should, the Framework proposes, inform practitioners, in regard to how they plan for the experiences of children in their care.

Under the Framework particular attention needs to be given to the Prime areas when working with very young children, which the Framework indicates will 'reflect the key skills and capacities all children need to develop and learn effectively, and become ready for school' (DfE, 2011, p. 6). The Framework also pays special attention to whether or not children have special educational needs or disabilities, which may call for specialist intervention. In this way links with families are made to assist them in accessing appropriate support from external agencies, where appropriate. In addition, the Framework gives special emphasis to the importance of assessment:

> Ongoing assessment (also known as formative assessment) is an integral part of the learning and development process. It involves practitioners observing children to understand their level of achievement, interests and learning styles, and to then shape learning experiences for each child reflecting those observations. (p. 10)

Included within the Framework is a clear emphasis upon the reduction of paperwork:

> Assessment should not entail prolonged breaks from interaction with children, nor require excessive paperwork. Paperwork should be limited to that which is absolutely necessary to promote children's successful learning and development. (p. 10)

The Framework also places significant emphasis upon the importance of child protection indicating, for example, that 'Providers must have and implement a policy, and procedures, to safeguard children' (p. 13). Similarly, the Framework also places significant emphasis upon the qualifications and training and skills level of providers as well as their need to engage effectively with the induction of new staff and offer suitable continuing professional development. The British Association for Early Childhood Education (2012) produced a very helpful publication, *Development Matters in the Early Years Foundation Stage (EYFS)*, which has provided clear guidance for providers and practitioners in an accessible format. It offers information regarding the learning of children in all of the Prime and 'Specific areas from birth to 11 months through to 40 to 60 months, offering providers as well as parents and other relevant professionals an indication of what they should expect from children at different ages and stages of development.

CHANGING LANDSCAPES IN THE PRIMARY YEARS

The extent to which schools in the UK and especially England have changed over the past decade is nothing short of extraordinary (MacBlain, 2014). Following the election of the current Coalition government in 2010 there has been a dramatic increase in the number of Academies and Free Schools with a growing emphasis being given to more formal learning in the primary school and pre-school settings. Alongside this has come a controversial decision by the Coalition government to move much of the training of teachers out of Higher Education Institutions such as universities and into schools (DfE, 2012).

Readers might wish to reflect upon the ideas and theoretical stances put forward by the enlightened thinkers of earlier generations and, more recently, earlier decades and consider the importance (and in some instances the lack of importance) given to learning, and more directly children's formal education by successive governments. Readers may, for example, wish to review the ideas put forward by Bronfenbrenner in Chapter 7 whose theoretical stance emphasized the constantly changing and dynamic cultures that shape education and schooling (Bronfenbrenner, 1979; Bronfenbrenner and Ceci, 1994). Readers might also reconsider the statement offered earlier in Chapter 8 by Smidt regarding Bruner's view of education: 'Bruner said that we should treat education for what it is, and for him what it was was political' (2011, p. 85).

It is also worth reflecting, at this point, upon the ideas expressed by the influential and controversial thinker Ivan Illich (1926–2002) cited in MacBlain only a few decades ago and how his ideas might offer a reference point for many of the changes that are currently taking place and that are influenced by social, economic and political interests:

> Illich ... expressed particular concern with regard to how large corporations might come to exercise considerable influence over what type of learning should take place in schools ... He argued, for example, that substantial parts of our lives are driven by institutions which lower individuals' self-confidence and self-esteem and adversely affect their abilities and their potential to take initiative and engage in solution-focused thinking and problem solving ... Illich also felt that in modern societies individuals are increasingly drawn into living their lives in institutionalized ways, a process that starts early when children begin their learning in large educational institutions. (2014, p. 27)

Shortly after the election of the Coalition government in 2010, Cox drew attention to the changing nature of teaching and learning in primary schools in the UK and the growing emphasis upon *assessment* and *outcomes*, often at the expense of other areas of learning such as creativity and social and emotional development:

> One point to be made, in any discussion of the curriculum and how it is to be taught, is that there is a difference between thinking about the material that is to be covered – the content – and thinking about what the children are intended to learn: between what the teacher is teaching and what the 'learning objectives' are … But to begin with, it is helpful to point out that the shift in focus from what is taught to what is to be learned clearly gives greater emphasis to assessment – it draws attention to what comes about as a result of the teaching – the outcomes. (2011, p. 163)

Cox further suggests that:

> when the emphasis is on covering content the material that is taught is arguably most readily conceived as 'information' – rather than, for example, skills or attitudes. This perhaps explains why the default approach to teaching can so readily become 'transmission' and why the simple recall of factual knowledge might seem to be the implicit approach to classroom assessment. (p. 163)

EMERGING LITERACIES

> **Example**
>
> Benjamin is 6 years of age and enjoys spending time on his digital tablet device, especially since his older brother has downloaded some new apps (computer applications) for him. He also enjoys spending time with his grandfather and takes great pride from the fact that he has been teaching his grandfather how to use his tablet and how to play with the new apps. Benjamin's mother is becoming increasingly concerned about the amount of time that he spends on his tablet. She scolds him from time to time about this but his grandfather tells her that Benjamin is, in fact, learning when he is using his tablet as some of the apps are very educational. Benjamin's mother is not convinced.

Benjamin is typical of many young children today not just in the UK but across the globe. Dunn (2015), cited in MacBlain et al. drew attention to the growing use of tablet technology across Europe:

> Recent data gathered in Europe suggests that 50% of Swedish children aged between 3 and 4 use tablet computers; 23% of children in Norway from 0 to 6 years old have access to touchscreens at home and 17% of families in Germany with children aged 3 to 7 have touchscreen tablets. In the UK the use of tablet computers by children has increased from 2% to 11% between 2011 and 2012 and the current rate of uptake is likely to be considerably higher than this (Holloway et al., 2013). (2015, p. 217)

Benjamin's experience of using his tablet is reflected in the many terms that have come to describe the increasing range of new literacies that rely on technology, for example, the term 'edutainment'. One commonly hears, for example, other such terms as 'technoliteracy', 'digital literacy' (Merchant, 2006, 2009, 2015) and 'multiliteracies' (MacBlain et al., 2015) and so on; new terms are emerging almost daily as digital technology becomes increasingly sophisticated and accessible to almost everyone. The recent rise in computer applications, or 'apps', for use by children has been quite astonishing, with whole companies being set up to provide educational applications for use even by pre-school children. Here, one is drawn to the work of more contemporary thinkers and philosophers such as Jean-Francois Lyotard (1924–98), Jürgen Habermas (b. 1929), Theodor Adorno (1903–69), Pierre Bordieu (1930–2002) and Hans-Georg Gadamer (1900–2002) who have offered differing explanations and insights into how western industrialized societies influence the learning of their children. Lyotard, for example, drew particular attention to how knowledge is understood and used and how this has evolved over time:

> [B]efore World War II, the pursuit of knowledge was seen as central to the pursuit of truth. However, since then it has been increasingly argued that knowledge is something that can be financially acquired and then sold within a widening and diverse range of markets, what Lyotard refers to as the 'mercantilization' of knowledge. (MacBlain, 2014, pp. 5–6)

One can, of course, relate this to the views expressed by Bronfenbrenner, in particular his ideas referring to the macrosystem in his ecological systems model, which reflects the child's cultural and societal values, legal structures and social institutions and so on. As young children grow from infanthood they are highly influenced by the behaviours of those around them (Cowie, 2012; MacBlain, 2014; Tizard and Hughes, 1984).

There are now levels of criticism being levelled in some quarters about the restricted nature of the way in which literacy is being taught and the continuing emphasis that is placed upon the use of books as opposed to wider literacy practices that are so common outside of schools such as Facebook, mobile phone texting, television and gaming technologies (Flewitt et al., 2014; Lankshear and Knobel, 2003; MacBlain et al., 2015; Merchant, 2006, 2009). There are, for example, a growing number of apps which are designed to support children with writing stories. Many of these apps permit children to use different fonts, add pictures and symbols and design their finished work. It is also possible, of course, for the children to start their stories in school and complete these later at home and to even email the finished product to their teachers or relatives and friends. Many of the devices children can use such as tablets also have built-in cameras that allow them to take photographs of people and items that are very important to them (MacBlain et al, 2015). In this way they can create more meaningful stories and texts now referred to as the 'pictorial superiority effect' (Stenberg, 2006). Indeed, there is now emerging evidence that written text ought to be paired alongside visual representations to assist in developing learning in young children (Frey and Fisher, 2010).

Reflection point

Readers may wish to access and then consider the following excellent article by Chaudron (2015), *Young Children (0–8) and Digital Technology: A Qualitative Exploratory Study Across Seven Countries,* which has as its abstract the following:

> Despite the growing number of very young children who go online and who are using a wide range of technologies, little is known about children's interactions with those technologies. This report presents a pilot qualitative study designed and implemented in collaboration with a selected group of academic partners in different European countries that aims at pioneering in Europe the exploration of young children and their families' experiences with new technologies. It presents its results and discusses the findings at cross-national level on how children between zero and eight engage with digital technologies such as smartphones, tablets, computers and games; how far parents mediate this engagement and their awareness on the risks-opportunities balance. The report concludes on recommendations to parents, industries and policymakers.

HOW PLAY AND CHILDREN'S INTERESTS ARE CHANGING AND IMPACTING UPON LEARNING

Through play young children learn to cooperate with others, to form and maintain relationships and understand the world in which they live. It is also through play that they develop their language skills and in doing so, their capacity to think (see Chapter 6 on the work of Vygotsky and Chapter 8 on Bruner). Play lies at the very core of children's development. Smith et al. have, however, drawn an important distinction between play and exploration in very young children, which can be located, they suggest, within the ideas of the behaviourists and the Piagetians:

> These were often subsumed together in earlier writings, perhaps because of the influence of behaviourism and learning theory. Both exploration and play were awkward for traditional learning theorists, as neither was obviously goal-seeking or under the control of reinforcers. It is also true that with very young children, during sensori-motor development ..., the distinction between exploration and play is difficult to make, as for young infants, all objects are novel. By the preschool years, however, the distinction is clearer. (2003, p. 218)

In emphasizing this distinction, Smith et al. have offered us not only a useful starting point but a very helpful conceptual framework through which we can go further in developing our understanding of this complex and appealing behaviour in young children. They suggest three kinds of play, namely: *locomotor* play, *sociodramatic* play and *language* play. The first of these, locomotor or physical activity play, includes exercise play and what is frequently described by parents as 'rough-and-tumble' play. The second type refers to play with objects including fantasy play and that type of play that is of a sociodramatic nature. The final type has language at its core.

With the first of these types of play, young children can be observed engaging in physical activities such as running and jumping. Here, readers might wish to consider how a lack of physical play might impact upon coordination, sensory integration and thinking. Readers might also consider the growth of Forest Schools over the last few decades and why Early Years practitioners consider these to be of value. One of the authors of this text (MacBlain) was fortunate enough to have worked at Bridgwater College in Somerset some decades ago when staff at the college were implementing their vision of Forest Schools. As a practising psychologist at the time, MacBlain was able to see at first hand the benefits of this new and visionary initiative and to observe not only the children's progress in many areas of development, but also the extent to which those experienced and highly expert practitioners at the college felt its benefits for the children with whom they worked.

Pellegrini and Smith (1998), cited in Smith et al. (2003, pp. 220–21) have suggested that in physical activity play three developmental stages can be identified: 'rhythmical stereotypes' such as the kicking of legs and waving of arms as found with infants; 'exercise play' such as running and jumping, involving the child's whole body, typically observed in preschool settings, which overlaps with the type of 'rough-and-tumble' play so commonly observed by teachers in the primary school playgrounds and by parents in their homes. It is worth considering how limited physical activity is for many young children today as they spend significant amounts of time prior to attending pre-school and primary school watching television for lengthy periods of time and later, sitting in front of screens whilst playing games on digital devices.

Smith et al. (2003) further propose that the second type of play, sociodramatic play, can be observed in children as young as 12 months, with the earliest type of pretend play involving such behaviours as directing actions towards themselves and largely dependent upon the use of objects such as those found in the children's homes. Again, it is worth considering the impact upon some children of not having 'play' objects in their homes where most emphasis is placed upon children being quiet and watching television. Here, one is reminded of the considerable emphasis that was placed upon 'play objects' by such key thinkers as Froebel who developed his educational 'materials' or 'gifts' and Montessori's notion of the *Casa dei Bambini* or *Children's House* (see Chapter 2). It is also worth considering how television and digital games have influenced the play of young children where, for example, they sometimes model the behaviours of those characters they see on television. The ultimate in imaginary play they propose is when young children have an 'imaginary companion'. Smith et al. have suggested that between a quarter and a half of young children between 3 and 8 years of age (with most giving up this behaviour by around 10) have some kind of 'imaginary companion'. Children with 'imaginary companions', they suggest, can frequently be observed to engage in very sophisticated pretend play with their 'imaginary companions'.

The final type of play suggested by Smith et al. is that of *language* play. At this point it is worth considering how visual play is for many children, and how few opportunities many children have to engage in verbal communication with other children. Drawing directly upon the work of Bruner, Brown suggests:

> Before the child can write or read he must be able to identify the symbols and the sounds they represent ... For written language the child must also have a high degree of motor coordination ... He [Bruner] suggested that the mind of a person who spent much of his time in these activities [reading and writing] might be 'profoundly different' from that of one who was involved in non-linguistic activities such as drawing or building, and perhaps even different from that of one who mostly talked and listened. (Brown, 1977, p. 119)

This is a hugely important point in regard to the nature of social activities of children such as Albert who spend little time reading and writing or communicating verbally with other members of their family. The implications would appear obvious. Brown goes further in drawing upon the work of Bruner:

> He [Bruner] suggested that there may be a minimal use of language in ordinary discourse which has little effect upon an individual's thought patterns, but beyond that level it may transform them. The most important step in this transformation he saw as instigated by the transference from speech into some form of notation such as writing or mathematical symbols. In this form it becomes more powerful. The rules which must be obeyed to construct written sentences may allow some people to analyse the products of their thoughts and to operate with formal operations (Piaget's term) in ways which would not otherwise be possible. (Brown, 1977, p. 119)

Children can be observed to gain much from listening to rhyming poems, riddles, nursery rhymes and so on. As children grow they move towards playing games that have rules as well as clearly defined structures. It is through this type of play that they learn to cooperate with others, the importance of boundaries, how to develop and manage relationships and so on. This type of play also provides children with opportunities to be active outside of the family home and to join local clubs such as cricket, football and tennis clubs. Again, it is worth reflecting upon the limited opportunities that some children now have as they spend more time in their homes watching television or playing with digital technologies.

Example

Albert is 4 years of age and has already been causing concern amongst staff at his playgroup. Unlike many of the other children, he prefers to play by himself and rarely involves himself in activities with the other children. Staff have observed Albert to have poor coordination, weak muscle tone and very limited vocabulary. They recognize that at home he spends most of his time watching television, and most nights stays up watching television until well after nine o'clock. His home life is dysfunctional; his mother suffers from depression and is now living with a third partner, having separated from Albert's father six months after he was born. Albert presents as being very immature, quick to get upset and to throw a tantrum. He becomes very upset each day when his mother leaves the playgroup and he appears inconsolable for some time even if she returns and lifts him up. Albert has an older sister who is 12 years of age and an older brother who is 14 years of age. Both of his siblings are known to Social Services and to the Educational psychology service in their area. Albert was recently given a mobile telephone for his birthday and at Christmas his mother arranged for him to have his own portable television in his bedroom, which he is allowed to watch after going to bed until he falls asleep.

Albert is typical of so many children nowadays who spend significant amounts of time engaged in passively watching television or computer screens at the expense of engaging in physical activity. On his current trajectory, as he grows it is likely that he will spend increasing amounts of time watching television and interacting with a computer screen. Back in 2006, the UK newspaper the *Daily Telegraph* published a letter signed by over a hundred teachers, psychologists and 'other experts' who were beseeching the government to 'prevent the death of childhood'. They wrote:

> Since children's brains are still developing, they cannot adjust – as full-grown adults can – to the effects of ever more rapid technological and cultural change. They still need what developing human beings have always needed, including real food (as opposed to processed 'junk'), real play (as opposed to sedentary, screen-based entertainment), first-hand experience of the world they live in and regular interaction with the real-life significant adults in their lives. (Fenton, 2006, p. 1)

Exercise

Identify what might be some of the key challenges facing Albert in terms of his language development. What steps could the practitioners working with Albert take to improve his language skills and develop his coordination? How might the behaviourist approach to learning (Chapter 3) help us understand the way in which Albert's learning and development is being shaped?

Summary

This chapter explored the developing nature of childhood in the 21st century, and the changing nature of the contexts within which learning in the Early Years and during the primary phase takes place, with particular attention being given to the growth of emerging digital literacies. The importance of play in children's lives was examined with particular reference being made to how children's interests are evolving and impacting upon their learning.

 # RECOMMENDED READING

Cowie, H. (2012) *From Birth to Sixteen: Children's Health, Social, Emotional and Linguistic Development.* London: Routledge.

An excellent and very insightful text on the significant challenges facing young people today through early childhood and the primary and post-primary stages.

James, O. (2007) *Affluenza.* London: Vermillion.

An excellent insight into the major challenges facing individuals in the 21st Century including children and their families.

Formby, S. (2014) *Practitioner Perspectives: Children's use of Technology in the Early Years.* London: National Literacy Trust.

A very interesting and informative text, which examines many of the implications of technology and its impact upon young children.

Department for Education (2014). Statutory Framework for the Early Years Foundation Stage. London: DfE. Available at: www.gov.uk/government/uploads/system/uploads/attachment_data/file/335504/EYFS_framework.

Eisenstadt, N. (2011) Sure Start: how government discovered early childhood. *RSA*, 26 October. Available at: http://comment.rsablogs.org.uk/2011/10/26/start-government-discovered-early-childhood/?_ga=1.45983012.168094431.1416479834 (accessed 11.12.14).

A very useful description and narrative of Sure Start, its philosophical underpinnings and its impact upon children.

REFERENCES

British Association for Early Childhood Education (2012). *Development Matters in the Early Years Foundation Stage (EYFS)*. London: Department for Education. Available at: www.foundationyears. org.uk/files/2012/03/Development-Matters-FINAL-PRINT-AMENDED.pdf (accessed 14.4.15).

Bronfenbrenner, U. (1979). *The Ecology of Human Development*. Cambridge, MA: Harvard University Press.

Bronfenbrenner, U. and Ceci, S.J. (1994). Nature-nurture reconceptualized in the developmental perspective: a bioecological model. *Psychological Review, 101,* 568–86.

Brown, G. (1977). *Child Development*. Shepton Mallet: Open Books.

Chaudron, S. (2015). *Young Children (0–8) and Digital Technology: A Qualitative Exploratory Study Across Seven Countries*. Brussels: Publications Office of the European Union. Available at: http://publications.jrc.ec.europa.eu/repository/handle/JRC93239 (accessed 27.1.15).

Cowie, H. (2012). *From Birth to Sixteen: Children's Health, Social, Emotional and Linguistic Development*. London: Routledge.

Cox, S. (2011). *New Perspectives in Primary Education: Meaning and Purpose in Learning and Teaching*. Maidenhead: Open University Press.

Cuthbert, C., Rayns, G. and Stanley, K. (2011). *All Babies Count, Prevention and Protection for Vulnerable Babies: A Review of the Evidence*. London: NSPCC.

Department for Education (2011). *Training Our Next Generation of Outstanding Teachers: Implementation Plan*. London: DfE. Available at: www.gov.uk/government/uploads/system/uploads/attachment_data/file/181154/DFE-00083–2011.pdf (accessed 20.1.15).

Department for Education (DfE) (2012). *Statutory Framework for the Early Years Foundation Stage: Setting the Standards for Learning, Development and Care for Children from Birth to Five*. Runcorn: DfE.

Department for Education and Department for Health (2014). Special educational needs and disability code of practice: 0 to 25 years: Statutory guidance for organisations who work with and support children and young people with special educational needs and disabilities, July, 2014. London: DfE. Available at: www.gov.uk/government/publications/send-code-of-practice-0-to-25 (accessed 20.1.15).

Dunn, J. (2015). New literacies in the classroom: forging culturally responsive curricula, in MacBlain, S.F., Long, L. and Dunn, J. (2015) *Dyslexia, Literacy and Inclusion: Child-Centred Perspectives*. London: Sage.

EYFS Statutory framework for the early years foundation stage. (2014). Setting the standards for learning, development and care for children from birth to five Reference: DFE-00337-2014.

Fenton, B. (2006). Junk culture 'is poisoning our children'. *Daily Telegraph*, 12 September.

Flewitt, R., Messser, D. and Kucirkova, N. (2014). New directions for early literacy in a digital age: the iPad. *Journal of Early Childhood Literacy*, 20 May.

Frey, N. and Fisher, D. (2010). Reading and the brain: what early childhood educators need to know. *Early Childhood Educational Journal, 38*, 103–110.

Holloway, D., Green, L. and Livingstone, S. (2013). *Zero to Eight: Young Children and their Internet Use*. LSE London: EU Kids Online Network.

James, O. (2007). *Affluenza*. London: Vermillion.

Jarvis, M. (2005). *The Psychology of Effective Learning and Teaching*. Cheltenham: Nelson Thornes.

Lankshear, C. and Knobel, M. (2003). *New Literacies: Changing Knowledge and Classroom Learning*. Buckingham: Open University Press.

MacBlain, S.F. (2014). *How Children Learn*. London: Sage.

MacBlain, S.F., Long, L. and Dunn, J. (2015). *Dyslexia, Literacy and Inclusion: Child-centred Perspectives*. London: Sage.

Merchant, G. (2006). A sign of the times: looking critically at popular digital writing. In J. Marsh and E. Millard (Eds) *Popular Literacies, Childhood and Schooling*. London: Routledge. pp. 93–108.

Merchant, G. (2009). Literacy in virtual worlds, *Journal of Research in Reading, 32*, 1, 38–56.

Merchant, G. (2015). Keep taking the tablets: iPads, story apps and early literacy. *Australian Journal of Language and Literacy, 38*, 1, 3–11.

Miller, L. and Pound, L. (2011). *Theories and Approaches to Learning in the Early Years*. London: Sage.

Newby, P. (2010). *Research Methods for Education*. Harlow: Pearson Education.

Office for National Statistics (2013). *Full report – Women in the Labour Market*. London: ONS. Available at: www.ons.gov.uk/ons/dcp171776_328352.pdf (accessed 20.1.15).

Office for Standards in Education (Ofsted) (2013). *What About the Children? Joint working between adult and children's services when parents or carers have mental ill health and/or drug and alcohol problems*. Manchester: Ofsted.

Pellegrini, A., and Smith, Peter K. (1998). Physical activity play: The nature and function of a neglected aspect of play. *Child Development*, 69, 557–598.

Smidt, S. (2011). *Introducing Bruner: A Guide for Practitioners and Students in Early Years Education*. London: Routledge.

Smith, K.S., Cowie, H. and Blades, M. (2003). *Understanding Children's Development*, 4th edn. Oxford: Blackwell.

Stenberg, G. (2006). Conceptual and perceptual factors in the picture superiority effect. *European Journal of Cognitive Psychology, 18*, 813–47.

Tizard, B. and Hughes, M. (1984). *Young Children Learning: Learning and Thinking at Home and at School*. London: Fontana.

Want to learn more about this Chapter?
Visit the companion website at **https://study.sagepub.com/grayandmacblain2e** to gain open access to selected SAGE journal articles, author podcasts and weblinks to help further your study.

GLOSSARY

Accommodation: This involves changing or adapting an existing schema, concept or idea to embrace new knowledge. Piaget believed that children learn by adaptation, which includes assimilation and accommodation.

Active learning: A theory proposing that children should be encouraged to learn by themselves rather rely on teachers for instruction.

Animistic thinking: The pre-operational child ascribes feelings to objects.

Assimilation: According to Piaget, 'assimilation is the integration of external elements into evolving or completed structures'. By this he means that new information is added into existing schemas or categories. Assimilation is an active and selective process.

Association: A relationship between two or more events.

Asymmetric relationship: A relationship which fosters the transfer of knowledge from a more knowledgeable peer to a less experienced learner.

Autism: A complex developmental disability that typically appears during the first three years of life and is the result of a neurological disorder that affects the normal functioning of the brain, impacting development in the areas of social interaction and communication skills. Both children and adults with autism typically show difficulties in verbal and non-verbal communication, social interaction and leisure or play activities.

Behavourism: A learning theory that focuses on objectively observable behaviours and discounts activities of the mind – how a child thinks, feels or interprets an event.

Behaviour theorists: These include Watson, Skinner and Thorndike, amongst others. Although Pavlov is often included as a behaviourist, he was a physiologist who described one aspect of learning.

Classical or Pavlovian conditioning: A learning process that occurs when an association develops between two events, sometimes after one or multiple pairings, and becomes fixed in a person's mind. For example, a child is sick on a long car journey. In future, the same child may become distressed at the thought of a car journey for fear of being sick. Mum gets a toddler's wellies ready to take to the park. She may have to repeat this a number of times before her toddler, on seeing the boots, makes an association between the wellies and the park.

Cognition: A broad term which includes, among other things, mental processes such as attention, perception, language, thinking and problem solving.

Cognitive development: The development of internal mental processes.

Computer assisted learning: Skinner developed computer programmes to teach skills such as arithmetic and spelling, based on operant conditioning.

Conditioned stimulus (CS): Previously neutral, a stimulus which now elicits a response. For example, you see the McDonalds's sign and then catch a whiff which reminds you that you are hungry. When you next see the McDonalds's sign, your mouth might start to water or your tummy rumble.

Conservation: The principle that quantities remain constant regardless of changes to their appearance.

Constructivism: A theory of knowledge (epistemology) that argues that humans generate knowledge and meaning from an interaction between their experiences and their ideas.

Cultural tools: The products of human, cultural and historical activity.

Culture: This is a complex concept. Put simply, it involves the socially transmitted behaviour patterns, arts and beliefs passed from one generation to another.

Egocentrism: An inability on the part of a child in the pre-operational stage of development to see any point of view other than their own. For example, Jamie is playing hide and seek with his granny. To hide, he covers his eyes assuming that if he can't see then he can't be seen.

Equilibration: This involves the child finding a balance between external (environmental) and internal thinking processes. Disequilibration is the result of a mismatch between the two.

Extinction: A reduction and eventual cessation of a behaviour in the absence of a reinforcer.

Generalization: Where a response generalizes to similar stimuli. For example, Little Albert generalized his fear of a white rabbit to cotton wool and white beards.

Halo effect: according to this theory, an attractive child or adult will be viewed as more intelligent, pleasant and kind than a less attractive child.

Higher order thinking: This includes logical and abstract thinking, ordering, classifying and so on.

Horizontal décalage: The term used by Piaget to describe inconsistent performance on tasks involving similar mental operations.

Instrumental conditioning: see **Operant conditioning**

Interpsychological: When information is transmitted between the child and others, including their parents, family, peers and Early Years professionals.

Intrapsychological: When the child internalizes knowledge gained from their experience with others.

Law of effect: Thorndike believed that actions are repeated for positive rewards and disappear when rewards are not repeated.

Learning: This is the permanent acquisition of knowledge or a skill.

Lower-order thinking: This involves innate factors including perception, attention and memory.

Meaningful event or happening: Lessons are centred on events which are highly meaningful to the child and touch their emotions. Subsequently, each lesson follows a plot relating directly to an event.

Mediated learning: According to Vygotsky, the interaction between the child and their environment is not immediate. Instead it is mediated through cultural tools (language, art, music etc.), psychological tools (mental processes) and social tools (social interaction).

Microgenetic approach: Examines change as it occurs, thus attempting to identify and explain its underlying mechanisms. For example, observing a child solve similar problems over a period of time will enable a professional to identify the child's progress or repeated mistakes.

Mores: Social, cultural and traditional influences that come to shape understanding, interpretation, attitudes and actions.

Negative reinforcer: Use of time out or the naughty step, loss of privileges such as sweets/television and so on.

Neo-Piagetians: A group of researchers who sought to develop and refine Piaget's theory.

Operant conditioning or instrumental conditioning: Learning which occurs when a behaviour is either rewarded or punished. Through operant/instrumental conditioning an association is made between a behaviour and a consequence of that behaviour.

Peers: For example, a child/ person who is equal to another in terms of age, ability, social status, qualifications and other factors that might determine a part of a similar grouping.

Perestroika: The policy of reconstructing a series of political and economic reforms in the former Soviet Union under the leadership of Mikhail Gorbachev which encouraged trade between Russia and non-Marxist countries.

Phobia: According to the American Psychiatric Association, a phobia is an irrational and excessive fear of an object or situation. In most cases, the phobia involves a sense of endangerment or a fear of harm.

Positive reinforcer: Use of praise, rewards, attention, money, star charts and so on.

Punishment: This varies in severity and length and may include the use of time out or the naughty step, the withdrawal of privileges, a ticking off, a severe scolding, a smack and so on.

Reinforcement schedule: The probability that behaviour will receive a reinforcer. Skinner identified four reinforcement schedules: a continuous reward is given every time the behaviour is displayed; with a fixed ratio, a reinforcer is given at set intervals, for example every third or fourth time; a fixed interval occurs at a specific time, for example every 5 minutes; with an intermittent or variable schedule, rewards/reinforcers are offered at differing times. The latter offers the most effective type of reinforcement.

Rigidity of thought: The child's inability to reverse sequences and their inability to adjust to changes in appearance.

Rote learning: The focus here is on committing facts to memory rather than on understanding.

Scaffolding: A metaphor coined by Wood, Bruner and Ross (1976) to describe the support that people need in learning new skills.

Scheme/schema: Piaget used the term 'scheme', most often referred to as a 'schema', to describe the basic unit of intelligent behaviour. It is an active process. Schemas are not fixed but evolve and develop with experience.

Social constructivism: Social constructivism emphasizes the importance of culture and context in understanding what occurs in society and constructing knowledge based on this understanding (Pagram and McMahon, 1997).

Socratic dialogue: a process of questioning and inquiry, termed, the soul recovers some aspects of knowledge.

Spontaneous recovery: This is the re-occurrence of a classically conditioned response after extinction has occurred.

Stimulus: An action or event that triggers a reaction. For example, if a teat is placed at the side of a baby's mouth, the baby will instinctively suck; the smell of food may cause your mouth to water; or you may find yourself humming along to a favourite tune.

Stimulus–response association: an association develops between a stimulus (passing McDonald's wafting smells at 7.00pm when you missed dinner) and response (mouth waters and stomach rumbles).

Symbolic: One object representing another, for example, a cardboard box represents a car.

Symmetric: A relationship which includes peers who bring the same level of knowledge to problem solving.

Systematic desensitization: This works on the principle that fear triggered, for example upon seeing a spider, can be reversed or unlearned. The person is first taught relaxation exercises, and then shown a picture of their feared object (such as a spider). Over a period of time they are introduced to a real spider. It is believed that relaxation will cancel out fear.

Transductive reasoning: As children progress from infants to toddlers, they also progress from the sensorimotor stage to the preoperational stage. The preoperational stage includes transductive reasoning. According to Piaget, transductive thought involves seeing a relationship between two things that are not actually related. Your child may be using transductive reasoning if she tells you that an orange is a ball. Because both the ball and the orange are round, her transductive reasoning tells her that they both must be a ball.

Unconditioned stimulus (UCS): A stimulus that naturally and automatically elicits a response. For example, hearing the theme tune of a favourite programme may cause a child to come running to watch.

Vicarious and self reinforcement: Vicarious reinforcement or observational learning occurs when a child witnesses the effects of an event and stores it in memory.

Zone of proximal development (ZPD): The distance between a child's actual developmental level, as determined by independent problem solving, and the level of potential development as determined through problem solving under adult guidance or in collaboration with more competent peers (Vygotsky, 1978, p. 86, cited in Wertsch, 1981).

APPENDIX: ANSWERS TO EXERCISES

Table A.1 Exemplar Learning Style

When you...	VISUAL	AUDITORY	TACTILE/KINEASTHETIC
Spell	Do you try to see the word? √	Do you sound out the word or use a phonetic approach?	Do you write the word down to find if it feels right?
Talk	Do you listen sparingly but dislike listening for too long? Do you favour words such as *see, picture,* and *imagine*?	Do you enjoy listening but are impatient to talk? Do you use words such as *hear, tune,* and *think*?	Do you gesture and use expressive movements? Do you use words such as *feel, touch,* and *hold*? √
Concentrate	Do you become distracted by untidiness or movement? √	Do you become distracted by sounds or noises?	Do you become distracted by activity around you?
Meet someone again	Do you forget names but remember faces or remember where you met? √	Do you forget faces but remember names or remember what you talked about?	Do you remember best what you did together?
Contact people on business	Do you prefer direct, face-to-face, personal meetings?	Do you prefer the telephone?	Do you talk with them while walking or participating in an activity? √
Read	Do you like descriptive scenes or pause to imagine the actions?	Do you enjoy dialog and conversation or hear the characters talk? √	Do you prefer action stories or are not a keen reader?
Do something new at work	Do you like to see demonstrations, diagrams, slides, or posters? √	Do you prefer verbal instructions or talking about it with someone else?	Do you prefer to jump right in and try it?
Put something together	Do you look at the directions and the picture? √		Do you ignore the directions and figure it out as you go along?
Need help with a computer application	Do you seek out pictures or diagrams?	Do you call the help desk, ask a neighbour, or growl at the computer? √	Do you keep trying to do it or try it on another computer?
TOTAL	5	2	2

Table A.2 Answers to Chapter 2 Exercise

Theorist	Philosopher	Educator
Pavlov	Locke	
Skinner	Rousseau	
Piaget	Froebel	
Vygotsky	Dewey	Dewey
Bruner	Montessori	
Bronfenbrenner	Steiner	Steiner
		McMillan sister

INDEX